T0367728

Management as Consultancy

The nature of management is changing: managers are becoming more like consultants, focusing on projects, functional integration, change and 'clients'. This timely book is based on a large-scale, international study of new management practices and examines the emergence of *consultant managers*. It breaks new ground in our understanding of this hybrid role, uncovering working practices, identities and occupational dynamics, to shed light on both management and consultancy. It unpacks the changing relationship between external consultants and management to reveal important implications for the future of consultancy. Both private and public sectors are covered, with a focus on managers in large and multinational organisations such as former consultants and those in specialisms such as HRM who adopt consulting roles. In addition to advancing our understanding of changes in management, this book offers a demystifying view of consultancy as a whole, from one of the largest-ever studies of this occupation.

ANDREW STURDY is Professor of Management at the University of Bristol, UK. His research interests focus mainly on issues of power and identity in the production and use of management ideas, especially in relation to management consultancy and organisational change. He has advised on consultancy to the UK Management Consultancies Association (MCA), Institute of Consulting, the UK National Audit Office and the media.

CHRISTOPHER WRIGHT is Professor of Organisational Studies at the University of Sydney, Australia. His research focuses on managerial and professional identity and organisational change. He has acted as a consultant and adviser to a range of private and public sector organisations on the use of consultants and organisational change.

NICK WYLIE is Senior Lecturer in HRM at Oxford Brookes University, UK. He researches the links between internal consultancy and the HR function and has published widely in this field. His work on internal consultancy received a best paper award at the 2010 Academy of Management Conference. He is an academic member of the Chartered Institute of Personnel and Development and has substantial management experience in a number of multinational financial services organisations.

Management as Consultancy

Neo-bureaucracy and the Consultant Manager

ANDREW STURDY
University of Bristol

CHRISTOPHER WRIGHT
University of Sydney

NICK WYLIE
Oxford Brookes University

CAMBRIDGE
UNIVERSITY PRESS

University Printing House, Cambridge CB2 8BS, United Kingdom

Cambridge University Press is part of the University of Cambridge.

It furthers the University's mission by disseminating knowledge in the pursuit of education, learning and research at the highest international levels of excellence.

www.cambridge.org
Information on this title: www.cambridge.org/9781107020962

© Andrew Sturdy, Christopher Wright and Nick Wylie 2015

This publication is in copyright. Subject to statutory exception and to the provisions of relevant collective licensing agreements, no reproduction of any part may take place without the written permission of Cambridge University Press.

First published 2015

A catalogue record for this publication is available from the British Library

Library of Congress Cataloguing in Publication data
Sturdy, Andrew.
Management as consultancy : neo-bureaucracy and the consultant manager / Andrew Sturdy, Christopher Wright, Nick Wylie.
    pages   cm
Includes bibliographical references and index.
ISBN 978-1-107-02096-2 (alk. paper : hardback)
1. Business consultants.   2. Management.   I. Title.
HD69.C6S89   2015
658.4'09–dc23

                                                        2014047085

ISBN 978-1-107-02096-2 Hardback

Cambridge University Press has no responsibility for the persistence or accuracy of URLs for external or third-party internet websites referred to in this publication, and does not guarantee that any content on such websites is, or will remain, accurate or appropriate.

Contents

Tables

Acknowledgements

We would like to acknowledge the following for their support of the management as consultancy research project and/or the writing of this book:

- The Economic and Social Research Council (ESRC) for funding the UK part of the research (grant number RES-000-22-1980-A).
- The Institute of Consulting and Chartered Management Institute, and Alan Warr in particular, who helped secure some research access and supported the presentation of our findings.
- Bill Trotter of the Association of Internal Management Consultants.
- Robin Fincham and Chris Grey for their helpful insights and Tasnima Islam for her contribution to the Australian research.
- The research participants who gave us their time and showed commitment to our work, but are made anonymous in the following pages.

Thank you.

I Management as consultancy – a case of neo-bureaucracy

INTRODUCTION – A BOOK ABOUT MANAGEMENT
AND ABOUT CONSULTANCY

> In place of the 'organization man' of corporate hierarchies emerges
> a new stereotype: the brash ... high-flyer, adept with the language of
> MBA programmes and big league consultants, parachuting from
> one change assignment to the next ... For less senior managers, the
> new images available are ... managers as coaches, teambuilders,
> facilitators and change agents.   *(Grey, 1999: 570 & 574)*

As the above quotation suggests, the popular image of managers has
undergone significant change over the last twenty years or so.
Management gurus and business schools have set these new images up
against the 'bad old days' of management as insular, hierarchical and rule
bound, as *bureaucratic*. It is claimed that managers are becoming change
focused, enterprising, project based, externally oriented and non-
hierarchical (e.g. Tengblad, 2006). This idea of the *post*-bureaucratic
manager continues to enjoy popular appeal. However, it has also attracted
significant academic criticism. In particular, it has been convincingly
argued that such a form of management is not as widespread, inevitable
or free of rationality and control as its advocates have suggested (Clegg,
2012). Critics have noted how changes in managerial work involve elements of *both* the new and the old, taking a hybrid or '*neo*-bureaucratic'
form rather than a *post*-bureaucratic one (Reed, 2011). What is striking
about this emergent hybrid form, which is a key theme of this book, is
that, in many respects, it is evocative of management *consultants*. As we
shall see, this parallel is not typically acknowledged despite being clearly
evident in the above quotation, with references to 'big league consultants'
and to teambuilding, facilitation and change agency.

We shall argue that significant aspects of managerial work are becoming like consultancy, leading to what we term *management as consultancy*. We see this as one way in which change within management is occurring and explore it through a specific 'extreme' case which is both an outcome and a mechanism of change – the emerging role of the *consultant manager*. Consultant managers, who may sometimes be former external consultants, are individual or groups of managers who recognise their roles as a form of consultancy (see Chapter 3 for a more detailed definition). These include those designated as 'consultants' in their job or unit titles, as well as other specialists providing advice and facilitation to others in the organisation, typically on a project basis, involving consulting skills such as client and change management. These are often hybrid roles, and this scenario has long been evident in the established positions of managers acting as 'internal consultants' but appears to be occurring much more frequently now. Managers and managerial occupations, such as accounting, information technology (IT) and human resource management (HRM), have adopted new roles, sometimes explicitly using the label of 'consultant'. Drawing on an extensive study of managers, this book examines how and why consultancy practices are brought into work organisations and with what effects, and what *management as consultancy* means more broadly for our understanding of emerging hybrid (neo-bureaucratic) forms of management.

At the same time as exploring management, our focus on consultant managers means this is also a book about consultancy. But it is one that shows consultancy in a different light to that of accounts of 'big league' professional service firms or external specialists with rare skills. As external management consultancy has become successful, it has also become quite commonplace in many organisational contexts and far from exotic. We shall examine consultancy as an activity, occupation and identity set *within* management rather than as an entirely distinctive professional group or project. By studying management as consultancy, we both explore a particular mechanism through which new management practices are established and simultaneously shed light on an otherwise neglected, yet widespread, form of consultancy. Indeed, we suggest that changes in *managerial* work towards a more hybrid form of neo-bureaucracy also have broader implications for our understanding of consultancy. The notion of neo-bureaucracy underpins the theoretical and empirical approach we adopt in this book, and so the remainder of this introductory chapter examines this in more detail. More specifically, we set out a general framework of neo-bureaucracy that is then developed in subsequent chapters. We also briefly summarise the book's structure.

TOWARDS A FRAMEWORK OF NEO-BUREAUCRACY

As we shall see in the following chapter, there is little agreement on what management is. This derives from its socially produced, contested and changing form. Indeed, the discourse of management now pervades almost all aspects of everyday life (Hancock and Tyler, 2009), suggesting that it needs to be located in a wider set of debates. For example, management is sometimes, and rightly, tied to its broader economic and social contexts, notably capitalism and modernity. Thus, changes in management are linked to ideas such as 'knowing capitalism' (Thrift, 2005), 'investor capitalism' (Morris, et al., 2008) or 'new spirits of capitalism' (Boltanski and Chiapello, 2005a), and to related debates on neo-liberalism, market rationality, globalisation and feminisation, for example. Management *work* therefore becomes a site within which new discourses around leadership, networks, new public management, knowledge work and enterprise reside (Martin and Wajcman, 2004; O'Reilly and Reed, 2011). Although each of these debates and discourses has its particular focus and nuances, many relate to *empirical* changes claimed of management work, such as around an increased emphasis on 'change, flexibility, leadership and culture' (Tengblad, 2006: 1438). In the study of management work, these empirical observations are typically related to broader discussions and critiques of changing *organisational* forms, including the notion of post-bureaucracy and/or other hybrid forms of organisation – such as neo-bureaucracy – to which we now turn.

From the 1980s to date, much has been written about the move towards post-bureaucratic organisations, where claimed characteristics include 'less rule-following, less hierarchical control, more flexibility, more coordination based on dialogue and trust, more self-organised units [e.g. projects], and more decentralised decision-making' (Vie, 2010: 183). Reed (2011), for example, outlines an ideal type of the post-bureaucratic organisation (PBO) as comprising *collaboration, flexibility, negotiation, dispersal (decentralisation), personalisation* and *individualisation*. This is typical of other accounts of post-bureaucracy (e.g. Bolin and Härenstam, 2008), although the term 'flexibility' probably under-represents the importance of organisational change, which has become somewhat fetishised in normative accounts of new management (Sturdy and Grey, 2003). Together, the dimensions are based upon an active and oppositional shift away from the familiar Weberian ideal type of the rational bureaucratic organisation (RBO) made up of, respectively, *specialisation, standardisation, formalisation, centralisation, depersonalisation* and *collectivisation* (Reed, 2011: 233). In short, the notion of a PBO represents a rejection of the perceived rigidities of the RBO's 'iron cage'.

However, how far rationalist and hierarchical traditions are actually being replaced by 'support, consultation and inspiration' (Vie, 2010: 183) has been hotly debated (Tengblad, 2012). There are those who see fundamental change in organisations and management towards post-bureaucracy (Heckscher and Donnellon, 1994; Kanter, 1989), but an even larger body of academic work has been devoted to challenging claims of bureaucracy's demise (e.g. Clegg, et al., 2011). Here, arguments point to its persistence, dominance and even intensification in different forms. For example, Hales argues that organisations have long been subject to minor changes or 'organic' variations, but still fundamentally retain 'hierarchical forms of control, centrally-imposed rules and individual managerial responsibility and accountability' (2002: 52). Likewise, McSweeney (2006) identifies an *intensification* of bureaucracy – for example, through the spread of measurement in the public sector. In setting out these three positions in the debate (change away from bureaucracy, no change and its intensification), we should also note that there is a long-established recognition of the limits in the extent to which bureaucracy or formal rationality was actually practised in the first place (e.g. Mintzberg, 1973; see also Chapter 4).

Nevertheless, over time, a general recognition has emerged in the literature, even among the most sceptical accounts, that while post-bureaucracy was barely evident beyond the hype, some change in organisations has indeed occurred (Harris, et al., 2011), resulting in hybrid forms of bureaucracy (Tengblad, 2006). The labels attached to these vary hugely according to analytical focus such that bureaucracy has become *soft* (Courpasson, 2000), *lite* (Hales, 2002), *selective* (Alvesson and Thompson, 2005), *accessorised* (Buchanan and Fitzgerald, 2011) and *customer oriented* (Korczynski, 2001). Following an emerging convention, and to avoid any implication that such changes necessarily reflect a *reduction* in bureaucracy, in this book we use the term neo-bureaucracy. As Clegg observes, 'whilst there can be little doubt that real and significant change is underway ... what has emerged is not the "end" of bureaucracy, but a more complex and differentiated set of post-bureaucratic or neo-bureaucratic possibilities' (2012: 69). Likewise, Farrell and Morris identify neo-bureaucracy as combining market and bureaucracy, centralised and decentralised control or 'new and more distributed modes of organisation juxtaposed with bureaucratic modes of co-ordination and control' (2013: 1389).

'Neo-bureaucracy' therefore implies the persistence of some features of bureaucracy, including various applications of rationality and hierarchical control, but also acknowledges changes and differences, resulting in organisational forms and practices which may include some features of what has come under the label of 'post-bureaucracy' (Alvesson and Thompson, 2005). Of course, hybrid organisational forms in which bureaucratic features are combined with others are not new (Adler and Borys, 1996; Ashcraft, 2001; Blau, 1955; Mintzberg, 1980). Indeed, accounts of changing organisations vary in terms of emphasis and comprise different features. For example, Hales (2002) stresses networks and leadership alongside hierarchical control and accountability, while others focus on careers (Farrell and Morris, 2013), project management (Clegg and Courpasson, 2004) or changing ethics (Clegg, et al., 2011). Similarly, hybridity can be evident in the coexistence of separate bureaucratic and post-bureaucratic structures in different parts of the same organisation (Bolin and Härenstam, 2008; cf. Lawrence and Lorsch, 1967). Nevertheless, these studies can be drawn together by way of a summary of the common features of the neo-bureaucratic organisation (NBO):

1. Relatively few hierarchical levels (decentralisation) combined with centralisation of control (e.g. through information technology and knowledge management) (Reed, 2011); the traditional hierarchical career becomes more lateral and insecure (Morris, et al., 2008).
2. Non-hierarchical *styles* of interaction (Diefenbach and Sillince, 2011), with control achieved through markets, self-discipline (enterprise culture) and/or peers as well as traditional hierarchy (Reed, 2011; Styhre, 2008).
3. The use of project planning and cross-functional integrative teams, which might result in parallel and temporary hierarchical structures (Clegg and Courpasson, 2004; Hodgson, 2002). Some fragmentation of organisations and relationships (e.g. through outsourcing, external networks and diffuse occupational boundaries), but not their dissolution (Alvesson and Thompson, 2005; Poole, et al., 2003).

This list is useful, not least because detailed and comprehensive accounts of neo-bureaucracy are rare despite the growing use of the term. Probably the most developed classification is by Reed (2011). However, his focus is not the same as ours and is quite specific – control logics, foci and modes. For example, he points to a combination of self- and peer surveillance of team performance, to how labour market competition disciplines workers and to employee participation through 'delegated autonomy'. Thus, the core hybrid features or combinations within neo-bureaucracy such as hierarchy–market and centralisation–decentralisation or, as Reed puts it, the bureaucratic 'cage' and the post-bureaucratic 'gaze' are evident, but not the breadth of organisational

Table 1.1 *Organisational ideal types*

Rational bureaucratic organisation (RBO)	Post-bureaucratic organisation (PBO)	Neo-bureaucratic organisation (NBO)	Example
Specialisation	Collaboration	*Functional integration*	Multi-functional projects
Standardisation	Flexibility	*Managed improvisation*	Change programmes and adapting methods
Formalisation	Negotiation	*Structured organisational politics*	Relationship, client and change management methods
Centralisation	Dispersal (decentralisation)	*Delegated autonomy*	Quasi-market structures, leaderism
Depersonalisation	Personalisation	*Networked 'meritocracy'*	Added value and personal credibility
Collectivisation	Individualisation	*Dual identities*	Conditional commitment, professionals as managers

characteristics such as those outlined above. This is unsurprising given his different focus; nevertheless, neo-bureaucracy as an organisational form is not compared with his basic RBO and PBO ideal types. What then might an ideal type of the NBO look like? In other words, based on the literature to date, how are bureaucratic and post-bureaucratic ideals combined in a hybrid form (see Table 1.1)?

First, both specialisation and collaboration can coexist by not completely breaking down functional or occupational divisions but by bringing specialisms together through multi-functional project teams – for example, *functional integration* (Table 1.1, Row 1). Indeed project management is a central theme of hybridised working more generally, with its focus on measurement, change and local accountability (Clegg and Courpasson, 2004). This is also reflected in the combination of standardisation with flexibility and change (Row 2), where change (emblematic of the PBO) is managed in a structured way by not only using but also adapting formal or bureaucratic tools – what we have termed *managed improvisation*. Likewise, informal negotiation and political relations with others can be achieved through formal structures or practices such as relationship and change management techniques and internal markets – a form of *structured organisational politics* (Row 3). Market structures within organisations, where colleagues become clients or internal customers, for example, also form part of the discipline sought partly outside traditional hierarchical control – *delegated autonomy*. This is also evident in the emphasis placed on the leader at the expense of the manager (O'Reilly and Reed, 2011) and, as noted already, can be achieved through distributed technologies such as knowledge management systems (Grant, et al., 2006) (Row 4). A hybrid form of depersonalisation and personalisation (Row 5) has not received the same attention as other aspects of the NBO. However, we will see how a form of this is evident in the practice of consultant managers having to demonstrate how they *objectively* 'add value' to the organisation, but in a way which relies on established networks of long-standing personal relationships and credibility – what we have termed *networked meritocracy*. Finally, between the collective identification of 'organisation man' and individualisation (Row 6) lies the prospect of *dual (or multiple) identities* such as that of the 'professionals as managers' (e.g. doctor-managers) in many public sector hybrids (Farrell and Morris, 2003), where *organisational* commitment may be partial, conditional or transitory.

Our ideal type of the NBO is then clearly linked to the established models of the RBO and PBO, and this adds to its analytical value. It is also grounded in research on contemporary organisational forms and provides a useful reference point in subsequent chapters. However, its neatness and relative simplicity means that some issues or complexities are hidden from view. For example, we have already highlighted how the importance of organisational change is insufficiently reflected in Reed's (2011) model of PBO. Likewise, the critiques of bureaucracy which helped inform changes in organisation and management practice extend into other areas. For example, Boltanski and Chiapello (2005a; see also du Gay, 2000) cite the perceived problems of bureaucratic management as being static, hierarchical, internally focused, tactical, 'excessively technical', limiting of autonomy and authenticity, open ended (ongoing) and lacking in commerciality or market discipline. Most of these are covered in our ideal type, but not all. In particular, we might add a greater external and strategic focus to the PBO as well as the need to lose an 'open-ended approach' and introduce some form of periodic 'closure'. This might translate into elements of a hybrid NBO form which combines internal and external orientations, short-term projects and long-term development, and attention to both strategic and tactical or operational concerns. Reed, for example, talks of 'a deft combination of remote strategic leadership and detailed operational management' (2011: 243). Similarly, post-bureaucratic conceptualisations of more fluid and varied portfolio careers contrast with the linear and organisationally based career trajectories of the RBO (Wacjman and Martin, 2001). In an ideal type of NBO, this suggests a more careful sifting of employee potential and attempts to retain those employees deemed as 'talent' within internal career patterns, while others are encouraged to pursue other opportunities (e.g. through 'up or out' and 'rank and yank' performance management systems or outsourcing; Reed, 2011). Such a feature of NBO might be termed *marketised careers*.

Thus, we might add these extra features to our model (Table 1.2), although there will always be scope for further development. Indeed, it is important to note briefly some of the uses and limitations of ideal

Table 1.2 *Neo-bureaucracy amended*

Neo-bureaucratic organisation (NBO)
Functional integration
Managed improvisation
Structured organisational politics
Delegated autonomy
Networked 'meritocracy'
Dual identities
Strategic/operational and long-/short-term foci
Internal and external orientation
Marketised careers

types more generally. Their value lies, in particular, in their use as an abstract, theoretical tool for comparison. While there is a risk of underplaying connections between types and complexities of form and process (e.g. how characteristics emerge), probably the greatest danger is one of misuse. In particular, ideal types are not designed to reflect reality. Rather they are useful for simplifying, synthesising and accentuating (Hekman, 1983; Höpfl, 2006). For example, in our case, empirical research shows how organisational forms such as post- and neo-bureaucracy are likely to vary significantly in practice, by sector or nation for example, and not match any ideal type (Bolin and Härenstam, 2008; Johnson, et al., 2009). However, our concern is not with *organisational* forms *per se* but with what neo-bureaucratic organisation means for *management* practices and outcomes. Before developing a framework of neo-bureaucratic management and of the relationship between management and consultancy in the next chapter, we conclude with a brief overview of the book as a whole.

AIMS AND STRUCTURE OF THE BOOK

As we have outlined, the aim of this book is to explore *management as consultancy* as a form of contemporary, neo-bureaucratic management practice. Thus, we seek to develop the ideal type of neo-bureaucracy set out in the previous section through considering the rationales and mechanisms of its introduction, and the outcomes for individual managers and their organisations. At a general level we seek to address the following questions: what might neo-bureaucratic management look like, how does it emerge and with what outcomes?

As we shall see shortly, we are not concerned with the question of the precise extent of neo-bureaucratic management practice or of changes towards it at a point in time. Rather, we are convinced that management as consultancy is an excellent site to explore neo-bureaucracy and emerging management practices given the parallels between them. We shall see how management as consultancy is both a means and an outcome of change. Furthermore, neo-bureaucracy not only co-opts much of the criticism of bureaucracy, but also incorporates and even reinforces elements of this form of organisation and control. As a result, we also argue that, rather than resolving key tensions and dilemmas of organisation, within and between market and hierarchy for example, this hybrid form of organisation and management both reproduces them and indeed produces new ones. In short, our analysis aims to show how widely discussed changes in management can be achieved while also reinforcing the contradictions of managerial control.

The study is not simply one of management of course. It could have a number of alternative occupational foci such as change or project management, but our secondary concern is with consultancy. Indeed, and as noted earlier, the book offers what we believe is a highly distinctive approach. Almost all consultancy research has examined consultants as independent and/or organisationally *external* individuals and groups. What limited literature there is on so-called internal consulting has focused on individual consultants in comparison with their external counterparts or the professions (e.g. Lacey, 1995; O'Mahoney, 2010). By contrast, our approach is to focus on consulting in relation to management and, thereby, demystify it, as opposed to accounts of consulting as special and elite (also Faust and Schneider,

2014). Similarly, we are not just concerned with individual consultant managers but with those organised in consulting units or departments rather than professional services firms. Likewise, we engage with their struggles for existence within organisations, rather than assuming consulting to be preoccupied with projects of professionalisation and to be otherwise largely successful as an occupational group.

The book is organised as follows. The next chapter continues the themes introduced in this chapter through a review of the literature. It extends our model of neo-bureaucracy as an organisational form by exploring what neo-bureaucratic management work might look like and the complex, contested and changing nature of the relationship between management and consultancy. Chapter 3 set outs out the context and approach of the research on which the subsequent chapters are based. It highlights how the research developed over time and outlines the choices that were made in terms of methods and focus and their implications for our subsequent analysis. In particular, it shows how we combined a focus on individual consultant managers and their units or groups in two contexts – the UK and Australia – to produce a unique and large-scale study of both management and consultancy. The following four chapters comprise our analysis and systematically explore management as consultancy using the analytical framework set out in Chapter 2 and pay particular attention to the practical tensions which emerge. Although closely connected, the empirical chapters can be read more or less independently. In Chapters 4 and 5, we begin to examine the various work activities of consultant managers and their units, focusing on the most distinctive. Here, we look at change and project/programme management and methods (Chapter 4) and lateral relationships with clients and sponsors in terms of 'added value', as well as external links with other consultants (Chapter 5). In Chapter 6, we consider some of the mechanisms through which management as consultancy occurs, including management education, but we focus on our data on the recruitment of former external consultants – a 'consulting diaspora' – and on the importation of consulting practices by occupational groups such as HRM. This creates congestion and conflict over work jurisdictions. Some of these issues are considered in the subsequent chapter (Chapter 7), which addresses the work identities and 'identity work' of consultant managers. Here, we explore the tensions of their organisational position as an *outsider within* in relation to various boundaries such as those concerned with structure, power and knowledge and whether a dual, ambivalent or hybrid identity can be sustained. In the conclusion (Chapter 8), we return to the themes and questions raised above and subsequently draw attention to some wider implications of the study for our understanding of neo-bureaucracy, management and consultancy. For example, does management as consultancy effectively exclude other, more participative, ways of organising; will it further commodify external consulting; and can it exist in anything other than a minority or specialist form in organisations? In other words, can all managers be neo-bureaucratic?

2 Neo-bureaucratic management and consultancy

INTRODUCTION

The *organisational* features of neo-bureaucracy outlined in Chapter 1 readily translate into characteristics of managerial work. For example, neo-bureaucracy can be seen as project and methods based; change and externally oriented; integrative/lateral and facilitative; and insecure and market based, as well as conventionally bureaucratic in other respects. In this chapter, we develop this further, by setting out a framework through which we analyse neo-bureaucratic *management*, rather than organisations, and one upon which the subsequent chapters are partly based. In particular, drawing on different, related traditions in the study of management, we consider neo-bureaucratic management in terms of *activities*, *occupations* and *identities*. Within each of these, we recognise the contested nature of management as comprising various tensions, contradictions and dilemmas of organisation and control. These are a central theme in our empirical analysis of consultant managers and are briefly discussed here by way of introduction. The second half of this chapter is devoted to introducing some of the mechanisms through which neo-bureaucratic management has occurred. In particular, we focus on the importance of management consultancy, above and beyond its traditional role, in diffusing new practices through client projects. This focus leads us to explore further the relationship between management and consultancy, including through highlighting the apparent contrast between bureaucratic managers and 'professional' consultants and the apparent parallels between the latter and neo-bureaucratic management. We conclude by highlighting differences, commonalities and changes in the perceived relationship between management and consultancy.

NEO-BUREAUCRATIC MANAGERIAL WORK –
ACTIVITIES, OCCUPATIONS AND IDENTITIES

While management remains at the core of much of the literature in organisation studies, it is rarely a focus empirically. There is, however, a long tradition of management studies being built around the aim of describing and classifying managerial work (Matthaei, 2010). Studies in this 'work activity' school, which we draw upon in our framework, vary considerably, but have tended to focus on three aspects or questions (Hales, 1986; see also Chapter 4 for further discussion):

1. What do managers do, or what are the *purpose* and *content* of their activities?
2. How do managers work, or how do they *organise* and *structure* their role?
3. With whom do managers work, or what is the nature of the *relationships* managers have?

These questions provide useful dimensions for identifying the different elements of management work which can be compared with the ideal types of organisations outlined in Chapter 1 and NBO in particular. For example, a range of studies have suggested that the *purpose* and *content* of bureaucratic management are mostly concerned with sustaining and controlling operational procedures – that is, maintaining the steady state (Hales, 2002; Hales and Tamangani, 1996; Mintzberg, 1973; Tengblad and Vie, 2012). Doing so often involves managers in work that is immediate and focused on the resolution of short-term problems that threaten to undermine this steady state or the achievement of short-term performance measures. Such a purpose leads to the criticism of the bureaucratic manager as prioritising means over ends, being bound by rules and procedures and lacking insight into broader strategic issues. By contrast, images of *post*-bureaucratic management suggest its purpose to be more strategic in focus and concerned with longer-term innovation and change – or even with deliberately upsetting the steady state by improvising. A hybrid, neo-bureaucratic form of management might therefore combine a longer-term strategic focus on change and innovation (through the use and adaptation of structured change models) with an (often shorter-term) operational concern with process efficiency and cost reduction. This position is expressed in the ideal type of NBO as both *strategic/operational* and *long-/short-term foci* and a form of *managed improvisation*.

The work activity school has also explored the related question of how managers *organise* and *structure* their work. In bureaucratic management, work is organised around clear functional demarcations with consequent challenges for integration and communication – the notion of silo-based management. Post-bureaucracy, on the other hand, is considered to be antagonistic towards traditional boundaries and so pan-organisational in scope, fluid in structure and collaborative in nature (Hales, 2002: 55). Therefore, the organisation and structure of neo-bureaucratic management might draw together these elements through a form of *functional integration* in which specialisms persist but are combined through the extensive use of project working (with tasks formed into highly planned, discrete and time-bound units of activity) (Clegg and Courpasson, 2004), as well as structured change programmes and project methodologies.

Of course, management is also crucially organised and structured hierarchically, even if this might sometimes be denied in post-bureaucratic discourse, where market discipline is emphasised. Neo-bureaucratic management, then, would continue to depend on centralised hierarchical structures, even if they might be less visible (Vie, 2010), and yet also seek a defined degree of independence within these hierarchical and market structures – an approach represented by the notion of *delegated autonomy* in our ideal type of the NBO (also Reed, 2011). This connects directly to the third question addressed in the management work literature, that of with whom managers work or the nature of their *relationships*. Once again, images of bureaucratic and post-bureaucratic management are polarised in this area. For example, Hales (2002: 55) documents the claimed shift to *post*-bureaucracy, whereby 'managerial attention switches from the vertical ... to the lateral – communicating, liaising, negotiating and collaborating ... across both internal and external organisational boundaries'. This characterises bureaucratic management as embedded within vertical hierarchical relationships and contained within organisational boundaries. Thus, neo-bureaucracy would not only retain some measure of hierarchy (as above), but managerial *orientations* would be both *internal and external* to the organisation. Similarly, while bureaucracy celebrates depersonalisation and formality in relationships, post-bureaucracy gives emphasis to their other, in the form of personal qualities and informal negotiation. These have long been recognised as a central feature of management activity (Burns, 1957; Pettigrew, 1973; Sayles, 1964) but not celebrated or legitimised nor placed within market contexts, for example. Thus, and as we suggested in the previous chapter, within neo-bureaucratic management, political relations emerge as being partly structured in formal client/relationship, project and change management techniques – *structured organisational politics*. At the same time, although not yet well documented, seemingly meritocratic measures of personal or group worth and credibility such as 'value add' can be combined with informal networks as *networked meritocracy*.

Despite a tendency in the literature to reduce conceptions of management to what managers do (Grey, 1999), it is important to recognise that management also comprises various *occupational and career dynamics*. This draws attention to management as a hierarchical function or level. Regardless of its activities, it is both a subject and an object of control (Harding, et al., 2014) and has historically been shaped by competition between different occupations, including professional communities ('within capital') (Abbott, 1988; Armstrong, 1986), resulting in varied practices in different industry and national settings (Guillén, 1994; Shenhav, 1999). At the same time, bureaucratic structures provide for a measure of commonality in terms of functional and hierarchical careers, for example. Here, some individual managers can progress in a linear and vertical fashion almost exclusively within a functional domain and often in a single organisation – 'organization man' (Whyte, 1956).

Of course, ideal-type post-bureaucracy rejects such rigid distinctions, emphasising, instead, managers operating across, and even undermining, traditional occupational divisions and jurisdictional claims over knowledge. Indeed, as we shall see, such a debate exists in relation to management as consultancy. Moreover, post-bureaucratic managers are more externally and market oriented, less constrained by organisational boundaries and so associated with fluid and typically insecure 'portfolio careers' where personal development is deemed as a matter of individual responsibility, external networks and enterprise (Morris, et al., 2008). Such characteristics are also likely to be evident within neo-bureaucracy, although alongside more bureaucratic features. Here, we might see both internal and external and horizontal and vertical career paths as well as combinations such as 'professionals as managers' in health care, for example, and 'corporate professions' (Muzio, et al., 2011) such as project management. As outlined in the previous chapter, we label these hybrids as *marketised careers* in our ideal type of neo-bureaucracy.

The domains of work activity and occupational/career dynamics both emphasise some fluidity or lack of permanence (as well as continuities) in neo-bureaucratic management. Considering how this is experienced by managers and, specifically, how it shapes, and is shaped by, their *identities* is the third dimension of management we examine. Such a focus is important in its own right, not only by way of exploring how practices and structures are mediated subjectively (Alvesson and Willmott, 2002) but also because it allows for an integration of the different features of neo-bureaucratic work and therefore a consideration of how they might act together. Furthermore, given the essentially contested and socially produced nature of management, we cannot rely solely on any claimed objective feature of management work (Thomas and Linstead, 2002). Rather, identity is constructed in a relational and situational way through various boundaries (e.g. organisational, knowledge and political) of inclusion and exclusion (Ellis and Ybema, 2010).

Multiple forms of identity can sometimes present challenges for individuals seeking to maintain a coherent sense of self, especially those in ambivalent positions (Brown, 2014). This has long been evident with middle managers set in an intermediate structural location (Harding, et al., 2014) and is also likely to be especially significant in negotiating a hybrid position between the ideal of a bureaucratic and post-bureaucratic management identity. In the case of the former this means being fully integrated politically and/or interpersonally within the organisation. However, post-bureaucratic ideals emphasise the importance of distinctive and shifting identities, often developed outside the organisation and so more capable of adapting to an environment of greater job and career insecurity (Morris, et al., 2008; Webb, 2004). Neo-bureaucratic managers therefore need to be both distinctive and integrated within the organisation. This position or *dual identity* as the cosmopolitan *and* local or the 'outsider within' (Meyerson and Scully, 1995: 589) resonates strongly with the ideal type of neo-bureaucracy. The question, and one that we begin to address in Chapter 7, is whether and under what conditions the tensions produced by such a hybrid position can be sustained as a coherent identity (see also Zabusky and Barley, 1997).

Having set out an initial basic framework of some of the core hybrid characteristics of neo-bureaucratic management in terms of *activities, occupations* and *identities* (Table 2.1), the natural next step would be to explore the extent to which they have been adopted, if at all. This then might feed into an assessment of how much change has occurred, assuming one had a point of reference to start from. However, given the extent of debate on the subject of management, there is remarkably little empirical research examining the nature and extent of change. Indeed, this is difficult to establish, for a range of reasons. First, many studies have been based on highly specific and diverse contexts in terms of geography (e.g. Sweden, Norway, Zimbabwe and Malaysia) and management level (e.g. CEOs and middle managers) and yet used to chart or question changes in general (e.g. Hales, 2002; Tengblad, 2006; Vie, 2010). Some larger-scale studies exist

Table 2.1 *Management and neo-bureaucracy*

Management dimension	Indicative neo-bureaucratic characteristics
Work activities (Chapters 4 and 5) *Purpose/content* *Structure/organisation* *Relationships*	Managed improvisation Strategic/operational and long-/ short-term foci Functional integration Delegated autonomy Internal and external orientation Structured organisational politics Networked 'meritocracy'
Occupational and career dynamics (Chapter 6)	Marketised careers
Identities (Chapter 7)	Dual identities

and suggest that there is considerable variation in the degree of change in management (Farrell and Morris, 2013). This fits with the findings of studies cited in Chapter 1 on related organisational developments (e.g. Bolin and Härenstam, 2008). It is also characteristic of management studies historically, even within national and sector contexts, where diversity of practice is the norm (Stewart, 1991). Furthermore, variation is emphasised in the very unusual case of longitudinal (time series) studies of management across levels and sectors (Poole, et al., 2001: 4).

In part, such contextual variation and methodological challenges inform our alternative focus on exploring a context where hybrid management practices are especially evident, rather than seeking to contribute to a debate on the extent of any general change in practice. As Thomas and Linstead (2002: 89) argue, we should be asking *not* what has become of management, but how are managers becoming?

This is not simply a matter of methods. The problems of establishing the nature and significance of change are compounded by variations in the perspectives on management taken in the literature, to which we now turn. Furthermore, and as we shall explore later in the chapter, any assessment of management as consultancy needs the relationship between them to be unpacked as well.

MANAGEMENT AND THE TENSIONS OF ORGANISING

As we have noted, much of the empirical research on management explores managerial work activities in detail. This tradition continues. For example, following the shift in the strategy literature towards studying it as a practice (Jarzabkowski and Spee, 2009), recent work focuses on 'management as practice' (Tengblad, 2012). Such an approach can be contrasted with another tradition in the literature – seeing management primarily as an abstract, collective process or function, in particular, as a control imperative within capitalism (Marglin, 1974). Here, management is not a set of universal, or even changing, activities (largely synonymous with organising), but embedded in specific historical and social relations whereby 'managers act to intermediate between those who deploy resources to dominate or exploit others, and others who are subordinated in such processes' (Alvesson and Willmott, 2012: 21). Even though our main empirical focus in this book is on management practices and their outcomes, our position, following Tsoukas (1994) and many others, is that *both* these foci are needed (cf. Hales, 1986).

Indeed, it is possible that the different positions in the debate mentioned in Chapter 1 regarding moves to *post*-bureaucracy can be partly explained by the perspective taken on management rather than empirics alone. For example, managerial roles and tasks are more readily linked to the varied and changeable *practice* of management, whereas more fundamental and systemic conceptions, notably linked to capitalist and patriarchal relations of production, point more to continuity. Furthermore, as Tsoukas (1994: 295) points out, there is a tension between perspectives in that 'the more one observes changes in the role of managers, the more one is inclined to disagree with an abstract conception' of management. By the same token, the more one sees management in abstract, systemic terms, the less significance will be attached to changing practices – 'old wine in new bottles' (cf. Hales, 2002). As Clegg observed with regard to related *organisational* changes, 'bureaucracy is both being superseded by post-bureaucracy and not being superseded by post-bureaucracy ... it all depends on whether one focuses on re-composition or decomposition' (2012: 74).

Tsoukas (1994) presents a meta-theory of management which goes some way to address this issue. Here, management is seen as layered from 'roles', 'tasks' and 'functions' to the more abstract 'causal powers', such as the need to *control* subordinates in the pursuit of efficiency and surplus. This is helpful and informs our approach, but what it neglects is how the layers are interdependent and implicated in management itself. In particular, and as Willmott (1996) points out, seeing management as a range of roles, tasks or functions itself operates at the level of 'causal powers', ideologically. It helps to legitimate management as a natural or 'neutral' series of activities. Rather than objective phenomena, management practices are themselves critical to the social renewal of capitalism. Indeed, following a long and continuing critical tradition of studies of management, a basic feature of its practice is seeking the legitimation of authority and exclusivity of control over employees and others (Bendix, 1963). More recently, new management practices have been seen in this way, as constituting an 'ideology that justifies people's commitment to capitalism, and which renders this commitment attractive' (Boltanski and Chiapello, 2005b: 162). So, for instance, it is claimed that the critiques and rejection of bureaucracy by advocates of new management have been appropriated and adapted to a 'new spirit' to justify, rather than undermine, modern capitalism. However, this ideological effect has barely been explored empirically, at least at the micro level (Ekman, 2013).

Indeed, the recent critiques of bureaucratic management may often be misguided, not least in ignoring its ethics (du Gay, 2000) but also in overlooking some of the long-established limitations identified in bureaucratic structures. These are very familiar within organisation theory and include those associated with the ideal type of bureaucracy outlined in Chapter 1 – *specialisation, centralisation, formalisation* and *standardisation* as well as *depersonalisation* and *collectivisation*. As we have seen, models of post-bureaucracy were held by some to address these issues (Heckscher and Donnellon, 1994; Kanter, 1989), but they remained largely an ideal. Furthermore, the classic *problems* of bureaucratic structures are better seen as *dilemmas* or tensions of organisation design, such as those between

- specialist expertise and integration/common goals;
- hierarchical and participative decision-making/discretion;
- written procedures and informal processes;
- standardised routines and personal initiative/flexibility; and
- stability/predictability and innovation/change (Child, 1984).

Likewise, others have pointed to dilemmas *within* each of these poles such as between change directed at short-term economic benefits – 'value add' – and that focused on long-term organisational development – 'Theory E vs Theory O' (Beer and Nohria, 2000) or specialisation pursued through internal or external expertise (see Menon and Pfeffer, 2003).

Dilemmas imply that there are no clear solutions, except perhaps through forms of hybridity (e.g. the classic 'solution' of the matrix organisation). Indeed, some have, tentatively at least, suggested that neo-bureaucratic hybrids of organising hold such a prospect. It is argued that they can resolve tensions between post-bureaucra and rational bureaucratic organisation. For example, Clegg (2012: 69, 71) observes that 'neo-bureaucratic possibilities have had the effect of undermining some distinctions previously deemed incontestable (e.g. market vs. hierarchy; centralization vs. decentralization; public vs. private sectors) ... domination and self-determination'. Similarly, Reed (2011: 245) maintains that neo-bureaucratic regimes attempt 'to blend, even achieve a partial synthesis between, selected elements of "the cage" (rational bureaucratic control) and "the gaze" (post-bureaucratic control) in order to deliver a configuration of regulative mechanisms that can effectively facilitate the practice of contemporary governance' (cf. Donnelly, 2009).

Of course, dialectical traditions of analysis such as labour process theory (e.g. Marglin, 1979; Ramsay, 1977) as well as those approaches which point to the hubris of modernity (Clegg, et al., 2011; Gabriel, 1998) would suggest that, far from solving problems, *new* structures and management practices are likely to generate *new* dilemmas. In other words, management is continuously seeking to 'contain and exploit the tensions, conflicts and inequalities' (Willmott, 1984: 363), but with only partial success. Indeed, dualities, contradictions and paradoxes are likely to be a 'normal condition of organisational life, not an anomalous problem to be removed or resolved' (Trethewey and Ashcraft, 2004: 81). These include both generic and particular tensions and dysfunctions of control, notably various forms of resistance and adaptation among employees, and other unintended consequences, including moulding new practices and ideas to improve or maintain one's occupational or sectional status (Armstrong, 1986; Erturk, et al., 2005; Tengblad, 2004). More generally, multiple systems or discourses exist in management contexts, in partial tension with each other such as those between occupation, gender and organisation (see Whittington, 1992). As intimated earlier, these present diverse opportunities and dilemmas in terms of identity work as well (Brown, 2014).

Given the productive, if not always positive, power of such tensions and contradictions, it is not surprising that some theorists of neo-bureaucracy suggest that it does not simply bring the prospect of resolution but that 'in such hybrid and often unclear situations, conflict and confrontation are inevitable' (Clegg, 2012: 71). For example, tensions have long been noted between, say, empowerment and rationalisation or hierarchy (Watson, 1994; Webb, 2004), and leadership as both rational-legal (e.g. strategic) and charismatic (Grey, 1999). Likewise, Clegg and Courpasson (2004: 545) note, with regard to project management, that 'it neither abolishes control nor those tensions associated with it. Instead, it has distinct modalities of control, each of which generates quite specific tensions. These are not so much an innovation in organisation form but a repositioning of some classic questions', such as the organisational design dilemmas outlined above. More generally, Bolin and Härenstam (2008: 559) speculate that the combination of bureaucratic and post-bureaucratic structures puts a 'particular strain and restrictions on ... employees, who are controlled according to two principles'. Finally, with respect to neo-bureaucracy specifically, Reed (2011: 243) highlights the need to recognise that 'of course, the potential for resistance, incompetence, confusion, and incoherence is very considerable and should never be underestimated in relation to any grounded assessment of how these hybridised control systems actually operate in practice'. This is a theme which will be pursued further throughout the following chapters.

Overall then, management needs to be understood not only in terms of various changing activities, occupational dynamics and identities but also in relation to dilemmas and tensions of control, crucially, but not exclusively, informed by capitalism and its legitimation. In the context of neo-bureaucratic management, some of these tensions have been highlighted but have yet to be fully explored in research on management work activities and its effects, where debate has focused largely on the nature and extent of change. Also lacking in the literature are detailed studies of the various individual *mechanisms* through which the new management practices arise, to which we now turn.

MECHANISMS OF CHANGE – TOWARDS MANAGEMENT AS CONSULTANCY?

We have seen how neo-bureaucracy is linked to changes in management practices, but that the precise nature, extent and significance of those changes are necessarily unclear. Likewise, accounts vary in the attention they give to the conditions and mechanisms of change. Typically, a wide range of generic conditions, in line with contingency theory, are outlined (Bolin and Härenstam, 2008). For example, with regard to *post*-bureaucracy, Alvesson and Thompson (2005: 488) refer to 'the usual suspects': 'intensification of competition, deregulation, globalization of production, rising rates of product innovation, new forms and increased significance of knowledge and information technology, differentiated and rapidly changing customer preferences, the dominance of intangible services, coping with and encouraging workforce diversity ... the sheer pace of change.'

These broad conditions provide some insight, but, as McSweeney (2006: 25) warns, there is a danger of overly deterministic accounts, especially as regards technology – 'absent is any consideration of interpretive space ... paradoxical effects ... diversity; interplay between the key "determinants"; or recognition that the named influences might intensify rather than dilute bureaucracy' (also Harrison and Smith, 2003). To compound these problems and as noted earlier, *neo-bureaucracy* is associated with and/or encompasses a wide range of related ideas such as downsizing, outsourcing, network or project structures, fluid or portfolio careers, interim managers, feminisation, corporate professionalism, boundary spanning, leaderism, enterprise, performance measures, new public management, project management, shareholder/ investor capitalism and knowledge work (see also Morris, et al., 2008).

Our concern is mostly at the organisational and individual levels, in terms of the specific ways in which hybrid forms of neo-bureaucratic management might develop while retaining features of bureaucracy. As we shall see, this has occurred in various ways, through different channels and agents of co-production. In particular, new knowledge and techniques have been acquired in the context of organisational restructuring. The following is indicative:

– *Education, training and knowledge transfer* (e.g. business schools, trainers, professional bodies, media/publishers, software houses). Management has 'professionalised', at least in the sense of managers becoming more familiar with case-based approaches and with abstract knowledge, methods and tools (Caldwell, 2005; Thomas, 2003). These include those associated with project and change management especially, as well as strategic, leadership, shareholder and enterprise discourses. The rise of the MBA, the associated 'flight from management' with its decline in status (Khurana, 2007) and the professionalisation projects of management occupations such as human resource management (HRM), purchasing and project management are a key part of this (Poole, et al., 2001), and so are in-house training and reward systems (Mueller and Whittle, 2011).

– *Restructuring and refocusing.* The restructuring and financialisation of organisations in terms of reducing hierarchical levels and headcount (cuts and outsourcing) and the development of technology and corporate governance to support such aims has helped reshape the orientations of managers. They are more focused towards shorter-term (project/career) goals, financial outcomes, change and horizontal and external networks than previously (Farrell and Morris, 2013; Khurana, 2007).

In addition to these direct mechanisms of change, there are partially unintended outcomes of neo-bureaucracy which have further contributed to its own development. In particular, the downsizing and de-layering of large organisations (and shift towards market rationality in terms of employment relationships) has fuelled both the demand for and supply of temporary expert labour (Grey, 1999; Kunda and Ailon-Souday, 2005; Wood, 2002). In short, managers and other experts are effectively re-hired on a short-term or project basis as interims or consultants. Indeed, we shall now briefly introduce how consultants specifically have played an important role in the development of neo-bureaucracy, but not just in the conventional sense of transferring knowledge to clients through projects.

Consultancy as a medium and exemplar of neo-bureaucracy

It is now well documented how management consultancy as an industry has grown rapidly, especially in the period of the emergence of neo-bureaucracy (1980s–) and in those nations where it is concentrated (e.g. UK, USA, Australia, Sweden) (see, e.g., O'Mahoney and Markham, 2013). Although its role is sometimes exaggerated and often contested

Table 2.2 *Mechanisms of creating neo-bureaucracy through management consulting*

1. Conventional diffusion of practices via consulting projects and 'thought leadership'
2. Emulation of consultants and firms as role models
3. In-house training of external consultants who then move to managerial roles
4. Colonisation of consultancy by *external* occupations (accounting, IT)
5*. Colonisation by *internal* occupations (HRM, auditing)
6*. Active recruitment of former externals as 'consultant managers'
7*. Partnering with external consultants outside of consulting project roles
8*. Practices of internal consulting units and individual consultant managers
    - Advisory style and relationship management
    - Project/change management methods and functional integration

in practice (Sturdy, 2011), external consultancy has been a key agent in these contexts in the promotion and diffusion of management ideas (see also Boltanski and Chiapello, 2005a; Kipping and Wright, 2012; Thrift, 2005). It is important to emphasise that this includes both bureaucratic and post-bureaucratic ideas and practices, such as performance measurement (McSweeney, 2006). Indeed, consulting is strongly associated with standardisation more generally (Wright, et al., 2012). However, this formal and conventional role of consulting as an active agent in knowledge flow, translation or diffusion is *not* our concern here (see Kipping and Engwall, 2002; Sturdy, et al., 2009). Rather, consulting has influence as an example *itself*, as a role model of ideal management practice. In particular, we aim to show that management consultancy is an exemplary case of new, neo-bureaucratic management and that management as consultancy is emerging through a number of mechanisms (see Table 2.2).

First, with the (often self-promoted) success and influence of consulting, client managers and project team members may emulate some of the practices and orientations of their consulting partners (Sturdy, et al., 2009). This has also occurred more formally and on a larger scale, including in the development of *bureaucratic* organisations historically. As McKenna (2006: 195) observes, 'the organization and culture of the leading management consulting firms would exert a powerful influence on large-scale bureaucratic institutions as executives began increasingly to model their organizations after knowledge-based, team-led consultancies'.

Influence also happens less consciously and more diffusely through former consultants becoming managers. Given the well-documented stresses of consulting life, consultancies' 'up or out' policies and the fact that many see consulting as only a short-term career, this flow can be quite significant (McGinn, 2013; Meriläinen, et al., 2004). Indeed, while training and education is seen as a key diffusion mechanism for management ideas in general, rarely are consulting firms identified as agents in this regard, as training providers. For example, in the case of McKinsey & Company alone, one estimate claimed that 80 per cent of consultants leave the firm in the first five years (O'Shea and Madigan, 1997: 261) and that there are now 27,000 alumni worldwide (Christensen, et al., 2013). While some leavers stay in external consulting or leave their consulting practices behind, many do not, and so, as we shall see further below, they bring consulting practices and orientations with them into mainstream management roles.

The adoption of new management practices in the form of consultancy has also been achieved more explicitly and directly through the proactive colonisation of management consultancy by particular *external* management occupations and professions, notably accountancy and information technology (Galal, et al., 2012; Greenwood, et al., 2002). Although sometimes undermined by tensions over conflicts of interest, in the case of accounting for example, such a process has been facilitated by a weak level of professional closure in consulting (Armbrüster, 2006). As we shall see in more detail shortly, such moves are in keeping with occupational dynamics more generally (Abbott, 1988), in seeking jurisdiction over a particular domain of activity, such as change management.

Our focus in this book is slightly different and more concerned with those developments in management towards consultancy that originate *within* organisations (marked with asterisk in Table 2.2). First, this is evident in the transformation of management occupations such as HRM or *internal* auditing to include consultancy as an inherent part of their work activity (Selim, et al., 2009; Wright, 2008). This relates both to a more general move into change management and the pursuit of a more 'strategic', less hierarchical, advisory or partner role (Caldwell, 2001). Second, while we have noted how consultancy practice is recruited in by default, with the appointment of those trained by consulting firms, this is also actively pursued by recruiters. The 'consulting diaspora' (Sturdy and Wright, 2008) comprises those who are seen as highly change and market oriented and skilled in relationship and project techniques. One practitioner-expert described this phenomenon, coining the term *consultant managers*, and saw their appointment as a partial threat to some of the business of *external* consultants (Czerniawska, 2011). Likewise, in a *Harvard Business Review* article on the consulting industry, it was claimed that 'precise data are not publicly available, but we know that many companies have hired small armies of former consultants' (Christensen, et al., 2013: 110). This group not only brings consultancy practices with it, but is especially likely to maintain and develop informal relationships with external consultants (including former colleagues) outside of specific consulting projects. Indeed, working closely or 'partnering' with consultants in this way is an established practice for many externally oriented managers, in order to keep up to date with management developments (on both sides) (Kitay and Wright, 2004). Again, this is a route through which consulting can be brought into management more or less informally.

In addition to these more recent, novel and less formal ways in which management roles come to incorporate consultancy practices, variously labelled consulting groups or units have developed within large organisations to assist in the management of change projects and programmes. Internal consulting has, of course, existed for some time, but was typically only seen in relation to its external counterpart and, as a result, as rather unfashionable (Armbrüster, 2006; Lacey, 1995). Currently, therefore, combined with the fact that management consulting as a whole sometimes has a stigma associated with it, the title 'consultant' or 'consulting' may be absent in internal units, even if many, if not all, of the core characteristics are evident. Indeed, it has been argued that 'internal consultancies have become major players; there are large numbers of managers who are, in fact, working as consultants ... without even realizing it' (Law, 2009: 63; Visscher, 2006). As we shall see in the following chapters, these units and the individuals who work in them exemplify many of the characteristics of neo-bureaucracy. For example, they may adopt 'non-hierarchical' styles of interaction within hierarchical structures, use consulting methods of change and project management and play a cross-functional integrating role, including through various forms of 'relationship management'. Furthermore, we shall show how the rationale for introducing such consulting practices often echoes critiques of bureaucracy although, as the following chapters demonstrate, their introduction, use and sustainability is far from guaranteed.

THE CHANGING RELATIONSHIPS BETWEEN MANAGEMENT AND CONSULTANCY

So far, we have suggested that the emerging hybrid form of neo-bureaucratic management resembles management consultancy and that the introduction of consultancy into organisations is one mechanism through which neo-bureaucratic management is developed. In order to explore this further in the following chapters, we need to examine the relationship between management and consulting more precisely, not least because some would argue either that consulting and management have always been equivalent or, by contrast, that they will always be quite distinct. These issues are made more difficult by the fact that both management and consulting do not have objective qualities, they are internally diverse, and their form and meaning change situationally and over time. Furthermore, and as we have already seen with management, their meanings are contested and shaped by different perspectives. But within a given social context, this does not mean that their identities are infinitely flexible (Kitay and Wright, 2007).

In short, then, we argue that management roles and identities, *at the middle levels at least*, often used to be quite distinct from those of the *professional* form of management consultancy. However, in becoming neo-bureaucratic, management has become more similar. At the same time, although not our focus in subsequent chapters, we shall note here how external consultancy has come to take on many of the traditional functions of management. First, however, we shall outline some of the different positions on, and forms of, consultancy.

Contrasting views and forms

We noted earlier how management has different and contested meanings. The same can be said of consulting, including whether emphasis is placed on its broad function and/or detailed practices. This will become evident below and poses definitional difficulties. Likewise, perspectives vary normatively in the sense of what management or consulting *should* be and, in particular, how inclusive or exclusive they are in membership (Grey, 1999). Such tensions are evident elsewhere such as in HRM (Guest, 1987) and project management (Hodgson, 2002), where exclusivity is typically associated with the professionalisation projects of different occupational groups.

Confusion and conflict also arise from the diversity of forms within an occupation and how these can provide the basis of multiple and optional objects of personal identification. Internal diversity is quite normal in occupations (Fine, 1996), but is perhaps especially applicable to both management and consulting, given their openness and ambiguity (Harding, et al., 2014; Kitay and Wright, 2007). Indeed, and as noted earlier, most accounts highlight variation (e.g. Poole, et al., 2001). In external consulting, one can compare and contrast, for example, the experienced sole practitioner providing niche or esoteric advice with the young 'blue chip' employee implementing standard models. But there are many other variations. A study by Kitay and Wright (2007), for example, found a wide range of activities and roles under the consulting label. These provided the basis for occupational rhetorics and social identities categorised into consultant as 'professional' (the most common), 'prophet' (elite), 'businessperson' and 'service worker'. Furthermore, these identities were drawn on by individuals selectively and strategically, according to the situation and context such as the consulting sector and hierarchical level. The 'businessperson', for example, was more common among the more senior consultants who had income-generating roles. We shall see, when considering the identities of consultant managers, that other identifications are also evident, including alternative occupations or disciplines such as HRM or organisational development, not least given the stigma sometimes attached to consulting (and management) (Brocklehurst, et al., 2010; Sturdy, 2009). Given such difficulties, analytically, we focus on dominant images of consultancy and management (see below), and empirically, we explore mostly those acting at the middle levels of management – those who recognise that their role can be seen as consulting even if they do not always actively identify with the occupation. We now examine different positions on the relationship between management and consulting in more detail.

Management and consulting as equivalent
To many, especially those who are directly affected by their work, there is little difference between management and consulting in a general sense. Both often perform very similar types of activity, sometimes directly on behalf of the owners of organisations, or, if not, consultants might simply legitimate management or act as a scapegoat for it (Sturdy, 2011). But consulting and management are seen as

equivalent in two more specific senses, one more aspirational than the other. First, to those who subscribe to or pursue a professional status for management, the roles are very close. For example, the early UK management pioneer Lyndall Urwick thought that management should be a third-party activity, independent from both capital and labour (Brech, et al., 2010; also Shenhav, 1999). Variations of this view have persisted, albeit with limited success (Khurana, 2007; Poole, et al., 2001), and are reflected in the fact that the professional body of consulting in the UK (the Institute of Consulting) is part of the broader Chartered Institute of Management.

Second, and more significant, management and consulting coincide in one of the two main definitions of consulting. This emphasises the practice of providing assistance directed towards organisational improvement. Here, *we can all be consultants* in particular contexts, regardless of our main occupation: 'Thus a manager can also act as a consultant if he or she decides to give advice and help to a fellow manager, or even to subordinates rather than directing them or issuing orders to them' (Kubr, 1996: 3). This is a highly *inclusive* view of consulting, derived largely from humanistic and process consultancy traditions (Schein, 1987), where the emphasis is on facilitation or, more simply, helping (Schein, 2009). However, and as we shall see shortly, this tradition of consulting is declining in contexts where it was once significant, even if some of the activities (e.g. superficially non-directive styles of change intervention) are not.

Management and consulting as different

The second main view of consulting is an exclusive one, typically favoured by professional consulting associations (and shared by many consulting researchers). It presents consulting as a special service for managers, which involves specific qualifications or skills and training, used to help identify and analyse problems and recommend solutions 'in an objective and independent manner' (Kubr, 1996: 3). This 'professional' and 'expert' model of consulting emerged in a particular way in the USA in the 1930s (David, et al., 2013). It is not the only model, nor is it without internal tensions (e.g. over routes to professionalism), but it conforms to a broader, still dominant image of consulting as a 'distinctive occupation' or profession compared to management (Kitay and Wright, 2007: 1615). As we outline below, this distinctiveness is evident in a number of respects, notably in terms of knowledge, relationships, work and career patterns and personal characteristics.

First, regardless of how 'objective' and 'independent' of managerial clients consultants actually are, they are seen as not being involved in the day-to-day administration of organisations and as having no direct responsibility for decisions or hierarchical authority to instruct. This echoes wider, long-standing distinctions between managers and experts both within and beyond the organisation (Brint, 1996). Given that, in most cases, there is no compulsion to use such experts, they have to rely strongly on persuasion and relationship building. *Within* organisations too, these 'staff professionals', as they were once known (Dalton, 1950; Daudigeos, 2013), were also considered distinctive from managers in terms of their lower organisational loyalty and greater commitment to specialist expertise and extra-organisational reference groups. They were more 'cosmopolitan' in their orientation or latent identity (Gouldner, 1957: 287).

With *external* experts, such as consultants, this distinction was reinforced by the short-term or project-based nature of assignments. Such a view of consultancy conforms to contemporary definitions used in the UK public sector, for example, which distinguish consultancy from 'steady-state' activities (and those of interim managers and outsourcing) (OGC, 2006). Likewise, a core area of expertise for consultants – change management – was long seen as being of only periodic concern to managers, and even then, their focus would be on implementation, rather than planning and integrating functional groups (Armbrüster and Kipping, 2002). More generally, since the start of professional consulting, relatively abstract methods and models have been used which were quite alien to managers, at least until the rise of the MBA (David, et al., 2013; McDonald, 2013). Such approaches were deployed for a range of reasons such as ensuring consistency and quality (Werr, et al., 1997). This became especially important as consultancies grew in size and geographical coverage and adopted the approach, started by strategy firms such as McKinsey & Company, of recruiting large numbers of young, relatively inexperienced graduates from elite universities and business schools (McKenna, 2006).

This shift in selection criteria, combined with the 'up or out' policy of many large consulting firms, generated an image and partial reality of consultants as quite distinct from their managerial clients in educational background, age, career dynamism and security (Kipping, 2011). In countries like the UK, for example, management careers traditionally would involve few, if any, changes of employer or function, and formal management education has only taken off relatively recently (Poole, et al., 2001). Indeed, for some it would still be 'contentious' to include management as an expert group (Fincham, 2012: 209). Rather, in keeping with the UK's standard occupational classification, for example, management is, once again, associated more with hierarchical levels and a control function than a specific occupational group. However, others do include management and its sub-disciplines in classifications of expertise. Reed (1996), for instance, in an influential study of expert labour, separates consultancy from management. Consultancy is classified (along with information technology (IT) and financial consultants) under 'entrepreneurial professions' or knowledge workers who may subject managers themselves to control on behalf of capital. By contrast, Fincham (2012) focuses only on specific management occupations, with consultancy again paired with IT as a 'business service', while HRM and project management are placed in a 'quasi-professions' group (also Muzio, et al., 2011).

Such contrasting classifications of expert groups serve to highlight the contested nature of occupational boundaries (at least within academic work), but they can be useful for specific analytical purposes – as ideal types. Indeed, while the distinctions outlined above are effectively stereotypes in that they are not presented as being especially sensitive to context or variation, they serve to highlight a central theme in our analysis. As we have already noted, the traditional, expert or professional view of the management consultant compares well with contemporary images of neo-bureaucratic managers. As outlined in Table 2.3, this contrasts with images of the manager in bureaucracies (discussed above and in subsequent chapters) in terms of work activities, occupational and career dynamics and identities (see also Donnelly, 2009, on contrasting employment relations between knowledge work, such as consulting, and bureaucracy).

Management and consulting: Both the same and different but changing

We have seen how, depending on one's perspective on inclusivity/exclusivity and empirical focus, consulting and management can be seen as either quite similar or distinct. This suggests that a more pragmatic position might be to see them as *both* the same *and* different. Indeed, others do implicitly adopt an intermediate position on the relationship. In the prescriptive literature, for example, Wickham (1999: 3) sees consulting as a 'special form of management'. More concretely, Fincham (2012: 215) sees it as the 'expert arm of management' or, by focusing on its agency role for managerial clients, as 'extruded management' – the 'agent's agent' (also 2003; Sturdy, 1997a). These are helpful from a broad structural perspective, but are also reflected in part, in studies exploring identity. For example, Sturdy et al. (2009) show how consultants seek to identify *both* with their managerial clients (as 'insiders') *and* as separate from them, according to the specific context such as the phase of a project (also Kitay and Wright, 2003). Indeed, it is important to highlight that, for all but the self-employed, *external* consultants are simultaneously employees themselves, often in bureaucratic organisations, and sometimes acting as managers (see Donnelly, 2009, for a study of this tension). For example, in stark contrast to the often elite, even glamorous image of consulting, those who are consultants as a result of redundancy from a managerial position can see *consulting as failed management*. Even those in seemingly elite consulting positions can regard them as merely stepping stones to (senior) management (also McGinn, 2013). Such observations not only contribute to a more

Table 2.3 *Traditional (stereotypical) distinctions between managers and consultants*

	Middle managers in bureaucracies	'Professional' consultants
Activities	Day-to-day administration; steady state; experience-based and sector-specific knowledge; change and cross-functional work is rare and has an implementation focus Relationships based on hierarchical level (and function) with high accountability – instruction (masculine). Internally focused	Short-term, project-based and integrative work; use of qualification-based and abstract methods to advise and influence; change focused Formally independent of (client) hierarchy with low/indirect accountability; reliance on persuasion and advice (feminine); cross-functional and externally networked
Occupation/ career	Low/no management education; single firm; progression by seniority; relative job security	Special training and management education (e.g. MBA); high job/ employer mobility/ insecurity ('up or out')
Identities	Bureaucratic/hierarchical and organisation based (local)	Professional, qualification/ occupation based; externally and change oriented and distinct from (middle) managers (cosmopolitan)

Table 2.4 *Varying conceptions of the relationship between management and consulting*

Same	Consulting as management work, on behalf of owners – agents or scapegoats (Sturdy, 2011) Process consulting (facilitation, helping) as integral to management (Schein, 1987, 2009) Management as professional, with an independent role (Khurana, 2007)
Different	Consulting as advisory (staff professionals or cosmopolitans) and management as a hierarchical level with day-to-day operational responsibility (locals) Consulting as knowledge work or an entrepreneurial profession, controlling management; management as comprising organisational professions (Reed, 1996)
Both	Special, expert and externalised arm of management – the agents' agent ('extruded management'). Competes with management groups for agency role for owners ('management in parallel') (Fincham, 1999, 2012; Ruef, 2002; Sturdy, 1997a) Identify variably with managers and consulting (Sturdy, et al., 2009). Both are expert labour of different kinds (Fincham, 2012; Reed, 1996)

sophisticated 'both/and' view of consulting and management (see Table 2.4) but also reiterate the importance of being more explicit about contexts. So, for example, the idealised contrast set out above might best be seen in terms of middle managers in bureaucratic organisations in the UK up to the 1980s, compared with middle- and junior-ranking consultants in large strategy or general consulting firms at the same time. However, specification also highlights how forms of consulting and management, and therefore the relationships between them, are subject to change.

Indeed, the close relationship between consulting and management is also illustrated in their historical development, where each has stimulated changes in the other. Kipping (2002), for example, has argued that at the macro or firm level, consultancy has followed management in terms of addressing its emergent needs in waves, from scientific management, to organisation and strategy to IT. Likewise, and as noted earlier, Wood (2002), among others, has shown how both the supply of and demand for consulting were increased by corporate de-layering and downsizing of management and of specialist in-house functions – consultancy became 'externalized management' (Ruef, 2002). Furthermore, we have seen how consulting has influenced organisational design and practices through its own management activities, rather than simply through client projects, in knowledge and culture management and project working (McKenna, 2006).

Clearly, shifts in the nature of consulting pose analytical problems although change is normal in occupations more generally (Fine, 1996). As Fincham and Clark (2002: 2) note, 'no sooner are the limits of the industry identified or the composition of consultancy skills articulated than these factors (unique tasks, skills and firms) become redundant because the nature of consultancy work has shifted'. Presently, for example, the process approach to consultancy is seen as transforming into business coaching, which, in Australia at least, is sharply distinguished by practitioners from what remains as 'consulting' (see Clegg, et al., 2007). Another interpretation of this is that although facilitation methods remain common in both consulting and management, the 'non-expert', humanistic tradition of consulting has been pushed out by a more 'professional' or expert approach (Butler, 2008).

However, this 'professional' model of consulting has also changed, not least with the rise of accounting and IT firms and, more recently, via offshoring and automating expertise and research; retainer relations with clients rather than projects; and challenges to the 'blue-chip' firms, including through consultant managers (Christensen, et al., 2013). Furthermore, although we have placed emphasis here on how management is becoming similar to consulting, through emulation and incorporation, the consulting industry has also shifted towards management. This is most evident in the now-established move towards consultancy being involved in change *implementation* rather than restricting itself to advice (Morris, 2000). It is also reflected in the expansion of consulting firms' services even if these do not always come under the label of consulting *per se*. For example, some carry out work that has been outsourced by clients, especially in IT-related activities, or offer interim (change) managers on a temporary basis. Finally, developments in consulting also arise out of client concerns or criticisms rather than simply their requirements for particular products or services (Sturdy, 1997b). For example, although still a strong source of recruits generally, some large firms have shifted away from appointing young MBA graduates with limited business experience towards specialists and former managers or even experienced consultants from other firms (Sturdy, 2011).

Together with the changes in management towards neo-bureaucracy outlined earlier (which incorporate much of what was once associated with both professional and process consulting), such developments have the potential to undermine or cloud the distinctions between consulting and management. One possible view of this de-differentiation is that, much as managerialism became so successful and widespread that the special status of management and of the manager declined (Grey, 1999), so too consultancy is becoming pervasive such that the consultant identity loses distinctiveness and prestige. Certainly, as we shall see, some management groups such as HRM see a consulting identity and role as a route to increased status, but it could be that this paradoxically might be self-defeating (Wylie, et al., 2014).

CONCLUSION

This chapter began by following on from the ideal types outlined in Chapter 1 to set out a framework for analysing neo-bureaucratic management. Its components of activities/relationships, occupational dynamics and identities will provide the basis of our empirical analysis in Chapters 4–7, but we have also argued that such a focus alone is insufficient. Management should not be seen solely in terms of practices and activities but also in terms of its wider role with capitalism and modernity, notably, as a form of control. While such a view can sometimes lead to masking seemingly minor changes in practices, it can also draw attention to some of the tensions and contradictions of organising out of which further change can emerge. At the same time, we have seen how, for some, the hybrid form of neo-bureaucracy has a potential to resolve tensions, between bureaucratic and post-bureaucratic forms in particular, although others see internal conflict.

Acknowledging the difficulty of evaluating the nature and extent of change in management, we then looked at the mechanisms of change more directly. Our particular focus reflected our concern with management consulting and those developments which are bringing consulting into organisations as management practice. These developments are creating changes, not only in management, but in the relationship between management and consulting. We outlined some of the different views of consulting and of its relationship with management, including the traditional view of consultants and managers as worlds apart. We argue for a position which is distinct from this and the other dominant perspective of consulting and management as equivalent. Rather, both positions were shown to be valid, not only because of changes in their form over time but also because of the importance of adopting a similar focus to that which we applied to management as a whole, where different dimensions are held at the same time, including those held by the actors themselves, to which we now turn.

3　The research study

INTRODUCTION AND PROJECT BACKGROUND

This chapter sets out some of the background and details of the study on which the book is based. Doing this is important for two reasons. First, of course, it helps readers to understand and assess the research findings and claims made. The particular context in which research is carried out, its methods and its assumptions all inform the nature and quality of the arguments. Second, it sheds light on research practice in a manner that is not generally possible in a journal article or final research report. Not only is there less space to outline methodological issues in these formats, but the sometimes *ad hoc* and frequently emergent nature of the research process is often played down or silenced. Even in the fairly conventional account presented here, research appears far less contained, planned and controlled than that expected by many journals. Such an experience of research will be familiar to many and indeed is evident in most research methods texts and guides (Becker, 1998; Bryman, 2004; Van Maanen, 1988) but remains largely invisible in research accounts. Therefore, before outlining features of the empirical context of the research and the methods used, we briefly set out the history of the project and how it shaped the focus of this book.

Our focus on management in the form of consultancy emerged after a long period of research studying *consultancy* rather than management specifically. This background will inevitably lead to a contrast with other accounts of management and managerial work which tend to draw from a different tradition of studies (based on managers in general or according to a particular hierarchical level) (e.g. see

Matthaei, 2010; Tengblad and Vie, 2012, for detailed reviews; and Chapter 4). Initially, our focus was directed towards *external* management consultancy, where different themes were pursued from the 1990s onwards, especially those of consultants' identity and their role in management innovation (e.g. see Kitay and Wright, 2007; Sturdy, 1997b). Partly on the basis of a research neglect of *internal* consultants, and the fact that they presented a potential policy alternative to externals, an initial exploratory research project was started by one of the authors in Australia, based on interviews with individual managers in internal consulting roles. This research revealed that many of these individuals were not explicitly or exclusively based in 'consulting' units or departments. Rather, they were often specialist managers adopting consulting practices and identities, particularly in functional areas such as human resource management (HRM), where consulting formed part of a broader professionalisation project (Wright, 2008, 2009). These initial findings provided the basis for our current focus on the broader issue of management as consultancy.

The focus on HRM informed a research proposal we prepared as a joint submission to the Australian Research Council (ARC) in Australia and the Economic and Social Research Council (ESRC) in the UK in 2007. Here, attention was placed on internal consulting *groups* rather than individuals, identifying the reasons for establishing an internal consulting approach to HRM, on the forms it took and on the perceived impacts it had (see Sturdy, et al., 2013; Wylie, et al., 2014). It also included a consideration of internal consulting as an alternative approach to organisational innovation. The proposal was funded by the ESRC as a UK-only project which started in 2008 and finished in 2012. The unfunded research on individual consultants in Australia continued while the new ESRC project was adapted, partly out of choice and partly through circumstance. First, as we shall see, when a sample of internal consulting groups was being selected, they were found to exist throughout various structural and functional bases of management in organisations, rather than simply HRM. This was partly a consequence of seeking some support for research access through the UK Institute of Consultants' internal consulting group, which (as part of the Chartered Management Institute) was not exclusively HR based. It was also a consequence of our concern to widen the remit of the research with the hope of identifying new organisational forms and practices. Still, however, the focus remained on internal consulting.

The shift to a more explicit focus on management emerged over time as the fieldwork, conducted in parallel in both the UK and Australia, progressed and as we continued to review emergent literature and write up our research – that is, through abduction (Van Maanen, et al., 2007). In particular, the following themes emerged as important:

- the identification of the *consultant manager* as quite widespread in the field and as emerging in practitioner literature (e.g. Christensen, et al., 2013; Czerniawska, 2011), especially managers recruited specifically for their external consulting background and skills (Sturdy and Wright, 2008);
- the diffuse nature of boundaries and identities between management and consulting staff and their roles and responsibilities in diverse organisational settings (see also discussion in Chapter 2);
- our recognition of an unacknowledged and strong parallel in the literature between some elements of emerging post-/neo-bureaucratic forms of management and various traditional and existing forms of management consultancy;
- our view of a narrowness or partiality in the management consulting literature arising from
  - seeing *internal* consultancy in relation to its *external* counterpart rather than to management;
  - understanding the organisation of management consulting in terms of *professional service firms* rather than internal consulting units (ICUs);
  - regarding management consulting as a *profession* or change specialism rather than a management occupation or set of practices for other occupations to appropriate; and

– portraying management consulting as *elite and privileged with a mystique*, rather than also as mundane, standardised and controlled/controlling.

Such an emergent process of research is by no means unusual, but is rarely visible. Indeed, additional research foci other than management as consultancy or those of the formal project objectives were also developed from this research, such as standardisation in innovation (Wright, et al., 2012), the uncertainty of consulting organisation (Sturdy, et al., 2013) and the nature of change agency (Wylie, et al., 2014). Nevertheless, the above experiences and developments contributed to seeing the wider significance of our research in relation to changes in the nature of management or, at least, as an extreme case of emerging management forms and practices. This was initially set out in a conference paper at the European Group for Organization Studies (EGOS) conference in 2010 (Sturdy, et al., 2010) and at a *Journal of Management Studies* workshop on the future of management (Sturdy, et al., 2012). This theme has been further developed (Sturdy, et al., forthcoming), with the following chapters bringing this work together empirically through a number of related themes.

RESEARCH DESIGN: THE SAMPLE

As noted in Chapter 2, there is a long tradition of research on management and the nature of managerial work activities, but for us, this focus was emergent. Therefore, we did not seek to add to existing studies of managerial work or make generalisable claims about management. Rather, our initial focus was on a largely neglected group – internal consultants – and therefore was exploratory in nature, developing into what we believe is the first ever study of consultant managers. In this sense, it is different from large-scale and wide-ranging studies of diverse management groups (Morris, et al., 2008; Poole, et al., 2001) but comparable with many other studies which have had a more focused approach, using R&D, project or interim managers, CEOs or particular sectors to provide insight into management in general (Hodgson, 2002; Inkson, et al., 2001; Vie, 2010). It is thus a study of both management *and* consulting.

Overall, our approach to analysing the role and perceived impact of management as consulting within organisations was qualitative, with a focus on both individual actors (mostly in Australia) and units (mostly in the UK). It comprised semi-structured interviews with internal consultants, as well as use of documentary data. In the UK study, this was supplemented with interviews with some clients and sponsors (senior managers supporting a consulting approach), especially within four case-study sites (financial services, health care, telecommunications and a government department), where a limited amount of observation was also carried out (see later sections and Wright, et al., 2012). In total, we undertook 136 semi-structured interviews (91 in the UK and 45 in Australia) of 45–120 minutes in over 50 organisations (24 in the UK and 30 in Australia). As we shall see, these included managers from a range of occupational and functional specialisms, including operational efficiency, strategy, organisational development (OD) and HRM, with the latter two being the primary focus in the Australian context and efficiency as dominant in the UK. The sectors in which they worked also varied and included multinational corporations in financial services and telecommunications as well as manufacturing firms, local and national government departments and health care organisations (see Table 3.1 for a combined summary and Appendices 1 and 2 for overviews of UK and Australian samples, respectively). The particular profile of our sample is by no means representative (and this was not the intention), with the public sector and financial services probably over-represented in the UK and manufacturing under-represented, and the public sector under-represented in Australia. In both contexts, we found no evidence of the consultant manager role in small- or medium-sized organisations although they were not specifically targeted. Nevertheless, in the context of studies of management work, very few have covered such a range of sectors or such a large number of respondents. For example, a detailed review and analysis of such research (Matthaei, 2010) identified only 19 from 70

Table 3.1 *Summary of research data*

Industry sector	Organisations operating in UK and Australia	Interviews	Indicative job titles	With external consulting experience
Manufacturing, mining and resources	Mining company (Australian MNC); oil processor (US MNC); pharmaceutical manufacturer (European MNC); engineering company (US MNC); automobile manufacturer (Asian MNC)	9	Best practice consultant; OD manager; learning and development (L&D) consultant; general manager HR	6
Retail	Supermarket chain (Australia); electricity retailer (Australia)	4	HR/OD manager; HR business partner; change implementation manager	1
Transport and storage	Rail firm (UK); equipment hire (Australia); airline (Australia)	8	Strategic analyst; business improvement consultant; change manager	5
Finance and insurance	Bank (UK MNC); building society (UK); insurance company (UK); investment bank (European	35	Org. change consultant; consultant people and performance; employee	13

	MNC); retail bank (Australian MNC); insurance company (Australian); global financial services (US MNC)		engagement manager; senior project manager	
Information and telecommunications	Telecom (UK); media (UK); IT company (US MNC); telecom (European MNC)	24	Leader culture and capability; group HR manager; OD and change director	9
Business services	Business support (US MNC); law firm (Australian); accounting and consulting firm (global partnership)	9	L&D manager; director people and performance; HR global services manager	3
Public administration	Local government (UK); central government (UK); government agencies (UK); local government (Australian)	25	Divisional manager strategy; business improvement director; corporate assurance manager; senior analyst	6
Health care and education	Hospital (UK); health care trust (UK); health institute (UK); private health care (UK); hospital (Australian); university (Australian)	22	Business consultant; team coach; project manager; manager L&D; OD manager	3
Total		136		46

studies involving more than 100 managers and 12 out of 62 covering both private and public sectors.

In the context of studies of consulting, this research is, to our knowledge, the largest ever exploration of internal consultancy and one of the largest of consulting in general. However, given that there is no general agreement on what constitutes internal (or external) consulting (Fincham and Clark, 2002) and no known database, the representativeness of the sample for even this subgroup of managers cannot be established precisely. There are some bodies which seek to organise internal consulting. For example, in the USA, the Association of Internal Management Consultants holds an annual conference and is seeking to develop internationally (www.aimc.org), while in the UK, there was a small expert group on internal consulting within the Institute of Consulting (IoC) (www.iconsulting.org.uk). However, both have very limited coverage. As a consequence, any estimates of the number of internal consultants should be treated with extreme caution. For example, Warr (formerly Chair of the UK IoC internal consulting group) estimated that 'around 30 per cent of large organisations have internal consulting functions' and that 10 per cent of consultants are internals (cited in O'Mahoney, 2010: 85). In Germany, Mohe (2005: 362) suggested that 'about 75% of German publicly traded companies employ their own consulting staff'. But in each case the source is not clear. As regards individual consultant managers, even less is known. Here, as noted earlier, Christensen et al. (2013: 110) suggest from a US context that 'precise data are not publicly available, but we know that many companies have hired small armies of former consultants' as managers. The problem is exacerbated by the fact that the stigma of the term 'consulting'/'consultant' in certain contexts means that numbers are necessarily uncertain. As we noted in Chapter 2, internal consultancy is increasingly hidden behind other labels.

In keeping with such observations, we adopted a liberal definition of consultant managers which included not only those who were clearly designated as internal consultants via their job or unit title (e.g.

'business improvement consultant') but also other specialist staff who provided advice, facilitation and expertise to operational managers and staff, typically on a project basis involving consulting skills (Scott, 2000). They would also recognise that their role could be seen in relation to consulting, even if they did not always or primarily identify themselves as consultants/consultancy.

This broad approach, combined with the fact that internal consulting is an activity which lacks clear definition, institutionalisation and standing, meant that the task of identifying individuals and consulting units was very difficult. Potential research sites were initially found through an analysis of articles in professional publications and websites, personal networks and, in the UK, through support from the IoC internal consulting special interest group (six organisations, including two of the case studies). However, difficulties also arose from the organisationally insecure nature of units and roles (see also Appendix 3; Sturdy, et al., 2013). This meant that they often had a short lifespan. For example, units would be identified, only to find that they had been disbanded (see also Chapter 7).

Following the tradition of organisational or 'staff professionals' more generally (Dalton, 1950; Daudigeos, 2013), our respondents typically did not have a formal line management responsibility for changes as some other managers in the organisations might have done. Of course, such a group could be classified as simply traditional internal consultants rather than as consultant managers as well, but this would be misleading for various reasons. First, at a general level and as discussed in the previous chapter, the common distinction between (external) consultants and managers is problematic or at least blurred (Sturdy, et al., 2009). Second, in our particular contexts, including in what might be seen as the strongest forms of management as consultancy, the individuals or units would not have such a title or define themselves primarily in such terms. For example, unit titles included 'transformation delivery', 'corporate assurance' and 'performance improvement', while individuals used labels such as 'project manager', 'business analyst', 'leader' or some kind of standard management title (see Appendices 1–3). Furthermore and third, individual respondents could be considered as conventional managers in terms of

- being continuing salaried employees who typically (but not always) saw consultancy as part of their managerial role;
- being mostly based within operational divisions and cost centre structures, not working with a free-floating or strict market-based approach (even if internal market language was often used such as 'clients');
- sometimes acting in a quasi-policing (effectively, a hierarchical) role, ensuring that strategic change objectives such as cost savings were met, including through involvement in change implementation.

As intimated above, there was both variation and commonality within our sample. This is illustrated in more detail in the following summary of both the ICUs studied in the UK and the individual consultants interviewed in Australia.

Functional focus of UK internal consulting units
The ICUs drew upon sometimes very different knowledge bases and/or consultancy traditions. Before outlining these, it is important to highlight how such traditions are broad categorisations and by no means always mutually exclusive. They can be combined as part of a range of services or even within the same project and consultant. We have divided the areas into those which were most commonly represented in our data: operational efficiency, organisational development, strategic analysis and project management.

In keeping with the claimed impacts around process improvement and cost savings, just over half of ICUs drew their identity from an *operational efficiency* background. This included practices which were focused around improving systems or processes so that information and/or material can be moved through the organisation more efficiently (Chase and Kumar, 2005). Inevitably, this can cover a huge range of interventions, although a typical example was for ICUs to be asked to evaluate what type of work was being undertaken by a specific team and how that might be either redistributed across the organisation, improved or outsourced. In other instances, ICUs were able to use efficiency-based methodologies to remove 'unnecessary' stages from a process to make it less complex. ICUs drawing on this tradition often required their consultants to have advanced skills in the use of formal systems improvement methodologies (e.g. Lean, Six Sigma).

A second tradition which ICUs drew upon was that of organisational development (OD), including the use of psychology-based analytical tools and, broadly speaking, more of an interest or focus on people rather than work processes (Schein, 1969; Worren, et al., 1999). Again, this term covered a multitude of different interventions, although some examples were specific attempts at conflict resolution or improving team-working skills across the organisation, through the facilitation of team away days and the like. Indeed, this tradition often explicitly (though not exclusively) drew on the process consultancy approach – the notion of 'helping people to help themselves' rather than providing expert advice. Consultants here were required to have developed facilitation skills which on occasion required them to use well-defined methodologies, but with outcomes likely to be more diffuse (e.g. team harmony and understanding) and localised. This tradition connected strongly with pursuing functional integration discussed in Chapter 1 with regard to neo-bureaucracy, although this was not always an explicit aim of consulting projects.

A third consultancy tradition, associated with a minority of cases, was that of *strategic analysis* and development (Nadler and Slywotzky, 2005). Those ICUs that operated in this area were often charged with analysing particular features of the organisation's external environment in order to make recommendations about strategic direction and plans. Alternatively, ICUs could be used to collate internal data. It was rare for them to engage directly in the strategy development process although many aspired to this activity, suggesting that internal consultancy as a whole may be perceived as something that operated in a different domain from the explicitly strategic.

Finally, a number of ICUs emerged from a relatively new explicit form of management consultancy – *project management*. Clearly, the ability to manage change programmes and projects is key in other consulting traditions (Caldwell, 2005), but ICUs embedded in this domain offered a set of skills as a service across the organisation – meaning that any project in any area requiring some form of coordination could be taken on. In some cases, project management was not simply offered as a management service, but as a skill to be transferred to clients through training. Also, project (and programme) management was typically structurally distinguished from other consultancy services. Indeed, many consultants would draw sharp distinctions between their expertise and someone who is 'just a project manager'. Key differentiators here were the greater emphasis on relationship management in consultancy and the greater accountability associated with project management.

Size and structural location of internal consulting groups

As well as variety in the work of ICUs, their size differed considerably (see Appendix 3). Staff numbers ranged from a solitary internal consultant, to a unit which included around 200 individuals. There were slightly more examples of smaller units (less than ten internal consultants) within our sample, although there was no obvious link between size and other features such as consulting tradition. Rather, the size of ICUs fitted specific organisational characteristics and dynamics.

A more pronounced form of variation between ICUs was their structural location – the hierarchical and functional base from which they operated. These were important to ICUs for a number of reasons, including the nature of their relationships with clients and how they were perceived politically across the organisation (see Chapter 5). Some practitioners feel that ICUs should have a free-floating role, not attached to a particular operational division. Our research found that that this was often not the case, certainly in large organisations where control over budgets and decentralisation of service functions meant that ICUs had to belong somewhere. Although typically complex in practice, we identified three broad types of structural location:

1. *Centralised and 'independent' – part of corporate function or CEO support unit*: 'Centralised' can often be a confusing term in modern network-based structures in that some organisations claim a number of centres or none at all. Nevertheless, some hierarchy is typically evident, and we categorised as centralised and independent those ICUs that had a clear association with the CEOs or had a pan-organisational remit. 'Independent' in this sense refers to the ICUs being separate from any specific managerial/operational or central service function and so potentially were more able to consider a wider range of activities. This was important to them because they were less constrained and often experienced greater credibility through links to the most senior management. However, and as we shall see in Chapter 5, senior sponsorship carried risks as well, in being seen as a compliance unit more than a professional service provider to clients.

2. *Centralised service function – part of a cross-organisational service function (e.g. HR, information technology (IT))*: A contrasting group of ICUs were centralised in the sense that they were able to operate across the organisation, but they were embedded in what might be termed a service function – that is, a department that offers specific services to operational or customer facing departments, with HR, IT and legal services being the best examples. Interestingly, there were some examples where being part of a service function did not necessarily match the perceptions that ICUs had of themselves, meaning it could come into conflict with their identity as consultants. In one organisation, a series of restructures led to the ICU becoming part of the HR function even though there were some concerns among the internal consultants that this was a long way from the process efficiency work the group were doing. In another case, consultants were located within IT, but worked in the fields of strategy and organisational change in order to enhance the wider credibility of, and demand for, the IT function.

3. *Divisional – located within an operational/customer-facing division*: A third group of ICUs were based in customer-facing or operational divisions. There were fewer of these cases, and each was in a large organisation (employing over 20,000 people). For the ICU, this meant that their role was limited to this division (although it is important to note that some of the divisions were larger than the whole organisation in which other ICUs operated). Although there were no clear advantages or disadvantages to being a divisional ICU, there was some evidence to suggest that the greater proximity to customers or service delivery ensured that the ICU was seen to be engaged in more overtly 'business critical' work.

Overview of individuals in the Australian sample

While the Australian data focused more on individual consultant managers, rather than those in designated internal consulting units, like the UK data, the Australian respondents came from a diversity of industries and business activities (see Appendix 2). Again, we focused on large businesses, including major corporations and multinational businesses in financial and professional business services, manufacturing, resources, telecommunications, retail, education, transport and industrial services. Respondents were selected on the basis of being specialist full-time managers who assisted other organisational employees in solving problems and implementing change through the provision of advice and expertise rather than direct authority. In many cases, respondents' job titles indicated their consulting role, while for others the concept of internal consultant or consultant manager was one they implicitly recognised and identified with. While the Australian interviews initially concentrated on those with a focus on human resource and OD issues, later interviews were broadened to include consultant managers engaged in other functional areas such as operational efficiency, IT implementation and business strategy. Building on the initial interviews, several small case studies of internal consulting groups were also developed which served to supplement the individual perspectives. This included an operational efficiency consulting unit in a global telecommunications company, a culture change group in a major bank and an IT implementation group at a food manufacturer (Wright, et al., 2012).

Given the focus on individuals in the Australian interviews, it was also possible to explore in greater depth individuals' job histories and careers. One important theme that emerged in this respect was the 'zigzag' nature of job changes and movement between external and internal consulting – akin to the marketised careers identified as part of the ideal type of neo-bureaucracy. For example, about half of the Australian respondents also had prior experience as external management consultants, either working for large global consulting firms or having spent some time as solo consultants and contractors, prior to their consultant manager roles. The relationship between consultant managers within organisations and external management consultants is a theme we explore in Chapters 5 and 6 in particular, with regard to relationship development and knowledge and the career and occupational dynamics of the consultant manager.

We can see from the above summary of both the UK and Australian samples something of their characteristics, and further detail will be revealed in the following chapters. This includes variation in the extent to which consulting was a central part of job/unit roles and identities and to which hierarchical responsibility for organisational changes was assumed. Likewise, there were differences in terms of whether consulting practices and units were set up explicitly in line with external consulting models and, similarly, whether individuals had previously worked as external consultants or simply saw consultancy as a convenient way to start, develop or end a managerial career. However, while cognisant and sensitive to such variations, our exploratory approach to researching a new group of actors led us to focus mostly on common themes in our analysis, an activity to which we now turn.

DATA ANALYSIS

The research team (the authors of this volume) were all involved in data collection and analysis, with UK–Australia collaboration achieved through email, occasional meetings (at conferences, for example, and short visits) and conversations using Skype. Interviews were conducted at respondents' firms, most of which were located in London and the South East of England in the UK and the metropolitan area of Sydney in Australia. Interviewees were guaranteed anonymity for themselves and their employer. The interviews were almost all recorded electronically and then transcribed professionally. In addition, handwritten notes were taken, including from some observations, and often supplemented by relevant documentary data. These included organisation charts, change methodologies, marketing materials, work programmes and reports, and were more extensive in the case studies than with one-off interviews.

We began by coding transcripts and fieldwork notes, focusing particularly on the broad research project objectives such as interviewees' perceptions of their structural position, work background, current work activities and impact. In the UK interviews, particular attention was also given to the history and organisation of their unit or group. In keeping with the emergent and exploratory nature of the research, later stages of coding involved a more iterative or abductive interrogation of the data (Van Maanen, et al., 2007). This led to the development of different conceptual themes and, ultimately, research outputs. For example, in the UK, the uncertainty of the units was explored and analysed (Sturdy, et al., 2013), along with the consultants'/units' need to secure internal credibility around change agency capability (Wylie, et al., 2014; see also Appendix 3). Similarly, with a focus on case-study data, we examined standardisation and innovation in both the UK and Australia (Wright, et al., 2012; see also Appendix 4). Finally, with the early Australian data, themes of interactions with external consultants and the recruitment of former externals were initially explored in relation to knowledge brokering and enterprise discourse (Sturdy and Wright, 2008, 2011).

As our focus on management emerged, we continued this iterative process of analysis, identifying key themes or higher-level categories within which to organise our coding concepts. For example, in terms of the higher-order category of 'work activities', a subsidiary coding concept involved the interaction of consultant managers with external actors or internal relationship management. Similarly, we linked our concerns with occupation, career and identity to a broad number of concepts from our coding and from literature on management and neo-bureaucracy (see also Sturdy, et al., 2014, forthcoming). These became organising themes within our interrogation of the data. In seeking a measure of construct validity or confidence, we reviewed each other's coding choices. Also, our overall interpretation of organisational cases was typically fed back to key informants. This was achieved in different ways and to different degrees. With the UK case studies, it was easier to conduct a dialogue as the research progressed and to amass sufficient data to feedback in an organisation-specific way. With individuals, this was more difficult, so feedback was sometimes given through open, interim and final project workshops on the aggregate findings and, ultimately, the distribution of a report for research users (see Sturdy and Wylie, 2011). In all cases, particular attention was given to protecting the anonymity of individual informants and their organisations as appropriate.

The interview transcripts and associated documentation resulted in an extensive amount of rich and detailed qualitative data amounting to over 4,000 pages of text. The subsequent coding and analysis organised this in different ways and added to the data set overall. We then had choices over how to use and present our findings and, in particular, which data to select to illustrate wider conceptual themes and claims. As is common in such research, only a fraction of the data and analysis is used in research outputs. For example, little of the documentary data collected was explicitly cited, but it did provide valuable background. Even in the form of a research monograph such as this one, where there is scope to go into more detail and depth, this selectivity remains. The choices made are important in shaping the subsequent account. For example, our focus on common themes leads to a more universalist style regardless of any cautions given about generalisability. To focus more on differences would strengthen the importance of context, but possibly at the expense of a clear and strong argument. It would also suit a less exploratory research approach. The following are four key choices we made in constructing this account and their associated rationales:

1. *Qualitative insight over explicit quantification and correlation*: Contrary to popular perceptions, quantification is evident in almost all qualitative research (Cicourel, 1964), reflected in the use of words such as 'sometimes', 'often', 'mostly' and 'rarely'. This implicitness could imply a lack of methodological rigour and does require a measure of trust in the researchers on the part of readers. We did engage in some quantification in our analysis in order to check whether or not our impressions from specific data were reflected more widely in the sample (see, e.g., Appendix 1). However, even within a positivist framing, any explicit or advanced quantification would be unwarranted and could perhaps give a false impression of generalisability. First, and as we have seen, there is no way of establishing the representativeness of our sample. Second, our research approach was exploratory and dual focused. Interviews were semi-structured, and many of our research themes were emergent. This all meant that the same questions or observations were not systematically addressed to, or revealed from, respondents. For similar reasons, we did not engage in analysis to relate or compare systematically findings by gender, sector or other categories. The result is that we offer a form of analysis directed at generating insight and emergent themes rather than statistically significant comparative findings.

2. *Integration of case study and other interview data*: As outlined above, in the UK research design, the aim was to combine a broad interview-based study with four in-depth case studies. This was achieved, although the level of access gained allowed only minimal observation of the direct work of consultant managers. What the

case-study research provided, however, was the opportunity to interview other participants such as clients and sponsors and to identify work practices and methods in greater detail. It also enabled continuing engagement with respondents, for over two years in one case. At the same time, in the Australian research, even though the focus was more on individuals, interviewing a number of them in the same organisation allowed for some case-study analysis. Thus, we were able to combine Australian and UK cases in an analysis of standardisation, with one case common across both contexts (see Appendix 4 and Wright, et al., 2012).

However, in presenting our analysis here (and elsewhere), we have chosen to integrate case study and other interview data. This is because the themes explored have been common across both approaches such that insights were often gained as much through one-off interviews as more intensive data collection. For example, we followed a specific consulting project in one case in depth for over two weeks and interviewed all the participants. This generated some insights into consulting work in general, but little on the nature of management as consulting. Similarly, if we had been more concerned with micro practices or engagement with the idiosyncrasies of contexts, an alternative approach would have been to present data in terms of an initial overview followed by an exploration of specific issues through the case-study data. Again, our exploratory and emergent approach did not allow for such control in generating data.

3. *Combining an individual/organisational focus with broad management functions at the expense of wider institutional and national contexts*: As outlined in Chapter 2, we have been concerned to explore management in a way which attends both to the details of its organisational practices and to its wider, more abstract role, in terms of control and tensions. In doing so, there is a danger of neglecting what lies between these levels of analysis, the wider institutional context in particular. This might be especially significant when considering data from different countries such as in this research. However, in our data analysis, we found no instances when differences appeared systematically to relate to the contrasting *national*

context. This could be for a range of reasons. First, the data were drawn from contexts that were highly varied in different ways. As we have seen, there was more of an emphasis on HRM and less representation of the public sector with the Australian respondents and so any nationally specific variations could be hidden within this variety. Second, in many and perhaps important ways, the two national contexts and research samples are similar. In particular, the samples comprised mostly large organisations, including many multinationals. Although such organisations are by no means socially dis-embedded, they are more likely to be sensitive to transnational practices. In addition, notwithstanding geographical distance and other important differences, the UK and Australia are comparable, in terms of language, culture, neo-liberal business ideology and institutional connections derived from a common colonial history (Robertson and Singleton, 2001). The final possible reason why national variation was not evident was because our chosen method of data collection, focused on the individual and organisation levels, prevented it from coming to the fore. However, it is important to emphasise that broad and common changes in management and organisations towards different elements of neo-bureaucracy have been identified across many 'advanced' capitalist economies, albeit to different degrees (Morris, et al., 2008).

4. *Selective use of data*: In the chapters that follow, given the wide scope of our empirical coverage, we use only illustrative quotes and examples (preserving organisational and individual anonymity) to provide insight into management as consultancy and, at the same time, some of the ways in which new forms and tensions of neo-bureaucratic management occur. As noted earlier, all research reporting (and data collection) is highly selective. However, here, our dual focus (on individuals and units) meant that we had to decide how best to represent the data against the different emergent themes. For example, one option was to segregate the data according to an area of research focus such as using the individual-based Australian data in relation to identities and careers, while using UK data in relation to work practices and methods. To an extent, this is evident in that data are concentrated

in this way. However, we also found considerable overlap in the data collected. As a consequence, we have not segregated the data between chapters and themes, but integrated them. There was only one theme which was not covered in some way in both contexts (consulting unit structures as outlined above), and this is not a key element of our concerns here and has been written up elsewhere (Sturdy, et al., 2013). Furthermore, although combining two distinct, albeit closely related, projects can be seen as problematic, it has the advantage of highlighting how observed phenomena are not restricted to one particular context.

CONCLUSION

In this chapter we have provided some of the background to the research projects upon which the following chapters are based, as well as details of the research methods used and research choices made. The main purpose in doing this has been to provide some contextual information for readers to draw on when assessing the research findings and conclusions. At the same time, we have emphasised how emergent and iterative the research process has been, especially in terms of the development of our principal focus on management as consultancy. This serves not only as further contextual detail but also to outline how research in practice can depart quite considerably from that found in formalised accounts such as in many journal articles.

Part of the process of developing an understanding of research accounts requires details of how the research was conducted, but this also allows for a consideration of the strengths and weaknesses evident in any research work. We shall return to these briefly in our concluding chapter, when considering the need for further research. However, here we can highlight some of the distinguishing features and foci of our project, including some weaknesses and implied areas of neglect. In particular, in the following chapters, we

- aim to explore management work through the lenses of consulting and neo-bureaucracy via an extreme case, as well as through critical traditions which examine contradiction and control. As a result,

practice perspectives and attention to other forms of management
are less apparent, including non-consultant managers in the same
organisations;

- seek to adopt a distinctive approach to consulting in general and
internal consulting in particular that departs from previous reference points in the literature such as elites, professional service firms
and *external* management consulting (see also Chapter 1);
- rely primarily on interview data, mostly with consultant managers
and on cross-sectional research providing wide-ranging insights.
However, this approach limits exposure to consultancy in action
and other voices, including those subject to control through management as consultancy;
- focus on diverse contexts covered with some additional depth
through case studies, but these data are not representative, generalisable or always comparable, especially given the diffuse nature of
occupational boundaries;
- adopt an exploratory approach and focus on common themes combined with a wide breadth of data sources. However, this means
limited attention was given to contextual variation within and
between research samples.

Notwithstanding some of the above limitations, the research offers
insights into contemporary management practice through a large-scale
study and the extreme case of the consultant manager. More specifically and theoretically, we hope that our account shows how neo-
bureaucracy as a hybrid comprises both new and classic tensions of
management and organisation, and how consultancy is intimately
connected to management.

4 The work activities of the consultant manager

INTRODUCTION
In this chapter we explore some of the activities of consultant managers and their relationship to the ideal type of neo-bureaucracy outlined earlier. The focus on activities is a key aspect of the position we have adopted in relation to the nature of management. To recap, we argued in Chapter 2 that seeking to understand what managers do ('management as practice') (Tengblad and Vie, 2012) can be contrasted with an emphasis on the abstract and political nature of management and its location within broader social and historical contexts (Alvesson and Willmott, 2012). These two approaches represent different perspectives on management. In the case of the former, there is a tendency for management to be seen as a set of more or less neutral techniques aimed at enhancing organisational efficiency, whereas in the latter it is considered a mechanism of control and exploitation and even 'a form of thought and activity which is being used to justify considerable cruelty and inequality' (Parker, 2002: 9). Although many approaches tend to revert to a view of management as its practices (see Grey, 1999), our position is that a focus on both dimensions is necessary, not least because management's 'causal powers' (Tsoukas, 1994) are legitimised by its activities, roles and tasks (Willmott, 1996).

In order to draw out some of the wider implications of management as consultancy (such as occupational connections and identities), we first need to explore the nature of consultant manager roles and responsibilities and the extent to which neo-bureaucracy might extend tensions and ambiguities within management and/or lead to new ones. To do this we develop the framework introduced in Chapter 2, which considers the purpose, organisation and relationships of management work. Using this classification, we then examine the aims and content of consultant managers' work and its organisation and structure. While there are some similarities with the picture of traditional bureaucratic management, we also identify significant differences suggestive of an emergent hybrid role of the neo-bureaucratic manager. This theme of similarity and difference in the work of consultant managers is further developed in the following chapters such as Chapter 5, which explores the nature of internal and external work relationships that consultant managers develop.

CLASSIFYING MANAGEMENT ACTIVITIES: PURPOSE, STRUCTURE AND RELATIONSHIPS

In Chapter 2, we argued that studies of managerial work vary considerably in terms of context and methodology, making it very difficult to build a coherent understanding of management activities (Hales, 1986). Indeed, attempts to draw overall conclusions about key features and the degree of change in these activities over time are inevitably broad and partial (Tengblad and Vie, 2012). Nonetheless, we proposed the following classification of management work activity which we used to set out key features of neo-bureaucratic management:

1. What do managers do, or what is the *purpose* and *content* of their activities?
2. How do managers work, or how do managers *organise* and *structure* their work?
3. With whom do managers work, or what is the nature of the *relationships* managers have?

Our aim in this and the following chapter is to use these questions to examine the work of consultant managers in more depth and contrast it with that of the traditional or bureaucratic manager. However, before we turn to the findings of our study, it is necessary to set out in a little more detail how existing empirical studies of management have described its purpose, structure and relationships.

The question of 'what do managers do' seeks to understand how the content or *purpose* of managerial activities can be categorised in terms of subject area or functional discipline. This is arguably the most problematic question to answer given the variety of approaches adopted in the managerial work literature. Differences in context (national, cultural and industry), participants (supervisors/executives) and methodologies (self-reporting, direct observation) produce differences in the categorisation of the content of managerial work. Some case studies use broad functional associations, allied with more specific distinctions from classical management theory. For example, Horne and Lupton (1965) asked their respondents to categorise any activity as either 'formulating', 'organising', 'unifying' or 'regulating', as well as to locate it within a functional domain (e.g. commercial, sales, accounting). Hales (2002) adopted a similar approach, asking managers to record activities as either staff administration (e.g. supervision and work allocation), general administration (e.g. work planning, problem-solving) or management of routine information (e.g. reporting and disseminating information). Other studies which closely follow Mintzberg's (1973) classification categorise the purpose of each managerial interaction (Martinko and Gardner, 1990; Tengblad, 2006; Vie, 2010). This includes such things as the giving or receiving of information, scheduling and negotiation, although the specific definitions of these are less clear – a problem of classification recognised within the literature (Hales and Tamangani, 1996).

Despite these problems, and more general concerns about the use of self-reporting data, there are commonalities across these studies in terms of the purpose of management activity. First, it is evident that management work is varied and involves a range of activities (Mintzberg, 1973; Tengblad and Vie, 2012). Second, across this variety, the general purpose of management work is mainly operational, routine and administrative and based around the reporting of performance data (Hales, 2002; Hales and Tamangani, 1996). Studies of management work have also consistently demonstrated that managers work primarily on short-term and immediate issues (Horne and

Lupton, 1965), with an emphasis on localised and technical concerns rather than developmental ones (Tengblad and Vie, 2012). Consequently, and taking account of the problems of categorising managerial work undertaken in very different contexts, the purpose or content of (traditional/bureaucratic) management activities can be characterised as low level, functionally based, administrative and concerned with sustaining operational procedures, at least at the middle levels.

The second question used to classify management activity considers 'how do managers work?' (Hales, 1986). We refer to this as the *organisation and structure* of management activity – meaning how managers arrange or order their work in order to deliver its content. Management studies have primarily considered issues of organisation by measuring the time allocated to different tasks (Burns, 1954; Mintzberg, 1973; Tengblad, 2006; Vie, 2010). This is mainly done to indicate which activities are the most common and can also be used to assess how far the purpose of managerial work may have changed over time (Tengblad, 2006). Other issues considered are the location in which activities take place and also the type of communication managers engage in (Mintzberg, 1973; Noordegraaf, 2000). Findings from the analysis of these aspects have consistently suggested that management activity can be frantic, with very little time spent on individual tasks and managers being required to deal with regular interruptions (Kotter, 1999). In addition, communications were primarily verbal and focused on short-term immediate problem-solving – what Mintzberg (1973) refers to as a preference among managers for 'live action' and which has been supplemented by the use of email and other IT-based communication media (Matthaei, 2010). The indication then is that management work is often fragmented, disorganised and involves little in the way of longer-term planning or innovation. Furthermore, Tengblad and Vie (2012) conclude that, contrary to the bureaucratic ideal, managers do not work systematically and are resistant to the use of rational models intended to allow them to work in a more structured fashion.

The third dimension of management activity is concerned with the *nature of relationships* – or the question of with whom managers work. Studies of management work have consistently explored how far different activities require managers to interact with others in the organisation, both vertically and horizontally (Horne and Lupton, 1965; Mintzberg, 1973; Noordegraaf, 2000; Tengblad and Vie, 2012). For example, Vie (2010), following Mintzberg (1973), measures the amount of time managers spend in verbal contact with subordinates, superiors, peers and clients. The themes that have emerged suggest that hierarchical relationships are a central feature of traditional management activity, with the majority of time spent with subordinates and superiors (Vie, 2010). Also, the expectations about the nature of managerial work, the priority given to certain activities and an emphasis on maintaining rules and procedures and reporting performance data have all been related to the demands placed on managers by hierarchical relationships (Hales and Tamangani, 1996; Noordegraaf, 2000). In addition, informally at least, lateral relationships impact upon management activity (Sayles, 1964). For example, a number of studies have stressed that management activity is reliant on networks within the organisation and that managers also operate in political environments where they compete with each other to secure promotions and advantage (Buchanan and Badham, 1999; Jackall, 1988; Pettigrew, 1973, 1985).

Table 4.1 summarises some of the features of traditional management activity based on the framework of *purpose/content, organisation/structure* and *relationships*. It is important to acknowledge that these dimensions are interconnected, meaning, for example, that the purpose and organisation of management activities may be derived from the nature of specific relationships in any given context. However, by making these distinctions, we are able to draw out particular aspects of management activities and provide a basis through which we can compare the activities of consultant managers with those of both the ideal type of a bureaucratic manager and the post-bureaucratic reaction to that view. In the following sections, we

Table 4.1 *Ideal typical features of management activity*

Dimension of management activity	Key question	Variables/measures	Main features of management activity
Purpose/content	What do managers do?	Functional categorisation	Low level
		Administrative activities	Functionally based
		'Core' management functions (planning, organising, coordinating, control of resources)	Administrative
			Concerned with sustaining operational procedures
Organisation/ structure	How do managers work?	Time spent on activities	Fragmented
		Location of activities	Disorganised
		Methods of communication	Limited evidence of long-term planning
			Resistance to systematic and structured methods
Relationships	With whom do they work?	Number of interactions – horizontal (e.g. with other managers) and vertical (with subordinates and senior managers)	Hierarchical relationships critical to expectations, prioritisation and emphasis on rules and procedures
			Lateral relationships dominated by political activity
			Few external links

explore the first two dimensions of consultant managers' work activities – that is, the purpose and content of their work, its organisation and its structure. The issue of relationships is developed in Chapter 5.

WHAT DO CONSULTANT MANAGERS DO? CHANGE, INTEGRATION AND STRATEGIC EFFICIENCY

As we have seen, the common response to the question of 'what do managers do' is to place emphasis on the variety of different managerial activities. At the same time, management work has been limited in terms of its scope, primarily focused on the maintenance of operating procedures. As outlined in Chapter 3, the consultant managers and their groups which we studied in both the UK and Australia were also involved in a broad range of activities, which included a focus on improving operational efficiency, organisational development (OD), strategic analysis and development and project management. Their structural location and number could also vary widely, and the initiatives they undertook ranged from small, one-off tasks for a specific internal 'client' manager through to organisation-wide transformations that might span years. Nevertheless, despite this diversity in activities, a number of central themes underpinned the work of consultant managers. These included the concepts of change and change management, the link to business strategy and project and broader programme management, themes which, as we outlined in Chapters 1 and 2, are closely associated with neo-bureaucracy.

Change management

Unlike the traditional model of the bureaucratic manager, a defining characteristic of the consultant managers in our study was an emphasis on *change*. In line with broader debates about the 'fetish' of change and change management (Sturdy and Grey, 2003) and the importance of innovation within post-bureaucratic discourse (du Gay, 2004), consultant managers expected to be engaged in activities that led to identifiable alterations in the operation of their organisation.

This apparent rejection of the status quo, or of steady-state activities, aligns with arguments about the need to shift away from the 'iron cage of bureaucracy' – a position represented in our model of neo-bureaucracy as a form of *managed improvisation*. Certainly among the consultant managers we studied, 'change' became a recurring justification or explanation for their role. This was summed up by Mike, a business consultant in CommsCo, who described his role as

> always thinking that it's about change and improvement, and
> the delivery of big, substantial pieces of work that are going to
> have some very clear end benefit for the organisation, be it a
> reduction in cost or be it an improvement in an aspect of
> service, whatever that clear end-gate is, i.e. facilitating and
> implementing change.

Change conceived in this way shifts from being an abstract notion of how an organisation needs to adapt to its environment to an observable activity which can form much of the content of a consultant manager's activity. Change management is often regarded as a central feature of management consultancy (Werr, et al., 1997), with large consultancy firms offering it as a specialist activity. In a similar vein consultant managers were considered to be in possession of distinct skills and knowledge required to deliver change – and were best placed to do this free from the operational constraints of traditional management roles and activities. For example, in ArtsCo, Alicia, a former management consultant, explained that the reason for her being asked to create an internal change team was that 'the board said, "We want ArtsCo to demonstrate increased capability around change, and we want to identify poor capability around change and we want you to drive that on"'. One of the outcomes of this process at ArtsCo was that change management became

an activity around which consultant managers could establish
some shared identity and internal networks, as Alicia went on to
describe:

> We've always run a change network [for] people who are heavily
> involved in change out in the business. They may not have a change
> management title, and therefore we need to bring them into the
> community. It largely stimulates debate and provides a place for
> people to come ... where they feel part of a movement of change in
> the organisation.

The implication of this was that activity involving change was distinct
from typical management activities and so indicative of emerging
forms of neo-bureaucracy. Indeed, an outsider status and one separate
from 'business as usual' was a key part of the identity of the consultant
manager (see Chapter 6).

In terms of change activities and, again, in line with the notion
of *managed improvisation*, consultant managers were often used to
bringing a degree of focus and clarity to the change process that might
otherwise not be there. For example, in HealthCo2, the internal
consulting unit (ICU) described its change-based activities in promotional material as follows: '[The internal consulting unit will] work
with organisations, teams or individuals to help them gain a fresh,
objective view of the services they themselves provide, and manage
change with clarity and confidence'. Here 'clarity', 'freshness' and
'objectivity' are all key justifications for the role of the consultant
managers with, in this case, a focus on change at the local level
working alongside individual managers. In other cases, consultant
managers worked on change activities that had a broader focus,
pursuing change agendas across the whole organisation. These
could cover a number of different issues or foci; for example, in one
large Australian financial services company, a unit of consultant
managers was established to reinvent the company's corporate culture and initiate a 'cultural transformation journey'. Working

alongside an external consultancy, this unit designed a range of corporate values, and organised training sessions to disseminate the values and develop consistent management styles.

Culture- or values-based change of this type was not the only purpose of change-based activities involving consultant managers. In other cases, organisation-wide change involved the development and implementation of new technologies (something which could of course have implications for organisational culture). For example, FoodCo, a large Australian food processing company, implemented a proprietary enterprise resource planning (ERP) information system. This involved a complex redesign process in which traditional organisational practices were 're-engineered' to better fit with the assumptions implicit in the software. This might include, for example, changes in the way production is planned, human resources are managed or financial activities are undertaken (Grant, et al., 2006). Indeed, a specialist functionally integrative group was established specifically for the project, which, in collaboration with external consultants, planned and managed the ERP implementation. This occurred through staged roll-outs of system modules and associated changes in working and management practices over a four-year period, something they claimed would 'revolutionise' the work of managers and employees.

Although change activities around culture and technology were evident, the majority of consultant managers in our study were involved in more operational/short-term change agendas focused on cost savings and/or efficiency improvements. Once again, and distinct from the functionally based focus of the bureaucratic manager, this work typically spanned organisational departments. The emphasis on cost savings and efficiency was often explicit; for example, in two different UK local authorities, it was central to the purpose of the activities of consultant managers:

> I'm trying to create an internal consultancy within the
> organisation and the overall thrust of that consultancy would

be to re-engineer our business processes to improve the
effectiveness for the customer, to get efficiency savings basically,
save costs.   (Ade, Customer Strategy Manager, LocalGov3)

The purpose of the [internal consulting unit] is to identify
improvements, which will help the service to deliver cash savings,
improve value for money and make sustainable service
improvements through a process of reviews.

(LocalGov2 promotional material)

The manner in which the focus on cost savings was described is
an example of management activities acting as a justification
for the wider 'causal powers' (Tsoukas, 1994) of management.
Through an emphasis on 'effectiveness', 'value for money' and
'sustainable . . . improvements', the objectives of the consultant manager's work are presented in a neutral fashion, suggesting an implicit
acceptability of this type of change activity, at least for the consultant managers involved.

Unsurprisingly, however, consultant managers' involvement
in delivering a cost-saving change agenda could be challenged
and created problems. In FinCo1, for example, Sam, a regional head
with overall responsibility for the ICU, argued that a previous
incarnation of the unit had become unpopular in the organisation
because

They had stop watches, clip boards, and they went around every
organisation and they said 'fuck all the management of the
organisation, we're going to stop-watch you, clipboard you, and
we're going to present you with a document that says you've got
to cut 15%'. That was what that organisation did.

In this case the consultant managers had to seek to extend the
content of their activities so that they were not entirely associated
with change agendas involving efficiency and cost savings. A similar
situation occurred in GovServ1, where Ray, assistant director of
continuous improvement, argued that a shift to a more explicit

consultancy role among consultant managers was a response to the limitations of an efficiency-based approach: 'There was an efficiency team set up here with the deliberate purpose of running an efficiency programme. The word "efficiency" became unpopular at some stage and that migrated into a consultancy service and people started acquiring the skills associated with consultancy, rather than doing pure "efficiency work".'

Linking change and business strategy

The ideal type of neo-bureaucracy would suggest that involvement in short-term operational change is combined with a longer-term strategic focus. This was borne out in our study, where the change-focused purpose of consultant managers' activities could afford these managers the opportunity to associate their work explicitly with broader strategic objectives of the organisation. This was an important distinction from the operationally focused manager concerned with the immediate allocation (control) of resources in a particular domain. In contrast, the consultant manager could claim to be active across the organisation and so to be directly enacting or implementing strategy. This is not to say that the purpose of consultant managers' activity was to develop organisational strategy. In only four of the twenty-four UK organisations that participated in the study were consultant managers involved in this. Instead, the majority of organisations required consultant managers to deliver large-scale or pan-organisational change projects, but did not include them in the overall initial design or objectives of those projects. Nonetheless, the link to strategy, or at least the impression that consultant managers were involved in strategically significant work, was often a central characteristic claimed of their activities. As we shall see in Chapter 6, this was also an important part of the identities they claimed or aspired to.

On occasion it was up to consultant managers to develop the specific content of the work that would be undertaken within a strategic framework. For example, in LocalGov2, Brian, a business service manager, explained how the CEO had established a cost-saving agenda for the unit and had then requested that the unit

> 'Go away and map and landscape and tell us which of the areas we need to be looking at as a priority, and then bring that report through to the Performance Efficiency Group, and we'll challenge it, tweak it, change it, and authorise it and let you get on with it.' So that's how we went forward with this idea of a team, the team would have a programme, the programme would then start to, if you will, tackle the worst bits of the organisation first.

This gave the unit a clear strategic connection for their work. However, not all consultant managers had such a clear direction from senior management and so they tended to connect to strategic objectives on a project-by-project basis. In GovAgency4, for example, Bruce, a consultant manager, explained how this was achieved:

> We ask four questions and if it doesn't fit at least one of those criteria the work won't get done. The first is, does it feature in the GovAgency4 business plan? Second, does it support one of the strategic objectives? ... The third is, is there a senior management team member supporting the work and if so does it fit one of their strategic objectives? ... The fourth thing [is] that we reserve the right to do a piece of work that fits our [internal consulting unit] strategic objectives.

In FinCo1, a similar approach was adopted, although based on a hierarchical scale, with projects meeting the higher criteria being more likely to be taken on. As an internal policy document outlined: 'Project selection criteria – business needs; contribution to FinCo1 P/L (new revenue from new and existing clients); revenue retention or revenue at risk; cost reduction; process re-engineering; client relationship; raising team profile; team skills/development'. There was a clear emphasis in this scale on financial or revenue-based criteria over and above a focus on more abstract skill development – 'Theory E' over 'Theory O' – a feature perhaps of work more generally in a financial services organisation in a period of rationalisation. Moreover, this list also shows that for the consultant managers, the purpose of their activities should be justified in terms of both a strategic (e.g. business needs/development) *and* operational (e.g. process re-engineering) focus. That said, a link to strategic objectives and outcomes could be packaged in a number of different ways – a point that we return to below in discussing the importance of *added value* in the relationship activities of the consultant manger.

In HealthCo1, the consultant managers passed responsibility for identifying the strategic relevance of projects to their client managers as part of the project-scoping stage:

> There's a form we ask them to fill in, and we ask them why they want us, why now, why us, what they want to achieve, and ... also link it to organisational objectives, so we ask them to think about which of the organisational objectives what they're asking us to do matches against.   (*Austin, Programme Director*)

To assist in the process, the form contained details of different organisational objectives allied to national health care standards. However, Austin was sceptical that this was a useful method of supporting the involvement of his team in strategically significant work, arguing that the process had been designed in response to a request from an executive and that asking for this information 'was actually not helpful at all, because everything sits somewhere in one of the objectives'.

A wider problem in other organisations was translating a strategic focus into genuine strategic work. For example, Colin, a principal consultant in GovServ3, argued that it was difficult to balance the volume of work with its relevance to the organisation:

> The issue I think is more about getting the right type of work, rather than getting the right amount. Because we get work in, our section isn't that huge, we've got a huge organisation to cover, so in terms of getting work it's not a problem, it's making sure the work is of the right kind of strategic nature and adding the most value to the business.

Similar concerns existed at GovDept1. Here, the ICU had compiled a report entitled *Death or Glory* in an effort to justify the purpose of their activities in the organisation. A number of significant themes around the challenging role of the consultant manager emerged from this document, not least the connection between the need to secure work of greater significance and the wider reputation of the unit among senior management: 'While on the whole enough work comes in, too much of this is low-level business. It also means that while [the internal consulting unit] may have a decent reputation at lower levels of the Department, it is not always well known or respected at more senior levels.' Indeed, the concern expressed in this extract was later justified given the closure of the unit soon after this report was written!

This example also illustrates the requirement for consultant managers to explain consistently or justify the purpose of their activities. The 'Death or Glory' report was an (ultimately unsuccessful) example of this and an attempt to overcome some of the ambiguities and tensions around the question of 'what do consultant managers do'. In other words, the purpose (and strategic significance) of their activities was not always widely understood given that they often required consultant managers to work outside of (or across) recognised functional domains. This appeared to contrast with the content of operational management activities, which not only involved short-term administrative concerns and were associated with clear functional responsibilities but also had an implicit strategic significance in terms of sustaining business operations. The purpose of consultant managers' activities (as a form of neo-bureaucracy) might be to combine a longer-term focus on innovation and change with shorter-term emphasis on efficiency, but this could also create uncertainty, particularly if the strategic relevance of this work was not evident. This suggests that they could be as much constrained as liberated by the hybrid neo-bureaucratic nature of their role (Sturdy, et al., 2013).

HOW DO CONSULTANT MANAGERS WORK?
PROJECT/PROGRAMME MANAGEMENT,
METHODOLOGIES AND CONTROL

Beyond the focus on change management and its link to business strategy, the way in which consultant managers carried out their work was also distinctive. In particular, consultant managers stressed a structured approach to the planning and delivery of work activities, which often involved other managers as both 'clients' and participants in their change initiatives. As we argued above (see Table 4.1), traditional management, contrary to its bureaucratic ideal, has in practice consistently been found to be unstructured, disorganised and prone to interruption. Moreover, there is some indication that contemporary managers are actually resistant to methods or techniques that attempt to systematise their work (Tengblad and Vie, 2012). Here, the contrast with consultant managers is stark, because organising their work along structured and systematic (neo-bureaucratic) lines was, for many, a defining characteristic of their activities, to the extent that this difference could be a source of tension within their role. Here, the characteristic of *managed improvisation* was also relevant in the emphasis upon project management too, including the use of branded methodologies to deliver innovation and change, as well as consultant managers' related responsibility for *functional integration* through programme management.

Project management

As we discussed in Chapter 1, the growth of project working and project management (projectification) is a central theme in debates about the emergence of both post- and neo-bureaucracy (Clegg, 2012). Here, projects are seen as a condition and consequence of shifts in organisational structures (e.g. network organisations), with the aim of managing organisational change and responding to fluid external environments. They also mark a breakdown of functional specialisation and of the open-ended nature of work activity. At the same time, project working is emblematic of the way in which changes in management activities have occurred *at the same time* as continuity in its 'causal powers' (Tsoukas, 1994). Thus, while project working is a different way in which managers organise their work, it also acts to legitimise control (Clegg and Courpasson, 2004) through the promotion of instrumental rationality and an 'ideology of predictability' (Hodgson and Cicmil, 2007: 432). As we shall see then, it both challenges and extends bureaucracy (Hodgson, 2002; McSweeney, 2006).

Project working is defined by the application of a highly structured and sequential approach to addressing a specific organisational issue. These features are typically considered to be absent in the fragmented and reactive nature of operational management in practice. Projects are typically expected to involve a sequence of discrete stages. In FinCo1, for example, Andrew, a business analyst, described a typical project process in these standard terms: 'We had the planning and initiation phase and the fieldwork and current state of analysis phase and then an element of joint diagnosis and recommendation creation, followed by the whole management reporting piece ... it is a pure project management framework.' Each of these stages contains different activities, with the shifts from one to the next, an indication of progress.

Establishing clear timescales for a project allowed consultant managers to run a number of projects concurrently and ensure they would not become tied to one specific piece of work – a concern that represented the need for flexibility and dynamism in neo-bureaucratic management. For instance, in LocalGov3, Johnny and Brian expressed concern about a project in which they had become involved because it could not be delivered within the time frame indicated above. Although this project was of strategic significance, both consultant managers felt they would have less control and would be unable to follow the sequential process that they had developed. The priority in this case was to be nimble in order to balance the quantity and quality of projects. Other consultant managers also expressed frustration with projects that, for different reasons, had not been completed within what was deemed a reasonable timescale.

One method for ensuring that projects were not open-ended and so were limited in terms of time was to articulate clearly desired outcomes prior to starting the project (also an important feature of the relationship management activity of the consultant manager – see Chapter 5). Establishing some form of pre-agreement around the 'scope of work' was a key component of how consultant managers structured and organised their activities. The methods used to achieve this varied in terms of their formality and the extent to which they were documented. Nonetheless, it was often crucial that, in one form or another, consultant managers established a degree of clarity around the specific expectations of any given project. In TransCo, Dan, the manager of the internal consultancy, explained the 'project charter' that his unit used to set out the core features of a project:

> This project charter sets out . . . what are the things we need to do, why do we need to do them, what are the success criteria, and who our key stakeholders are . . . And we give that to the client and we ask the client to sign off on it. I want to stress though that it's a really short document. We're not talking about a ten- or fifteen-page project initiation document. We're talking about one, one-and-a-half pages.

The desire to prevent this charter from being a burden for clients to complete was clear, although having a mechanism for clarifying project outcomes also further justified the involvement of consultant managers in such activities. In addition, a charter or pre-agreement provided some certainty for the consultant manager that they were working to an agreed process and that the client managers had demonstrated some commitment to the project.

The role of project-based methodologies

A further element of project working that was important to consultant managers was the use and adaptation of defined methodologies to manage their analysis and generate insights within a project. These methodologies were typically branded as management techniques such as 'quality management', 'lean', 'Six Sigma' or 'process re-engineering' – which enabled a seemingly systematic process of analysis that sought process improvements within specified time-scales. Adopting a specific methodology enshrined the systematic approach consultant managers were keen to adopt. For example, at PhoneCo, an internal consulting group of over sixty consultants applied a Six Sigma methodology to business improvement popularised by companies such as Motorola and General Electric (Pande, et al., 2000). As Roy, the originator of the approach, noted:

> I mean the beauty of Six Sigma is that first of all we are able to train a set of competencies that we know ... They've [Six Sigma Black Belts] also got a series of templates and tools they can apply without having to go and look them up, so you just get through the whole process a lot quicker. You also can monitor the progress, so if you go through the DMAIC [define, measure, analyse, improve and control] five-phase problem-solving process and they've said we want two weeks for this, one week for that, you can control it very simply ... We know exactly what to expect with each of those.

In this example, Six Sigma was a methodology used to structure project working as a whole. A similar approach was adopted at CarCo, where Keira, the 'Best Practice Consultant', outlined her role in facilitating and training staff in a codified kaizen methodology favoured by her firm:

> The [company] kaizen methodology is PDCA – Plan, Do, Check, Act ... First of all, you set the thing, then you define the problem and get your statistics, conduct interviews, go to the source of information. Then you do a resource analysis, you ask yourself the question 'why do these problems happen', and then go through to finding solutions to the root causes that you've found, and of course implementation, confirm, check your measurements, see if you've actually improved things, and then standardize the process.

Methodologies could also be used to support specific analytical techniques within the standard project cycle. For example, in CommsCo, Anthony, an analyst in the Continuous Service Improvement team, explained how he used statistical process control in order to identify problems:

> It's a technique that you use to collect your data from an output of a process or an activity or whatever the performance of that process. But basically it plots on something called 'an upper and lower control limit' which are basically control lines that are derived from the data itself. So everything that sits within those lines, based on the dataset, is normal, you'd expect it to be there, and anything that falls outside of those lines, something's happened within that process to cause that data point to do that, it's abnormal, it's an exception to the rule if you like. So then what you do is you investigate it, you identify the root cause, remove the root cause of failure and generally you improve the process.

In these examples, the identification and resolution of 'root causes' indicated the extent to which the use of methodologies was based on claims to objectivity through measurement and control. This was important for consultant managers in that it reinforced the sense that their activities considered existing processes as being removed from the immediate and time-pressured concerns of other managers.

Indeed, the desire to apply a systematic approach within project work was often valued more by consultant managers than adherence to one specific methodology. So the majority of consultant managers we interviewed drew upon a range of tools that could support a variety of activity. As Pete, a change partner, and Christine, head of the Continuous Service Improvement team at CommsCo, noted, it was important to adopt a flexible or improvised approach in the use of different change methodologies:

> Within CommsCo, there are any number of methodologies that people say we follow ... just put your fingers in your ears and decide the tools, my approach is to take the tools that I think fit. You do come across people who say, 'Well you haven't got a

> project definition here from PRINCE2 so we can't progress.'
> <Pause> It drives me a little bit crazy! *(Pete)*

> It's understanding [that] not one size fits all, we don't use the
> pure methodology of Six Sigma just out of the textbook, we have
> to understand which tools will benefit those people, at what
> level and the way in which we deploy it will be slightly different
> but the fundamentals of it are the same. *(Christine)*

It was 'the fundamentals' that Christine referred to which were a key aspect of the use of methodologies to structure the work of consultant managers. In a number of organisations, these fundamentals were important in drawing consultant managers together through internal networks allowing them to develop a shared identity (see also Chapter 6). In CommsCo, a large number of consultant managers belonged to project management job families or professional communities which established connections between individuals with similar roles across the organisation. The OD and Change Director in ArtsCo, Pippa, also explained how she saw methodologies as being much more than a rigid set of techniques to be applied universally:

> Well I think methodology holds you together. I'm not a great
> advocate of having one change management methodology and
> pursuing it doggedly, but at least ... training all your change
> managers in one methodology helps enormously. They get one
> language, they have one set of tools, they may not always use them,
> and they certainly won't use them all necessarily in the sort of order
> that you might get from a change management methodology, but
> just that common language and common understanding I think
> helps enormously, and I think you have to invest a lot in building
> and maintaining a community.

This indicates how knowledge of a specific methodology could be an important indicator of the expertise of the consultant manager such that they could be distinguished from traditional managers. This is a theme that we pick up in more detail in the following chapter, but in the context of a discussion around the organisation of the activities of consultant managers, methods-based expertise had an impact on their involvement in knowledge transfer activity. In other words, consultant managers had to consider how far they would become involved in disseminating particular *techniques* to other (non-specialist) managers. There was a tension in how consultant managers should respond to this because, on the one hand, dissemination could detract from the mystique of the consultant manager, whereas not doing so could undermine the principle of continuous improvement that was hardwired into many methodologies (e.g. Six Sigma). Ray, also part of the Continuous Service Improvement team at CommsCo, acknowledged this tension:

> My whole job is to do myself out of a job! But I think the whole point
> of the philosophy is to allow people to have the tools at the very
> lowest level so that anything they work on, anything within
> [CommsCo] they can use some tools and methodologies to help
> them improve what they're doing.

Despite this view being acknowledged elsewhere, most ICUs we studied did *not* have knowledge transfer as a standard or conscious part of their activities (see also Sturdy, et al., 2009, on external consultants). Instead, a more typical approach was for consultant managers to support other managers or offer skill development on a more *ad hoc* basis. This was sometimes driven by resource constraints rather than OD-oriented motives. For example, in GovAgency3, Diana, the head of the Performance Improvement Unit, explained that

> what we're trying to do with our limited resources is set up a
> service to project teams. We can't give you a project manager,
> we can't come and do the project with you, but what we can
> do is help you go in the right direction, give you some key
> document templates, quality assure what you're doing and
> be very hands-off on it.

In FinCo4, Ian, the head of the Change Management Department, described a similar *ad hoc* approach:

> The other problem that you get sometimes is that you're seen
> as an additional resource and you have to be a little bit
> careful around that one too. But what we would do is we'd say,
> 'Well we can't support you on this one, unfortunately.' We have
> a prioritisation pipeline and we've pushed everything through
> the prioritisation pipeline, 'what we can do is we can work
> with some of your people and do a skills transfer across to them,
> so that you will be able to do it, and we'll mentor those people
> through'.

This concern with general dissemination of skills in certain method-ologies was indicative of a perception that expertise in these techni-ques remained relatively rare and distinctive in order to legitimise the activities of the consultant manager. However, these concerns came into conflict with the organisational belief that such skills should be a part of all managers' roles. In short, the use of pre-defined or branded methodologies as a source or expertise (and a mechanism for organis-ing their activities) for consultant managers was not always easy to sustain given the relevance of the values inherent in those method-ologies to all managers.

Project-based methodologies – operational managers' resistance

In addition to concerns about the knowledge transfer of branded meth-odologies, consultant managers also experienced other difficulties in organising their work via structured techniques. These difficulties highlighted both new and persistent tensions and ambiguities within management and so question assumptions that neo-bureaucratic activities are in some way a *solution* to the tensions inherent within and between bureaucratic and post-bureaucratic management. Many of the difficulties facing consultant managers were a result of resist-ance from operational managers who often reacted against structured and analytical methods, even in adapted forms, and so against the *managed improvisation* associated with neo-bureaucracy. This was neatly summed up by Pippa, who noted that managers 'hate methodologies, they're really very suspicious of them'.

In many of the organisations we studied, managers' suspicions stemmed in part from the association between methodologies and external management consultants (see also Chapter 5). In other cases, managers were concerned about the seemingly obscure or abstract nature of methodologies and how outcomes were to be generated. This was particularly evident during an observation of a small project within FinCo1. Here, the consultant managers were required to measure and evaluate the nature of work undertaken by a specific team in order to recommend if it should be relocated to an alternative division. In order to do this, activity within the team (including phone calls and emails) had been tracked over a two-week period, which was then followed up by a two-day visit, during which the consultant managers interviewed team members and observed their work. At various stages in the project, the operational manager expressed concern with the nature of the data that were being collected and how these were being categorised. During two conference calls, this manager consistently challenged the potential for simplification, arguing that 'we need to add some depth' in the data that were collected. As a result, the two consultant managers repeatedly reassured him about the process, how information was being captured and also how any outcomes would be handled, saying 'we will always look back with you over the data before any conclusions are drawn'. Although the team manager had no choice other than to accept the 'advice' of the consultant managers in this analysis, it was clear that he remained highly sceptical about the techniques applied and the overall value of the exercise.

Suspicions around techniques and outcomes were not the only challenge facing consultant managers in their efforts to apply and adapt structured models of change. In other cases, the practical limitations of methodologies (e.g. time) could be far more problematic for operational managers. Bob, a procurement consultant in CommsCo, gave a graphic image of these limitations: 'Of course, the Six Sigma approach isn't always supported when someone is standing on a burning platform. So if the flames are round their ears and someone says, "Let's just understand that true root cause" they say, "I don't give a shit! I just want to find a bucket of water!"'

Here, again, the underlying philosophy of methodologies such as Six Sigma came into conflict with a long-standing crisis management or reactive culture. In GovAgency2, Isaac faced similar problems due to a reluctance from other managers to engage with the structured approach of identifying project outcomes:

> We try to retain some structure. So if they ask us to do a piece of work we say 'Right, let's just agree what you want us to do, and let's just sign it off in terms of right, so you want us to improve that to that level. Let's just consider what the risks might be.' They don't want to get into all that, so part one of the tools that we bring is project management, a very light touch, but I think if we're going to commit some resource, what are the benefits we're going to get from it before I commit any resource to it. 'Oh, I don't know, we just need to do so and so.' Well, I'm not happy to proceed on that basis. So because they don't want all the faff of going through thinking why we ought to be doing stuff, they'd rather just get on and try and do something.

The preference suggested here among managers for immediate action over a planned and considered approach resonates with repeated findings detailing the nature of managerial work historically (Tengblad and Vie, 2012). Furthermore, structured methods can be felt as a restriction on autonomy in decision-making and action more generally.

Managerial resistance to methods also occurred if they had been widely used – a case of 'familiarity breeding contempt'. In HealthCo1, the ICU deployed a team facilitation method that had been introduced to the organisation by an external organisation. The unit became synonymous with this methodology to the extent that the group had developed a reputation for the excessive use of Post-it notes, which were used as part of the process. Although the unit was well regarded within the organisation more generally, there was a concern among its members that the methodology could undermine their reputation. As Ursula, one of the 'coaches' within the unit, noted, 'there are some teams who have done that so much they're sick of it'.

The case of Six Sigma in CommsCo was another example of a methodology losing its appeal. As we noted earlier, the organisation had trained large numbers of employees in this methodology, leading to a series of Six Sigma teams being established in each division. However, the ICU remained the only group which used the methodology across the whole of CommsCo. As Christine, the head of the team, explained: '[other divisions] had decided they no longer wanted to use the methodology, and this is so typical in CommsCo that we go through these cycles of, "We like it, we don't, we like it, we don't". And it can be flavour of the month.'

Part of the reason for Six Sigma going out of fashion lay with the concerns expressed above about the nature of the methodology. Colin, who was part of Christine's team, argued that

> The feedback that we received was certainly that Six Sigma
> has a bit of a stigma attached that it takes too long, it's analysis
> paralysis and actually it takes such a length of time to get
> to a point where you're delivering improvements that
> people kind of lose faith and lose the ability to come on board
> with you.

In part then, consultant managers were constrained by aspects of their hybrid neo-bureaucratic role to move from the ideal-type bureaucratic manager – namely the formalisation, standardisation and even depersonalisation implicit in their use of structured methods. Indeed, in some senses, rejecting the use of project methods suggested that operational managers were seeking to be *less* bureaucratic than their neo-bureaucratic colleagues. In any case, the response of the Six Sigma team was to make no mention of the methodology when working on projects, to the extent that they referred to themselves as 'The Secret Six Sigma Society'. As Anthony explained, this allowed him and other consultant managers to continue working with the key principles of the methodology without having to overcome the stigma or assumptions associated with it:

> Everything that we've done has always been based on Lean and Six Sigma, but we haven't actively rammed it down people's throats. We've kind of delivered benefit and then said, 'Oh, by the way that was this'. Because what we've found is a lot of people just got turned off by catchphrases and acronyms and the naming conventions, so it was much easier just to get on, deliver what people were asking for and actually then to almost de-brand it as Six Sigma.

While this 'de-branding' potentially allowed this group of consultant managers to sustain their interest in Six Sigma, the tensions of organising their activities in this way continued. Their preference for the relatively systematic approach offered by project methodologies stood in contrast to the reactive and day-to-day focus of managers who were sensitive to at least some of the dysfunctional outcomes of structured and time-consuming approaches.

Programme management: coordination and integration

A further dimension of the projectification of work involves the combination of individual projects into wider *programmes* of activities. This was also a key feature of how some of the consultant managers organised their activities, claiming that it explicitly connected their focus on change and organisational objectives. As we have seen, the particular goals of these programmes could vary in terms of not only their content (e.g. culture change, technology, efficiency) but also their scope and significance. For example, in CommsCo, the large internal change unit (approximately 180 employees) was established in order to deliver a two- to three-year programme targeting a 45 per cent cost reduction within one division. This helped give a sense of cohesion to otherwise disparate projects, although, as we shall see, the system of reporting that went along with this created problems with other managers. Another example occurred at LocalGov3. Here, a much smaller unit established a system of governance to create a shared purpose around work being undertaken in different parts of the organisation. Dennis, the customer strategy manager, described this system as follows: 'Projects are within the directorates [departments/divisions], but they are being brought together by programme governance . . . under the programme board we have sub-boards which manage the actual project, and that brings in various stakeholders across the organisation.'

Placing a programme structure around their project management activities also had a number of claimed advantages for developing the role of the consultant manager. One of the most significant was that it allowed them to act as an *integrating* force within the organisation, facilitating and coordinating various projects. As with project working, but on a larger scale, this ability of the consultant manager to work outside of function-based roles and responsibilities was an important point of distinction and clearly represented the notion of *functional integration* within the ideal type of neo-bureaucracy (see Chapter 6 for a more detailed discussion of the 'outsider' status of consultant managers). This was also a role that was particularly valued by 'client managers' and sponsors. For example, in HealthCo1, the ICU managed a pan-organisational programme seeking to improve the process for assessing patients in advance of operations. This had been an issue of long-standing concern within the organisation, but it had not been addressed given the scale of the changes and the number of stakeholders involved. Emma, a client manager involved in the programme, explained the complexities of the work involved:

> it's a massive project, because of the fact that it involves so many people, the staffing, the levels of staffing, the capacity, and trying to change orthopaedic surgeons, general surgeons, vascular surgeons,

cardio-rectal surgeons, ENT surgeons, max-fac surgeons, all of these people have got their own slightly different way of doing things in their allotted time.

Despite these challenges it was deemed a success, one attributed to the coordinating role of Austin, the programme director. Austin was a medical (rather than management) consultant and manager who had a high degree of credibility with both medical and non-medical professionals in the organisation. This allowed him to establish a system of control for the programme and bring together the relevant experts while maintaining an oversight of progress. Rhianna, one of the non-clinical managers, argued that this was critical: 'They needed somebody to be able to have an overview of it, and ... the reason it hasn't changed [previously] is because there were so many people involved, nobody was in charge of it to be able to look at it, to do something about it.'

The importance of a horizontally integrative role was also evident in FinCol, although here, consultant managers tended to underplay how much clients valued it. In one specific case, the consulting unit became involved in a programme of activities aimed at increasing the product knowledge of front-line sales staff, including an understanding of how different products had to be adapted to different national contexts. Although the specific innovation did not stem from the ICU, according to Fabio, a regional head of operations, their coordinating role was significant:

> My organisation supplied the entire intellectual content to it ... and the internal consulting organisation pulled that together in terms of a programme framework ... driving meetings forward and driving projects that have sat across the piece of FinCol Division, so not in Operations, not in Product, not in Technology, but looking at it from end to end, which has been good.

This was significant both in terms of its perceived contribution to the organisation and also because this integrative role had enhanced the credibility and identity of the unit. As Fabio went on to note: 'So as a user I think the exercise was a good exercise because it brought people together, and it was actually one of the first ... in fact it was the main project that cemented the consulting group, if you like, as an organisation.' This suggests that structuring work in programmes that could integrate different functional interests across an organisation could give consultant managers an opportunity to stabilise their role within the organisation and demonstrate a clear identity to others.

Programme management as control: tensions and ambiguities

Organising work into coherent programmes gave consultant managers some measure of work security by providing longer-term assignments. Also, by assuming governance and monitoring responsibilities, such *functional integration* was a means of establishing control over change agendas and projects across the organisation. In effect, some came to adopt a hierarchical role, even if temporarily. For instance, in FinCo3, Dean, an IT-based consultant manager, argued:

> What we're doing effectively is governance ... we're attempting to ensure that any decisions made, fit with our general strategy. And then people just don't [normally] work like that, well, certainly in our organisation, it's quite silo-based. And we're there to integrate the different domains and make sure that we coordinate them. Certainly with the projects I've been on, it's talking to different areas to make sure that they can all deliver.

Control over change agendas was also important for consultant managers as a means of avoiding confusion and duplication and achieving consistency in the approach to change in organisations:

> Because we've got to sort out programme management, we've got to sort out the fact that we have 120 change projects ... I can think of several projects which are overlapping, duplicating, actually maybe

working against each other, and some of them you begin to ask the
question, well why are we doing it now?

(Nate, head of performance management, LocalGov1)

However, perhaps inevitably, seeking (or being tasked) to assert control
over change projects could generate resistance from other managers,
among others. Control would often take the form of an apparent need
to report on the progress of different projects as part of governance
mechanisms. For the consultant managers, these allowed them to
track the progress of different activities against objectives, again signi-
fying their desire to pursue a systematic and structured approach and
focus on longer-term concerns. However, for those managers required
to report via these mechanisms, it appeared to be an additional layer of
bureaucratic control and an unwelcome interference in their domain.
This tension was most clearly illustrated in CommsCo. Here, given
the size of the change programme, a specific team was created within
the ICU with exclusive responsibility for governance. James, a programme director working within this team, explained the key task
facing the team:

> We had over 300 projects and programmes. Given we had less than
> 300 people actually working on these initiatives, you have to
> question really what's the progress being made! <Chuckles>
> Considering some of them were quite significant pieces of
> work, my reality was over half of those projects and
> programmes were going nowhere. So at that time a decision
> was made, we would focus down ... on a minimum number of
> activities.

This rationalisation of change projects required a system of reporting
that was based around the typical 'consultancy cycle' of scoping,
diagnosis, piloting, implementation and evaluation (Lippitt and
Lippitt, 1986). James' team asked divisional managers to provide
them with standardised data against each of these stages and then
used a 'traffic light' measurement system to highlight whether

projects were progressing in line with the required timescales. This had a number of clear advantages from a governance perspective. James argued that it created transparency and efficiency by cancelling those projects that were making no progress. It could also provide senior management with an understanding of the interactions of major projects and programmes (rather than seeing them as independent activities). However, these advantages did not seem to be widely accepted at CommsCo. The governance role was treated with suspicion by divisional (operational) managers, as an unnecessary interference that challenged their authority. This caused problems for James, who recognised that 'I have the infinite capacity to make myself extremely unpopular! And that's one of the challenges I have. Without [political] sponsorship, even within my own line structure, I can come away very poorly at the end of quarterly reviews. "James' team are a right pain in the arse." They keep marking us down.' For example, James went on to describe a particular situation he was facing where a senior individual was not reporting the progress of a programme:

> I have an individual reporting to an executive board member, saying 'I do not wish to update' what effectively is a programme definition document ... But this is a very senior person. There's a lack of awareness of need for effective governance, because they have inherited a feeling that governance is purely bureaucratic, where it should be a fairly snappy 'get the information you need to make an informed decision'.

This charge of increased bureaucracy was critical to the problems of governance – something that was acknowledged by Matt, another programme director and consultant manager in CommsCo:

> The governance side of it just becomes noise with people, because like bureaucracy, [they say] 'what am I getting from this? I'm giving you [governance team] loads of stuff, I'm taking time out of my day ...' It gets fed into the poor guys in the central team [who] have to

do the governances. It's a really hard job to get right. It's very important, but the organisation just isn't mature enough to execute it in the right way.

Thus, programme management introduced not only a structuring of managers' work, much like the methodologies of project management, but also a measure of non-standard hierarchical control and a high-level visibility, which created tensions with operational managers. They could notionally be responsible for a change activity, but the programme governance role of consultant managers formed an overlay of control which was not always welcomed. In this way, we can see that the neo-bureaucratic characteristics of *managed improvisation* and *functional integration* are by no means straightforward solutions to some of the traditional dilemmas of management outlined in Chapter 2.

CONCLUSION

In this chapter, we have begun to explore some of the work activities of the consultant manager. Drawing on the managerial work literature, we examined these along two interconnected dimensions: first, the content and purpose of their work (what do consultant managers do?), and second, the organisation and structure of their work (how do consultant managers work?). In each of these areas, we focused on how consultant managers operated in line with neo-bureaucratic dynamics rather than traditional conceptualisations of management as bureaucratic or reactive, for example. In particular, we have seen how they are concerned with strategic and long-term change and functional integration through various change and project management methodologies and programme governance. This presents a challenge to the bureaucratic emphasis on vertical/functional hierarchical divisions. However, neo-bureaucracy is a hybrid, and this has been most evident in the way in which change, project and programme methods take a highly formalised, if also adapted, approach in direct tension with the apparent preferences of many operational managers for informality and reactivity. Furthermore, the activities act as a form of control, sometimes in a way which belies consultant managers' formal status as lacking operational responsibility. Such an approach is in keeping with the need to assess management at both the level of practices and wider 'causal powers' and our view of neo-bureaucratic management as containing evidence of both change and continuity in managerial work.

Table 4.2 summarises the key observations along each of the two dimensions. In terms of *what consultant managers do*, we found that the main content of consultant managers' work was both change oriented, in areas such as culture, technology and process efficiency, and strategically informed, meaning it should emerge out of, and contribute towards, wider organisational objectives even if specific projects were more operational in focus. This can be contrasted with the steady-state, routinised and short-term emphasis of the operational manager. However, the difficulties for consultant managers of securing strategically significant work and becoming associated with an agenda of cost-cutting combined to create uncertainty in fulfilling their role.

In terms of *how consultant managers worked*, again, our evidence indicates that they used and adapted structured approaches to integrate and coordinate cross-functional change projects – something they were often well positioned to do from a position of quasi-independence. This *managed improvisation* typically involved organising work into a programme of activities containing a series of individual projects in which consultant managers often used branded project methodologies. These methodologies were based on the need to identify objectives in advance and divide work into a series of discrete stages. The contrast here with traditional managerial work as functionally specific and reactive was such that consultant managers often faced resistance to their approach to achieving change. In addition, their involvement in change programmes often implied a governance role in which their authority could be challenged and which threatened their independence.

Table 4.2 *Content and organisation of consultant managers' activities*

Consultant managers' activities	Main features	Distinction from managers in bureaucracy	Tensions, ambiguities and uncertainties
Content What do consultant managers do?	Strategically informed change agendas focusing on culture, technology and process efficiency (cost savings)	Longer-term focus and less concerned with maintenance of production/steady-state activities	Efficiency focus could create suspicion
	Some involvement in developing change focus/management across organisation	Strategic links have to be made explicit rather than implied in functional responsibilities	Difficulty of securing high-level strategic work and building credibility with senior management
Organisation How do consultant managers work?	Systematic and structured programme and project management	Cross-'silo' and broader in scope	Resistance to structured methods and use of branded methodologies
	Integrative approach coordinating different functions/departments	More structured working within defined timescales to agreed outcomes	Methodologies lose their relevance
	Use of branded project methodologies.	Less concerned with reactive and immediate problem-solving	Governance role in programme management undermines advisory role – creates resistance
		Punctuated vs ongoing	

Taken together, the activities of consultant managers reveal complexity and contradiction and certainly show that the suggestion, noted in Chapter 2, that the hybridity of neo-bureaucracy can reconcile bureaucratic and post-bureaucratic models is problematic in practice. More specifically, we suggest that neo-bureaucratic management (in the form of consultant managers) is often *paradoxical* in that many features are both a source of apparent *liberation* from the limitations of traditional management work and of *constraint* in still being subject to uncertainty and resistance. For example, consultant managers' desire to use project methodologies was, broadly speaking, an opportunity to eschew chaotic and unplanned management work, in favour of a structured and analytical approach to process improvement. However, being associated with a particular methodology could constrain consultant managers by preventing them from securing projects, either because the methodology was no longer fashionable or simply because operational managers were resistant to the systematic (and often time-consuming) approach inherent in their use. Likewise, programme governance provided an opportunity to control projects and yet also came up against more traditional hierarchical dilemmas in rendering performance and progress more visible. As a consequence, neo-bureaucratic management could be *more* uncertain and ambiguous in some contexts, a point we develop in the next chapter in considering the nature of consultant managers' relationships with both internal and external stakeholders.

5   Managing relationships as a consultant manager

INTRODUCTION

Beyond the questions of *what* consultant managers do and *how* they organise their work lies the critical issue of *with whom* they carry out such work. In this chapter, we explore the relationships of consultant managers in greater depth. As we noted in previous chapters, for managers, organisational relationships have been traditionally conceived as predominantly internally focused and hierarchical – vertical in direction with functional subordinates and superiors. Where lateral relationships are acknowledged, these have typically been seen as political, with managers seeking to take advantage of *informal* networks for the advancement of their own sectional interests (Buchanan and Badham, 1999; Sayles, 1964). By contrast, our model of neo-bureaucracy makes both lateral and external relationships more explicitly central to management work, especially in relation to *structured organisational politics* and, as we saw in the previous chapter, in relation to governing organisation-wide change programmes, *functional* integration. Both are also linked to *delegated autonomy* in the sense of combining vertical or hierarchical structures with a degree of independence from them or, at least, an additional concern with horizontal and external relationships. In this chapter, we shall see how consultant managers seek to mitigate some of the tensions of organising laterally through managing internal 'client' relations and senior sponsors, and how they engage externally through 'boundary spanning' (i.e. *structured organisational politics* and *internal and external orientation*). Furthermore, the notion of 'client management' indicates how consultant manager relationships are based on a market discourse, which translates into a concern with demonstrating merit-based indicators of 'added value'. Such concerns can have a significant effect on the ambiguity and uncertainty of the consultant manager role and stress the importance of *networked meritocracy* within neo-bureaucratic management – meaning consultant managers have to maintain their personal credibility within their relationships, often through careful management of supportive (often informal) internal and external networks.

In order to examine these features of neo-bureaucratic relationships, we focus on a number of issues to emerge from our study of consultant managers. In the first part of the chapter, we consider how consultant managers seek to structure their relationships with other internal, operational managers as clients or potential clients. We consider how consultant managers adopt relationship management techniques associated with external management consultancies, before highlighting some of the tensions to emerge from these activities, namely the problems of demonstrating added value, maintaining a quasi-independent status by rejecting involvement in implementation, a persistent reliance on senior management and the presence of competing or alternative sources of advice and support within the organisation. Drawing on this last point, the second half of the chapter considers the different mechanisms consultant managers use to manage their (sometimes competitive) relationships with external consultants.

THE CONSULTANT MANAGER AND 'CLIENT RELATIONS' – RELATIONSHIP MANAGEMENT

Beyond the focus on organisational change and project/programme management, a key feature of the consultant manager role was the redefinition of work relationships around the concept of 'client relations' (Anderson-Gough, et al., 2000). The internal market is a key feature of both the discourse of *post*-bureaucracy and the practice of *neo*-bureaucracy in the shift claimed from hierarchy to markets or their combination as hybrids. And indeed, the related idea of other managers and other employees as 'clients' is by no means restricted to consultant managers (Malone, 2004). However, it was pervasive among those we interviewed. It was central in how they represented their work and, as we shall see in Chapter 6, their work identity. This is perhaps unsurprising in that characterising other managers, divisions and departments as 'clients' derives not just from neo- and post-bureaucratic discourse but also from framing their work as consultancy as opposed to more operational management activities. It underpinned the idea that, rather than performing an ongoing administrative task, they were providing an advice- and project-based service. As Cherie, a learning and development manager in a large Australian university, pointed out, the use of the 'client' discourse was in fact preferred by both her team and those they worked with: 'we use "client" or "customer", probably more so "client". One does have to be careful about what the culture around you accepts or not accepts.' For others like Karli, the head of OD in a global IT company, the representation of the client relationship might take other forms, 'We treat managers and executives as our clients. We don't use that language with them, *per se*; we like to work with them as "business partners".'

However, embracing the commercial and professional discourse of 'client relations' also brought with it a different understanding of power relations and a realisation of the need to carefully manage these relationships if consultant managers were to maintain their legitimacy, standing and even employment within their organisation. Consequently, consultant managers actively sought to build productive and sustainable relationships through which they could justify and even extend their role. For instance, Lauren, an OD manager in a large Australian insurance company, highlighted how it took time to develop relationships which she could use to build her work presence: 'In an organisation like [an insurer] that is very relationship based and has been around for a long time, it takes time to build that relationship before they pretty much say, "yeah, come and diagnose, come and tell me what's wrong, tell me what you think we need to do"; to really build that level of trust.'

In so doing, consultant managers often mimicked the formal, structured and tactical relationship management activities of external consultants, in which relationships are explicitly based on market or contractual principles (see Karantinou and Hogg, 2001). Indeed, even if consultant managers' work was not formally based on an internal market mechanism, operational managers typically had discretion over whether (and in what way) they used their services. This meant that consultant managers, like their external counterparts and staff professionals more generally, had to use a range of techniques to influence these choices. For instance, the absence of formal procedural relationships meant that links between operational and consultant managers often relied on establishing some form of contract. As we saw in Chapter 4, contracts were used to ensure not only that the content of a consultant manager's work was linked to strategic objectives but also that the specific outcomes of any project could be agreed in advance. As Della, the human resources director in a large Australian industrial services company, outlined: 'As an internal consultant I don't have service-level agreements. I have a project plan ... because we agree to things in writing, but it's a compromise ... it's more informal in a corporate environment than it is as an external consultant.'

Contracts would often be the outcome of work generation or business development activities by consultant managers during which they sought to build an understanding of the core issues facing potential and existing clients. A formal mechanism for doing this was to have regular structured meetings with client departments in order to better understand their strategic priorities and anticipate where interventions could be beneficial. As Isaac in GovAgency2 outlined, 'I had four consultants attached, one to each business unit. So they'd go along to the monthly meeting of the unit to sit in, to prick up the ears if there are particular issues and say "Do you want any help with that?"'

While formal mechanisms could provide some measure of predictability around work generation, informal mechanisms were equally and, at times, more important. More specifically and in keeping with the work activity school view of managers in general, consultant managers took advantage of informal, *ad hoc* encounters or 'corridor conversations' to identify potential projects. At the same time, they would also develop and draw upon long-standing relationships to scope out work. As Leah, the new OD manager in a large Australian retailer, outlined: 'so it's really just about networking as much as possible, getting on the phone with people, trying to meet with them, getting on committees with other people, trying to influence them around to my way of thinking'.

At the same time, however, active relationship management of this type was also reported to have drawbacks, in the form of some loss of control over the quality and quantity of different projects. Colin, a principal consultant in GovServ3, explained how this situation might occur:

> Each of my Principals has a number of [divisions] with which they regularly visit. They phone them up and say, 'Can I come and see you? You know what our portfolio is, or if you don't because you're new, can I introduce myself, this is our portfolio, how do you think we can help you?' The danger then is of course you get floods of requests for work which you can't do.

To deal effectively with this problem of attracting too much work, consultant managers needed to ensure that they were able to refuse jobs. However, turning down projects risked undermining relationships, and thereby the long-term sustainability of the consultant manager's role, but they often had to say 'no' to work because it did not fit with their wider programme of work or available resources – although both of these factors were also cited when the decision to say 'no' to work was based more on a lack of interest or enthusiasm.

Saying 'no' was a key factor in relationship management because it allowed consultant managers to retain control over their workload (arguably in a way that was less available or legitimate to the managers whose work was more determined by their functional role) and to ensure they were not simply beholden to client needs. Moreover, as Kate, a resourcing manager in FinCo2, claimed, rejecting work was part of 'the nature of building a credible relationship. Saying "yes" all the time isn't being a proper business partner or a proper consultant.' Of course, if consultant managers were not perceived as willing to meet client requests, then, within market-based relationships, they could soon become obsolete. Inevitably, then, consultant managers would be cautious in what and how they turned down work, leading Dale, a colleague of Kate's at FinCo2, to observe that 'we probably don't say "no" enough sometimes ... I think we do need to become more selective about the type of activity that we do and more focused on what's the return on investment from this particular piece of work?'

ADDING VALUE

This last point was critical because it brought into focus the emphasis placed upon identifying commercial significance or 'added value' as being key to successful relationship management. According to both Graham at TransCo and Celia at HealthCo2, 'adding value' was fundamental to their role and credibility across their organisations:

> It's very, very important that the business [internal clients] perceives us as value adding, and that's something we work really, really hard at, to make sure that the business constantly thinks 'yeah, these are good guys to have around'. *(Graham)*

> Because I've always been clear with [the CEO] that unless we can add value to what the organisation's trying to achieve, then, you know, I know that if push came to shove, internal consultancy could be the first thing that went. *(Celia)*

A desire to demonstrate 'added value' on the part of consultant managers connected with the purpose and structure of their work. For example, and as we saw in Chapter 4, they typically aspired to do strategically significant work (where 'added value' is an important badge) and to work through projects, with clearly defined outcomes. Having said that, consultant managers often struggled to produce metrics which gave a clear indication of the level of value being created. For instance, most consultant managers (like their external counterparts) relied on client perceptions of their added value, typically measured through post-intervention feedback and by demonstrating performance against agreed objectives (see also MCA, 2010; Sturdy, 2011). However, such attempts to quantify the impact of consultant managers' interventions and establish some form of meritocracy did not always produce convincing information, as Simone, a coach at HealthCo1, explained: 'I bang on about it all the time 'cause it's so important and we struggle with it. We have invented several evaluation forms trying to capture both quantitative and qualitative stuff. We really struggle to nail it'.

Even where explicit cost savings and efficiencies were claimed, the specific role of consultant managers in this process (especially if they had played more of a facilitation role) was important yet, at the same time, difficult to establish politically as well as practically – who takes the credit in a joint activity? As Celia at HealthCo2 said of outcomes to emerge from projects in which her team had been involved, 'we didn't know, and still don't know, the extent to which that's got anything to do with us'.

This issue is mirrored in external consultancy where a common method prescribed for assessing impact is some form of cost–benefit analysis such as return on investment (Gable, 1996; Wright and Kitay, 2002). One of our expectations early in the research was that internal consulting units (ICUs) would use such approaches and charge for their services as a way of establishing their value. However, as noted earlier, this was rarely the case, with the majority reluctant to go to this extent in commercialising their activities with client managers. This is not to say that consultant managers rejected the premise that added value (and so their credibility) could be more easily identified through charging their clients. For example, Neil, the head of a consultant manager unit in HealthCo3, argued that the failure of consultant managers in general to use charging mechanisms meant

> Their work in many organisations isn't used to get the traction or to get the juice out of it, because the organisation that's the recipient

hasn't had to go through a process of deciding what they regard as the value of this process and doesn't necessarily engage with it as seriously as they would if they were paying.

Interestingly, where clients were asked to pay, this could be effective and accepted across the organisation. In HealthCo2, for example, the ICU charged a daily rate for the use of their consultant managers. Each division in the organisation was allocated a set number of 'free' days, but once this was exceeded, they then had to pay for additional days out of their operational budget. Importantly, this ICU had high credibility, had not experienced any problems in securing projects and had actually expanded its range of services, including engaging in external consultancy work with other health care organisations. Similarly, Peter, the learning and development director in a large Australian accounting firm, charged company managers for the use of his group's training and consultancy services: 'So we have a charge back system whereby most of the divisions have their own training budget and they buy the training services from us. If I can't sell my training services, I can't make budget.'

Nevertheless, in the majority of cases, consultant managers did not adopt such an approach and were often sceptical about doing so. A number of explanations for this were presented, with the complexity and administration of a charging mechanism the most common – a view summed up by Alan, a principal consultant in GovServ1: 'The sponsor incurs no costs. So he is not buying consultancy; it's centrally funded ... So there is all sorts of scope for money zipping all over the place. So it's very unlikely that we can have a sensible mechanism for doing it.' Other concerns were the difficulty of establishing a coherent cost base for the consultant manager (and one that would be lower than that of an external consultant). Also, as Graham, a business consultant in TransCo, explained, the marketisation of their work could be *self-defeating* for the organisation – because ability to pay did not necessarily equate to need for consultancy:

there are pros and there are cons, and the pros are obvious, that you get an immediate measure of value and you know what you're worth, you get the equivalent of a market signal. The cons are that, for example, it may cause the sort of behaviours which actually go against the reason for setting up an internal consulting unit in the first place, and for example, if we know that there are areas where we can add great value, but actually that area doesn't have any money to pay for the consulting this year, it's not necessarily that efficient a market mechanism for getting consulting in the areas where it's most needed.

An alternative to direct charging as an indicator of added value was to provide clients with a summary of the costs of a project (including time sheets), which could then be set against any efficiency savings. In addition, some units produced comparisons based on the likely relative costs of employing an external consultancy to do similar work. Matt, a specialist marketing consultant manager in GovAgency1, explained how this worked: 'Our team produces a statement every month to say, "This is what it's cost in terms of internal costs. This is what similar work would cost in the outside market." So we have that comparison with the outside market in terms of what we're doing.' However, this could also be problematic as it assumed that internal and external consultancy were considered equivalent and might portray the former as a 'cheap' alternative (see also Chapter 6). Overall then, clearly establishing merit-based indicators of the value of consultant managers work was both an imperative and yet often problematic – a further indication of the potential tensions and ambiguities in neo-bureaucracy more generally.

MAINTAINING INDEPENDENCE AND AUTONOMY FROM RESPONSIBILITY

Such tensions around the ability to demonstrate added value were often exacerbated because consultant managers typically had limited control over how far their recommendations were implemented. Clearly, implementation can be defined in a number of different ways, and a traditional view of internal consultants is that they are *more* likely than externals to be involved in it. However, a common reaction across our study (and in keeping with traditional manager–staff professional and manager–external consultant distinctions) was that operational managers should take responsibility for making changes that emerged from the analytical work of the consultant managers and their client project teams. There were practical reasons for this. For example, Diana, a programme director in CommsCo, argued that 'implementation *per se* works faster, a lot faster and [at] a lot less cost when it's in the direct line management of the unit'. In LocalGov2 as well, Brian claimed that his team could not afford to become involved in implementation, although he accepted this could have a detrimental impact on project outcomes:

> When we were set up, our boss was clear that we were not going to implement all the things that we identified. If we started to implement things people would have sat back, let us do it ... But that in itself causes some problems in that we can work quite hard and [identify] detailed actions, but sometimes it's the capacity of the individual we leave behind to actually do things [that is important] ... It's quite easy for them then, if we don't detail the actions, to confuse what we said ... [and] to give that as an excuse for not bringing the change about.

For Brian, the solution to this problem was to maintain some control over project outcomes by deliberately tasking client managers with responsibility for implementation and offering them ongoing support. This suggests that implementation remained a key concern even though consultant managers remained resistant to becoming too involved. For example, in GovServ1, Ray, the assistant director of continuous improvement, feigned disinterest in implementation as a means of encouraging client managers to take ownership of actions and recommendations:

> We then hand over. We say 'phew, you developed all this, we didn't, we just supported you to develop it. If you don't achieve those

actions ... Phew, couldn't care less, that's your problem!' Of course it isn't, 'cause I've got this wider remit to [maintain] the culture of continuous improvement. But basically they then take the credit, they implement, they get on with it.

Elsewhere, the consultant manager's role in implementation was a matter of debate as Geoff, a principal consultant who managed the ICU in GovServ2, explained:

Well my team and I disagree on this. If you were to ask the team, they want to be involved in implementation, they want to take it to that next stage. But I've resisted that for two reasons. First of all implementation is often long-term, heavily involved, difficult to extract yourself from, so I don't think that's us. I don't think implementation requires consultancy skill in the same way that researching and coming up with solutions does. And I actually think that it's part ... this is my perspective, part of being a consultant is recognising that it's the business owner that's the key player.

Such a debate or tension can partly be linked to the fact that achieving client credibility relied on consultant managers being able to demonstrate added value. This would be more likely if they were able to directly influence the implementation of their recommendations. Thus, consultant managers (as with the external counterparts) were both enabled and constrained by the advice-based nature of their relationships. Indeed, the tension was most explicit when clients downplayed or rejected the expert, advisory role of consultant managers in favour of seeing them simply as an additional resource – a 'body shop'. This meant not only using consultant managers for implementing tasks but also that the work of the consultant manager would be more tightly controlled by the client managers. In FinCo1, Davina, a divisional managing director to whom the ICU reported, reflected on this issue:

Some [managers] just want an extra pair of hands and I say to Belinda [internal consultancy manager], 'never appear willing to be the

> minute taker, the admin, I do not want the group doing that'. And
> I think I've been very strict on that because I also think it does our
> reputation no good at all if we're seen as that ... I don't like them
> doing that sort of work, I think their brains are better than that ...
> I think there's always a fear maybe the pipeline [of new business]
> will go away.

As this last point reveals, the need to undertake 'genuine advisory work'
was key, although not always possible – something Belinda herself discussed, explaining her concerns that her unit might be perceived as the

> service engine, the implementations engine. I think we do have to be
> careful about being seen that we can be an equal partner, that we are
> not just the resource, because what I hear more and more is, 'The
> consulting team are helping us', [and] that's not really what we
> want to be.

Instead, Belinda wanted her team to be seen as a genuinely independent group responsible for delivering valuable objective advice to their
clients. However, doing so meant establishing a position outside of
the political context in which managers sought to protect and expand
their own resources as identified in the management work literature
(Luthans, 1988). This was a significant issue in CommsCo, where
there was some debate about the value of a centralised change agency
unit. This unit was used (in part) as a 'body shop' from which senior
divisional managers could request consultant managers to work on
specific projects, although, as Valerie, one of these divisional managers, insisted, only as long as the lines of authority remained clear:
'As far as I'm concerned, as long as I've got control over the people and
they are fully capable of doing the role they're doing, I don't really mind
whether I line manage them or whether the central [ICU] team line
manage them.'

This desire to establish control over consultant managers was
a means by which divisional managers could also ensure that they
controlled and were responsible for – 'owned' – any change agenda in

their domain. For example, Matt, a consultant manager, described the view of a senior divisional manager towards the central change unit: 'He said, "So you give me the people, I know I applaud the people, but don't tell me [ICU] is delivering my transformation, it isn't, *we are*".' Inevitably, this view was a source of frustration for the consultant managers, who saw themselves as a key independent and objective resource for developing the change agenda in CommsCo. However, and once again, it was this very independence that undermined the ability of consultant managers to achieve credibility. As Diana, another divisional manager, explained, 'I think we try to make those people [consultant managers] be change agents, where in my view, they cannot be very successful change agents due to the fact that they sit outside of the line. So their ability to earn the trust and credibility of the sponsor would take a significant amount of time.'

Consequently, despite the efforts consultant managers put into relationship management, their outsider status or ambiguous location in the formal structure could still act as a barrier to developing credibility – almost regardless of whether they were able to demonstrate added value. This indicates that a notionally independent status and market-based relationships did not prevent consultant managers from being subject to the political nature of management in which individual or functional groups of managers compete to protect and extend their sphere of authority (Armstrong, 1989). Indeed, in one, albeit extreme, example, Geoff in GovServ2 had been directly confronted with political pressure to adapt findings which challenged his and his unit's independent position:

> there was one incident where the [operational manager] actually asked me to stop the study and throw it in the bin because he didn't want us to record the answer we were about to record, and there was an awful lot of pressure to re-write the report, which we refused to do. But that generated a lot of ill-feeling. There's one division here who will probably not use us again because we didn't manipulate the findings [for them].

Such an incident highlights again the challenges of the hybrid nature of neo-bureaucratic management and in particular the characteristic of *delegated autonomy*. Here, consultant managers sought to operate partially outside of this political (i.e. hierarchical and functional) environment in an almost free-floating role, yet it was clear that it remained a key factor in deciding with whom they worked and could be a source of significant uncertainty and conflict.

SENIOR MANAGEMENT SPONSORSHIP

These tensions of *delegated autonomy* and the need for consultant managers to engage explicitly with the politicised context in organisations – *structured organisational politics* – were most evident in their relationships with senior management. As we have seen, working partially outside of traditional hierarchical structures is a key feature of neo-bureaucracy, highlighting the extent to which, by contrast, traditional management is bound up in tightly controlled systems of reporting and accountability (Hales, 1986). Indeed, consultant managers took a pragmatic approach which involved working with and around existing hierarchical systems. In CommsCo, Steve, who was head of governance in the change unit, reflected upon this:

> People will hate me for saying this, [but] CommsCo is still quite hierarchical and it is quite command and control still, and I think the truth is that you need to see the guy at the top say 'it's important' and then you need to see him model its importance by investing time and effort into it, in order to believe that it's going to happen.

In short, within this context, it was critical for consultant managers to build relationships with senior management because they were very often reliant on them for patronage, authority and legitimacy (see also Pettigrew, 1975).

As outlined in Chapter 2, some ICUs reported directly to CEOs, but more generally they were associated with one or a small number of specific individuals. In HealthCo2, the CEO was seen to be central to the success of the ICU on account of the value he attached to its role.

Celia, the director of the ICU, argued that this support distinguished her unit from others:

> I know that if [the CEO] hadn't supported the internal service, it wouldn't have worked. And I know, talking to other internal consultants outside of HealthCo2, that internal consultancies have failed because one, they hadn't been able to maintain their independence or they hadn't had the support of the Chief Exec, and he is utterly convinced of the value of internal consultancy within the organisation.

The role of the CEO here helped to ensure that the ICU was working in line with his priorities and, crucially, was able to highlight this when seeking to persuade different areas to use its services.

Such a relationship could also work to the advantage of the CEO if he/she needed an 'independent' source of advice and insight which could then be employed in or imposed on any area of the organisation. In TransCo, for example, the ICU was established by the deputy CEO (who subsequently became CEO), and he used them to address wider issues within the organisation, as explained by Dan, the head of strategic analysis (the ICU):

> I think part of the benefit of having us there for [the deputy CEO] was he could maybe scare [other] people a bit sometimes, in terms of he would say, 'Well I'll give this to the guys who sit around the corner [the ICU] and they'll sort it out for me', and that would cause everyone [else] to go off and work a little bit harder.

Clearly, this often helped to ensure that the unit was considered credible across the organisation, so long as the CEO remained credible. However, Dan was not entirely comfortable with being used in this way because he felt that it undermined his unit's independence. Indeed, a similar situation occurred in FinCo4, as described by Ian, the head of the change management department:

> we actually became almost seen as that deputy CEO's eyes and ears around the organisation, which was actually quite detrimental to

> what we were trying to do, and we fought that quite long and hard ...
> We were almost – every opening conversation you had with
> somebody was about the fact that 'no, we are independent, we just
> happen to fall under them [the deputy CEO] in the structure chart'
> and all this sort of thing.

In LocalGov1 too, Nate, the head of performance management, also recognised the potentially problematic nature of his team's links to the CEO, claiming that 'some people are suspicious of us' and that it also 'closes some doors because we're close to him'. As a consequence, consultant managers faced a paradox whereby their dependence on the status and sponsorship of a senior manager was, on occasion, a source of uncertainty and insecurity – particularly if the consultant managers had few other sources of credibility such as respect for expertise or agreed measures of added value (see also Sturdy, et al., 2013). Such dependence was starkly illustrated in the case of FinCo4, where the unit was effectively disbanded after its sponsor and executive director retired and was replaced by one who, according to Dan, 'Took one look at it and said, "What you're doing, the HR department ought to be doing, and the other bit that you're doing, the managers ought to be able to do for themselves. I don't want an internal consultancy anymore."'

MANAGING COMPETITION: INTERACTIONS WITH EXTERNAL CONSULTANTS

Competitive threats did not only exist *within* the organisation from operational and other managers, but for many of our respondents, an ongoing challenge also was to maintain their legitimacy against rival *external* management consultants. For example, as Angela, a consultant manager in the OD field in a large Australian resource company, confided, 'there is no mandate that says, if you want facilitation, you have to go through OD to get it. You can pick up a phone and call your mate ... [an external]. We're none the wiser.' Such a threat was a common refrain in many of our interviews and was a key element of their neo-bureaucratic status in that it required them to combine both an *internal and external orientation*, that is, awareness of both the needs and expectations of client managers and how to position themselves in relation to external suppliers. This dual orientation led to different responses from outright competition through to more collaborative 'boundary-spanning' relationships in which consultant managers engaged in relationships outside the organisation, including drawing on external consultants as service providers and even collaborators in their activities.

One response to such external rivals was for consultant managers to act as organisational *gatekeepers*. Here, respondents described their efforts to control the entry stages of the external consulting process by way of quality control and/or protecting self-interest. Hence, Peter, a consultant manager based in a large accounting firm, spoke about the constant 'cold calls' from external consultants and his role in deciding who would be allowed to pitch for work: 'At least three or four external consultants contact me each week and I would probably maybe talk to one of them. I mean the other three they ring on the phone, I just say "sorry, not interested".' In this role, consultant managers often highlighted their ability to see beyond an external consultant's convincing sales pitch and distinguish those with the required expertise. Hence, Della emphasised her rational approach to selection: 'I have limited time. I don't want to be sold at. I want to assess who is the organisation [consultancy firm] that's going to come closest to meeting my requirements, not who is the organisation that are best at selling their skills.'

To be a successful gatekeeper relied to a significant extent on the consultant manager's personal reputation and legitimacy as an internal expert. As Daniel, the learning and development manager in a global investment bank, noted, he could sometimes use his subject expertise to prevent senior managers from hiring externals: 'I'm quite confident to say to the MDs [managing directors] in my business that I don't agree with that. Quite often that's the point at which they'll start to doubt themselves, so if I can get that seed of doubt in there, then I can often stop it.' Indeed, several respondents questioned whether externals posed a competitive threat at all, given their own strength in this gatekeeping role and their superior technical expertise. Hence, Sophie, a consultant manager from a global engineering firm, dismissed the potential for what she termed 'rogue buying' of external consultancy by colleagues without first gaining her approval. In this sense, she played a role similar to that of central purchasing departments in client firms, which control and sometimes frustrate both external consultants and operational managers in client roles (O'Mahoney, et al., 2013; Werr and Pemer, 2007). Others stressed a demarcation between the strategic activities of the consultant manager (implying a superior knowledge claim), and the use of external consultants as extra resources or 'body shops', engaged in more routine tasks. However, where the competitive threat was clear, some consultant managers used more direct strategies. As Daniel outlined:

> So when the external tries to become intimate with my managers [clients] and starts cutting me out of the game, I have got a problem with that. So I sit them back on their backsides. I will phone them and I will berate them for what they have done ... 'You are eating into my game. I want to know what you are doing with my managers' ... if they break that agreement too many times I will isolate them and move them out.

An alternative response to the competitive threat of external consultants was for consultant managers to seek to insert themselves as *intermediaries* between internal client managers and external consultants. Here, the consultant manager is engaged in the classic boundary-spanning role of sourcing and managing external consultants for their internal colleagues. Often this involved a brokering role in which consultant managers stressed their ability to scan the firm's environment and identify and oversee the adoption of external knowledge (Tushman, 1977). In these situations, they acted as 'intermediate' clients intervening within established consultant–client boundary relations and became the 'contact' client with the external consultant (Schein, 1997). For instance, Peter spoke about how offering himself as a broker of the external consultant–client relationship proved an effective form of intervention where senior partners in his accounting practice had a track record of bypassing him:

> so a tactic that I've taken on is that there is one division I know who were using an external consultant. So I heard about it and went along to the business head and said . . . 'Alright, well I'll tell you what we'll do, we'll take over the management of that [project] . . . ', and he was just delighted to actually give that away. So now it is advertised as a 'Learning and Education' [internal] product and we manage the external provider.

In such circumstances, consultant managers often co-branded with external consultants, thus extending their involvement to the diagnosis and implementation stages of consulting projects. Beyond acting as structural intermediaries, in these brokering roles, consultant managers also served as *interpreters* between external consultants and internal colleagues. For example, several interviewees emphasised the need to brief carefully and closely monitor external consultants in their interactions with other internal employees to ensure consistency with their organisation's activities. For example, Dimity spoke of her time as an external consultant when her expertise in business process re-engineering relied upon consultant managers in client firms acting as translators of the client organisation's norms and customs; 'in terms of the culture I was blind and he [the consultant manager] was my guide'. This conforms to the established view of the value of consultant managers more generally – their organisational knowledge – as well as echoing the few available accounts of managers who work closely with external consultants in the liminal space of project teams (Sturdy, et al., 2009).

Here then, consultant managers acted as a cultural and political bridge, actively mediating between the external consultants and operational managers using their hybrid internal and external orientation.

This boundary spanning was achieved by becoming partially removed from their regular organisational context and identifying with the project tasks and even the consultants. Indeed, such identification was especially evident in another aspect of the brokering role of the consultant managers – translating the 'realities' of external consultancy to internal managers. Hence, Keith, a consultant manager in a food company, spoke about how he sometimes had to chastise his colleagues for their treatment of external consultants. Similarly, Faye, a consultant manager in HR in an insurance company, noted how she had to engage in 'damage control' and stand up for the external provider when things had gone wrong. However, associating closely with externals, including through co-branding, carried some reputational risks. To mitigate these, interviewees spoke about how they laid out strict governance mechanisms for the behaviour of external consultants, which often linked to the evaluation of consultant performance in terms of 'value for money' and 'knowledge transfer'.

COLLABORATION AND CO-PRODUCTION: SOCIAL TIES AND PARTNERSHIP

While gatekeeping and brokering were common approaches to the competitive threat of external consultants, consultant managers also outlined more cooperative relationships, most specifically by partnering with externals as collaborators in organisational interventions and projects and knowledge exchange. Such interactions provided them with a means of learning and professional development and, as noted above, ensuring external providers understood the internal culture and political landscape of their organisation. Moreover, collaboration allowed consultant managers to take on a greater 'front stage' role with their internal clients.

Consultant managers' use of the imagery of partnership highlighted varying levels of engagement in external relations. For some, a controlling influence persisted, while others saw external consulting partners more as peers and colleagues in the design and implementation of organisational innovations. For Daniel, this involved issues of trust and knowledge sharing such that the organisational boundary was downplayed:

> So I think of them [externals] being part of my extended team . . . It is a true deeper relationship and that means total transparency. I share all information with them. Organisational information, we share on an emotional level and a psychological level, so they know how I feel about things in the organisation. I might tell them about things that I don't agree with.

The co-production of management knowledge in such relationships was also stressed. As was the case in the brokering role, at a basic level this involved characterisations by consultant managers of the blending of their detailed organisational knowledge with the consultant's external expertise or methodologies, resulting in a more customised organisational solution. At a deeper level, however, interviewees provided examples of a more open process of collaborative *exploration* where the boundary distinctions between internal and external knowledge blurred. Here, in keeping with the more positive images of joint consultant–client project work (Kitay and Wright, 2004), interactions were presented as a 'meeting of minds' in which internal and external consultant brainstormed and bounced ideas off one another. Hence, Sam, the director of a boutique external strategy consultancy, talked about how after half a day working with the consultant managers in a client company – 'I'm not sure whose idea is on the whiteboard anymore'. Similarly, from a consultant manager's perspective, Teresa spoke about how her partnering with a trusted external consultant often involved egging each other on and taking risks in pushing the limits of what might work in presentations to senior internal managers. Such an image suggests elements of creativity, enterprise and innovation which do not sit easily with bureaucratic forms, traditional boundaries and internally focused activity.

Knowledge partnerships between consultant managers and external consultants typically developed over time, often beyond a single consulting project. Accounts were rich in the imagery of reciprocity, trust and strong interpersonal ties – social embeddedness (Das and Teng, 1998) – rather than the formality of some brokering relationships described earlier. For instance, external consultants spoke about how they would go 'the extra mile' and never abuse confidences. Similarly, consultant managers spoke about standing by their external counterparts even in situations where things had gone badly and internal colleagues were unhappy. In particular, the image of 'true partnership' was raised by several of the respondents who had relationships with externals as implying a sufficient level of trust for one party to challenge and confront the other without harming the underlying relationship (see Nooteboom, et al., 2007). For external consultants, this was often represented as being frank and fearless in breaking bad news or 'holding up the mirror' to their consultant manager counterparts, although, as Daniel pointed out, this had its limits:

> There are times when Charlie [external consultant] is the chap with the leadership role, and you try and push something and he says 'shut up, you are just carrying on like a dill, I've got to tell you this is what's happening'. And he'll be right and I'll have to listen … So there will be times when he's in the power seat and I'm going to comply with what he's advising me to do. And then there will be times when I will say, 'hang on Charlie, don't forget who is signing the cheque here son!' So it does move back and forward.

The imagery of consultant managers and external consultants as partners therefore highlighted a far more symbiotic and open relationship than was the case in brokering roles or more conventional boundary spanning. Furthermore, the discourse of partnership with externals could add to the status and knowledge claims of consultant managers. Partnership implied security in both their role as organisational representatives and cosmopolitan professionals who were willing to share their knowledge and were open to learning with their trusted external colleagues. As noted above, however, such relations were dynamic, involving risks and tensions and the potential for a return to more competitive interaction, that is, control through the market rather than hierarchy.

CONCLUSION

In answering the question of with whom do consultant managers work (see Table 5.1), we have focused on operational and senior managers as clients and/or sponsors, along with external relations with consultants. In each case, the fact that the work of consultant managers is typically based around market principles, if not always strictly in practice, is key. In particular, clients have significant discretion over how (and how much) they use the services of consultant managers. As a consequence, consultant managers are obliged to engage in more and less formal relationship management activities in seeking to generate work through knowledge of the priorities of client managers and by pointing to the value they could add within any given project. Consultant managers also sought to regulate their involvement in implementation work as this could undermine their advisory relationship, even if it could also add to credibility. The need to source work through a market approach and engaging in lateral and external relationships distinguished them from bureaucratic managers whose relationships are often characterised as primarily hierarchical, functional and/or based around informal (and politicised) networks.

However, the notion that consultant managers operate outside of a hierarchical and therefore politicised context is misplaced, in that their advisory role as independent experts is not automatically accepted by operational managers, highlighting again the ambiguity of their hybrid neo-bureaucratic role. Their 'staff professional' status lacked traditional authority relations, so they needed to use political and influencing strategies to try and ensure acceptance of their expertise and services by internal managers as potential 'clients'. In a similar vein, their quasi-independent status and advisory role meant consultant managers were keen to contract work directly with client managers through market mechanisms (e.g. based on a cost–benefit analysis or direct charging), freeing them from open-ended work embedded in

Table 5.1 *The nature of relationships in consultant managers' activities*

Consultant managers' activities	Main features	Distinction from managers in bureaucracy	Tensions, ambiguities and uncertainties
Relationships With whom do consultant managers work?	Advisory/lateral relationships based around market mechanisms	Less emphasis on hierarchy/political relationships as a source of work	Difficulty of identifying measures of added value
	Limited involvement in implementation/delivery	Able to exercise more choice over work (i.e. saying 'no')	Hard to guarantee outcomes from advisory position – need to be involved in implementation
	Active relationship management activity to generate projects	Added value has to be made explicit – cannot be assumed	Used as additional resource rather than experts
	Focus on added value (e.g. cost–benefit analysis) to build credibility	Not responsible for day-to-day delivery – implementation delegated to operational managers	Reliant on precarious senior management for credibility
	Varying relationships with external providers and consultants ('gatekeepers', 'brokers' and 'partners')	Focus on being 'enterprising' and 'boundary spanning' regarding external relations	Potential for competitive relations with external consultants, and/or reputational risk from external partners' activities

functional processes and allocated through traditional hierarchical procedures. However, in requiring operational managers to act as clients, consultant managers were constrained by the need to remain credible and ensure that their work was *perceived* as adding value in order to secure both the right quality and quantity of work. In the absence of widely accepted metrics for demonstrating added value and with some client managers seeking to use them simply as an additional resource – a body shop – consultant managers relied on senior management sponsorship to validate their role, leaving them more vulnerable to being disbanded when personnel changed and to losing any status they might have acquired as independent. In short, and in keeping with the hybridity of neo-bureaucracy, they faced *both* hierarchy and market relations.

Consultant managers not only had the prospect of being disbanded in favour of delegating responsibilities to operational managers or some other form of internally organised change specialism, but they also experienced the competitive threat of internal managers bypassing their services and using external consultants as a source of advice and/or change facilitation. Here, consultant managers developed various responses including attempts at 'gatekeeping' the entry of external competitors and offering to source and broker external providers for internal managers. They also developed collaborative relationships and strong ties with external consultants as part of a cosmopolitan orientation and external boundary-spanning role, sometimes resulting in innovation.

In taking on the roles of 'gatekeepers', 'brokers' or 'partners', consultant managers engaged in another form of political manoeuvring. Those who managed it most successfully emphasised their personal reputation as internal experts to external consultants as well as their boundary-spanning role as a source of social capital and new knowledge for internal clients and sponsors – both 'cosmopolitan' and 'local'. Hence, like external consultants who rely upon a form of 'networked reputation' in their interactions with corporate clients (Glückler and Armbrüster, 2003), consultant managers are also continually engaged in reputation building within their organisations or, at least, are conscious of the need to do so. This tension of being to some extent an 'outsider within' is a theme we return to in greater depth in the following chapters in considering the occupational and identity characteristics of the consultant manager.

6 The occupational and career tensions of the consultant manager

INTRODUCTION

Examining the core activities and relationships of the consultant manager in the previous chapters drew attention to a series of tensions and ambiguities associated with this neo-bureaucratic form of work. In this chapter, we explore some of these tensions further by locating them within an *occupational* framework in which (external) management consultancy is emulated, diffused and appropriated within organisations. As we argued in Chapter 1, management consultancy is not only a form of neo-bureaucratic management but also a key mechanism through which management has become more neo-bureaucratic. As intimated in the previous chapter, this is partly achieved through consultant managers partnering with external consultants. However, this is probably less significant than other mechanisms of change.

In this chapter, we shall initially discuss how the spread of consulting across management occurs through shifts in management education and, more recently and directly, the active importation of consultancy practices and skill sets into various managerial and professional groups (e.g. accountancy and information technology (IT)), including through directly hiring former external management consultants into (consultant) management positions. We then examine one outcome of this importation, namely the further blurring of managerial and consultancy career paths and occupational boundaries. Indeed, the experiences of consultant managers in our sample indicate that this can lead to occupational contestation and congestion as different groups seek jurisdiction over the activities and expertise associated with management consultancy. This creates a fluid set of occupational and career dynamics in which neo-bureaucratic managers develop *marketised careers* where personal responsibility for career development is applied to internal and/or external career paths. As we shall argue, this has the effect of increasing the ambiguity and uncertainty of the consultant manager's role and reinforces our key theme that neo-bureaucracy extends, rather than resolves, the dilemmas and contradictions within and between traditional or bureaucratic management and post-bureaucracy.

OCCUPATIONAL SEGMENTATION AND THE BLURRING OF MANAGEMENT AND CONSULTING CAREERS

As we saw in Chapter 2, traditional definitions of 'professional' management consultancy have stressed differences with management (Kubr, 1996). Key points of differentiation exist around issues of expertise, formal authority and career development/stability (see also Table 2.3). At the same time, a few have stressed or prescribed commonality (Schein, 1987), leading us to adopt an intermediate, 'both/and' position, where there are structural similarities at the same time as a shifting relationship according to context, for example (see Table 2.4). Indeed, we have shown how the development of consulting roles within organisations, combined with the redesign of managerial activities around project-based work, client relationships and the management of organisational change, further challenges the distinctive occupational status of consultancy. If we understand occupations as combinations of job activities which define an economic role – 'the work that one does' (Hodson and Sullivan, 2002: 47) – then the emergence of the 'consultant manager' appears to minimise many of the differences asserted in traditional accounts of management and consultancy.

Of course, there is debate about whether management consultancy, or for that matter management, should be considered an occupation at all. The wide diversity of the work activities and specialisations that fall under the rubric of 'management' has led some to question whether this is a meaningful occupational categorisation or primarily a hierarchical level or control function (Brint, 1996).

For instance, a range of writers have stressed the way in which management historically evolved from diverse professional backgrounds including engineering, accountancy and psychology (Rose, 1990; Shenhav, 1999). Here, different managerial functions including production engineers and finance and personnel managers have competed for organisational status as distinct 'managerial professions' (Armstrong, 1986). Similarly, Fincham (2003) has questioned whether management *consultancy* is an occupation or a combination of occupations, with distinct work activities and identities (e.g. strategy, operational efficiency, systems and IT and organisational change consultancy).

However, against this fragmented perspective, others have highlighted the common-sense understandings of those who work within these fields and their representations of themselves as 'managers' and 'consultants' (Grey, 1999; Kitay and Wright, 2007). Furthermore, the historical evolution of management as an occupation and an aspiring 'profession' has been evident in the creation of professional associations of management, distinct forms of managerial education and the popular culture of 'the manager' as a recognisable work persona (Watson, 1994). In a similar vein, the 'persona' of the management consultant has become increasingly evident in popular culture and discourse (e.g. TV series such as *House of Lies*) and in management education (e.g. specialist training and courses in consulting skills). Moreover, leading consulting firms have stressed an image of an elite profession, in order to maintain their legitimacy in the eyes of their clients and their employees – a form of 'corporate professionalism' (Kipping, 2011; McKenna, 2006).

Our analysis of the internalisation of consultancy within corporate and public sector organisations through individual managerial roles and consulting groups provides further insights into the interrelationship between consultancy and management. While we by no means suggest that the occupational concepts of 'manager' and 'consultant' are redundant, we find evidence of an increased blurring of this distinction, both through former external management consultants moving 'in-house' and taking up what could be considered a more conventional managerial role and by existing managers seeking to adopt the language and practices of consultancy. Three particular themes are evident here: first, the appropriation of consultancy by different managerial specialisms; second, the diffusion of consulting skills in management education; and third, drawing more directly on our data, the career dispersion of former external management consultants into organisational roles.

Occupational appropriation of consultancy

As noted in Chapter 2, Kipping (2002) has argued that the history of management consulting has been closely tied to the development of management as an occupation and the changing demands of industry or capital. For example, the 'first wave' of management consultants derived from the field of engineering and developed 'efficiency' techniques for the burgeoning factories of the early twentieth century (Wright and Kipping, 2012). The 'second' and 'third waves' of consulting firms were strongly influenced by alternative occupational and professional groupings, including law, accounting, personnel management and more recently information technology and project management (David, et al., 2013; Kipping, 2002).

However, the relationship between these 'managerial professions' (Armstrong, 1986) and management consultancy has in fact flowed both ways over time, as the activity and discourse of consultancy has also been appropriated by different occupational groups. This has been particularly evident in the development of the major accounting and audit firms which are among the largest global providers of consulting services. Indeed, McDougald and Greenwood (2012) characterise consultancy as the 'cuckoo in the nest', raising conflicts of interest that fundamentally challenge the traditional business model of audit work. The appropriation of consultancy as an activity has become so pronounced in managerial accounting that it led to the break-up of major accounting practices and the creation of new business enterprises from their original accounting parents (most evident in the famed separation of Andersen Consulting from Arthur Andersen in 1989 – the former renaming itself Accenture in 2001) (Niece and Trompeter, 2004).

In a similar manner, consultancy has also been appropriated by IT, where not only specialist consulting firms have developed, but the language and identity of consultancy has permeated to IT practitioners in organisations more generally. This led to existing management consulting firms providing IT-related services, but as computer technologies have changed (e.g. personal computers, networked systems, the Internet and online businesses), technology companies have also increasingly adopted consulting approaches (Galal, et al., 2012; Nolan and Bennigson, 2005). In particular, the evolution of often standardised practices of change management in the development and implementation of IT systems highlights how consultancy concepts have become a core part of the occupational identity of IT professionals. This adds to a long-standing shared tradition in *project* management, perhaps derived from the non-continuous nature of the work and a common history of engineering.

The field of human resource management (HRM) provides further insight into how the appropriation of consultancy is evident not only in the establishment of consulting businesses but also at the level of practitioner thinking and managerial practice. Perceived for decades by its own practitioners as the 'poor cousin' of the managerial professions, during the 1990s HR writers advocated the need for a reinvention of the function around the concept of a 'business partner' and 'trusted adviser' to senior management (Ulrich, 1998; Ulrich and Brockbank, 2005). Implicit within these depictions of a new model of the HR practitioner was an emphasis on consultancy skills (Caldwell, 2001; Hunter, et al., 2006; Kenton and Yarnall, 2005; Robinson and Robinson, 2005). As an 'internal consultant', the HR practitioner was seen as advising senior managers about key strategic issues and facilitating major organisational changes. Rather than relying on the power of their bureaucratic position, the HR 'business partner' was seen as a skilful 'change agent' using his/her political and interpersonal skills to influence change (Kenton and Moody, 2003; Robinson and Robinson, 2005). While the actual uptake of such a strategic view of the HR function is debated (Caldwell, 2003, 2008; Wright, 2008), the adoption of the language of change agency and consultancy amongst HR practitioners further indicates the occupational appropriation of consultancy discourse and practice (Wylie, et al., 2014). As we shall see shortly, such a move was evident among those of our research participants in HR roles but resulted in various tensions and dilemmas.

Management education and management as consultancy

While different managerial functions have actively sought to appropriate consultancy, a second path for the development of management into a (neo-bureaucratic) form that is similar to consulting has been through changes in management education. As noted in Chapter 2, a key differentiator between management and consultancy was access to abstract and formalised management knowledge. Such knowledge was traditionally the preserve of only the elite of management but was more common in consulting. However, over the last thirty years, the expansion of business school education and the master of business administration (MBA) course in particular have served to spread formal management knowledge to a much wider audience, even if they have not (yet) succeeded in addressing the hopes of those wishing to professionalise management (Khurana, 2007). This has meant that a larger group of managers are exposed to the generic tools and methods of management *and* consultancy. Although formal education is not the only way of acquiring such knowledge, such a development led Belinda in CommsCo to observe that 'If I look at what the ... knowledge gap between managers then [15 years ago] and managers now is – it's .... closed. There are some really good line managers, directors and so forth who have got as much knowledge as some of the consultants that are out there peddling their wares.'

However, management becoming more like consulting is not simply a consequence of more managers receiving the same kind of education as consultants, or of them being exposed as consulting clients to formalised management techniques learned in business schools. Rather, sections of the consulting industry have actively shaped the nature of business education, and the MBA in particular, and, certainly, there has been a reciprocal relationship between the top business schools and consulting firms (Engwall, 2012). Indeed, some have argued that the influence of management consulting has been so great that 'by the end of twentieth century, the leading professional service firms had first captured, and then redirected, the elite business schools to serve the specialized needs of their own quasi-professions' (McKenna, 2006: 2). While this redesign of management education towards management consulting, and aligned professional services (such as investment banking), might have served to reinforce the contrast with more conventional management careers in industrial and service organisations, we argue that this has also been critical in reshaping how managers conceive of their role, activities and marketised careers.

For example, the history of management education has involved an ongoing contestation between those who have promoted the need for 'practical' skills and others who see university-based education of managers as the path to the true professionalisation of management (Daniel, 1998; Khurana, 2007; Mintzberg, 2004; Pfeffer and Fong, 2002). Management consultancies were key players in this process, with prominent consultants serving on the faculty and governing bodies of leading business schools, such as Harvard, Wharton and the University of Chicago (Engwall, 2012). This was crucially linked to firms such as McKinsey & Co. redesigning their hiring practices away from experienced managers and towards young business school graduates (David, 2012; McKenna, 2006). This approach not only reinforced the importance of business schools as sources of future consulting labour but also provided an image or 'ideology of professionalisation' for consulting firms that was critical for client legitimacy and employee loyalty (McKenna, 2006: 209). The influence of management consulting on management education increased during the 1980s and 1990s as consultancy became the leading career choice of most business school graduates. As Lemann (1999: 209) noted, for the 'best and brightest' graduates of America's leading business schools:

> Management consulting in general and the McKinsey Business-analyst program in particular have been the plum post-college jobs of the nineties . . . The general feeling is that in all the big wide world there are only two default fields of endeavour, as far as postgraduate employment is concerned: investment banking [ever so slightly fading] and management consulting [on the rise].

Business schools recognised the critical place of the consultancy industry as a destination for their graduates as well as a source of students. For example, Northwestern University's Kellogg Business School and INSEAD have around 40 per cent of their MBA graduates accepting jobs in management consulting (Byrne, 2012). In terms of curriculum, the pervasive presence of the business case study in much 'B-school' teaching further engrains a consulting mindset on graduates from an early stage (Armbrüster, 2004). Such cases put students in the position of a senior company executive or adviser faced with a business problem and set them the task of diagnosing the problem and suggesting a solution based on the provided data. At Harvard Business School, which pioneered this method with the explicit support of McKinsey (Edersheim, 2004; McDonald, 2013), there is a strong emphasis on the case method as the dominant pedagogical strategy. Up to 50 per cent of a student's final grade is based on their participation in such exercises, and students are said to study over 500 cases during their two-year MBA programme (HBS, 2013).

It is worth noting that the need for consultant managers to possess recognised management, and even consulting-specific, qualifications was apparent in many of the organisations in our study. Often, this was linked to a desire to increase the perceived quality and professionalism of the staff in their internal consulting group. In the UK public sector, for example, Geoff, the manager of the internal consulting unit (ICU) at GovServ2, pursued a deliberate strategy of improving the skills of his team and placed significant value on prior education, 'So we are now getting the right people. I'm getting people who already have master's degrees; I'm getting people who already have MBAs in particular; I'm getting people who have perhaps developed themselves as project managers, or programme managers who want to come here and build on their skills.'

The focus on management education was also apparent among individual respondents as part of their development of a neo-bureaucratic marketised career. For instance, a majority of the Australian consultant managers interviewed for this study had undertaken some form of business-related postgraduate education, with the MBA a common touchstone. Indicative of this career trajectory, Garry, a senior supply chain manager in a major Australian manufacturing firm, reflected on how the MBA was a necessary step in building his managerial career:

> and then I came upon a time that I thought I needed to do more if I was going to become a more senior person and get paid for what I wanted to do. So I then tackled the MBA. I did an Exec MBA, so it was about 12 years ago now, and then have just moved through more and more senior roles.

For many, this was also linked to earlier career choices such as working in management consultancy, which was seen as adding to their formal management education in providing practical application of the knowledge they had learned. As Barry, a group HR manager in a major Australian resource company, reflected, his career in a major global consulting firm provided a valuable add-on to his formal MBA education:

> so you do learn a lot and it's a really good – in fact one of the MBA professors talked about it a while ago while I was there – consulting – it's a good finishing school for an MBA because you come out of there with lots of theory, lots of latent skills but consulting is a really good way to refine that and it gives a focus.

Such concerns to ensure that consultant managers are suitably skilled and that this can be achieved through formal university education merely hints at the larger relationship between management and business schools that we have briefly outlined above. As noted earlier, this is not just a question of managers now acquiring the same abstract management methods and case-study-based approaches as their consulting cousins once did almost exclusively. Rather, consulting has shaped business school provision partly in its own image, including through reframing it on a model of consultancy problem-solving. Crucially then, this means not just that business schools are a recruiting ground for both managers and consultants but that a key theme in the education of managers is the acquisition or development of consultancy skills and approaches.

A consulting 'diaspora': the organisational importation of consultancy

A third and quite direct mechanism through which management has imported consulting practices and orientations and thereby developed a more hybrid neo-bureaucratic form has been the conscious recruitment of former external management consultants into management roles, as consultant managers. In many contexts, this can still bring quite a clash of cultures and practices, which is often precisely what is hoped for by those advocating bringing in outsiders. As we saw in Chapter 2, traditional managerial careers based upon strong internal labour markets and long job/employer tenure helped form part of the conventional distinction between management and consultancy. While the early management consultancies often hired experienced, senior managers from engineering and accounting backgrounds, and senior consultants sometimes moved back into executive positions in major corporations (Wright and Kipping, 2012), these were limited in extent and failed to affect the vast majority of managers whose careers relied upon years of loyal service and steady intra-organisational progression (Donnelly, 2009). In contrast, and as we have seen, the neo-bureaucratic manager is considered to experience much greater flux and churn in their careers as a result of organisational restructuring, downsizing and de-layering (Hassard, et al., 2012; Martin, 2005).

Indeed, neo-bureaucratic managers lack much of the job security of their predecessors and are encouraged to adopt an enterprising work identity, branding themselves as a marketable commodity, and constantly open to new job opportunities and a 'portfolio career' (Peters, 1997; Pink, 2001; Storey, et al., 2005).

While such changes have sometimes been exaggerated as part of claims surrounding '*post*-bureaucracy', various studies have pointed to greater job insecurity among managers across a range of sectors (Farrell and Morris, 2013). In many respects these features of neo-bureaucratic management echo those of management consultants. For example, and as we have noted already, job mobility has been an ongoing feature of management consulting. Indeed, various industry surveys suggest that more than half of all consulting staff leave the industry within seven years of entering it (O'Mahoney and Markham, 2013: 367). As Maister (1993) has documented, the leverage structure of consulting firms (the proportion of juniors to seniors) is maintained through a constant turnover of staff – 'up or out'. Such turnover has also been shaped by the high work demands placed on junior consulting staff, with long working hours, job stress and travel demands making it something of a young person's job (Carroll and Moore, 2013).

These issues were relevant to those of our respondents who had had an earlier career in external management consultancy (e.g. 60 per cent of our Australian sample and 20 per cent in the UK). For instance, Kim talked about how as a young external consultant she had 'burnt out at the age of 24' after end-to-end projects, long hours and constant travel. In CommsCo, Matt explained that he had moved into a consultant manager role because 'in my previous role as an external consultant I probably spent five/six days a week away from home … [and] I didn't want to be all over the place'. Others expressed frustration with the repetition of consulting assignments and methodologies and the need to broaden their skills beyond project-based organisational change. As Sophie outlined, 'we were just getting the same work constantly … so it's not really exciting when you're doing that for project after project after project'. In a different vein, Garry expressed the frustration of failing to see his interventions through to completion: 'I wanted to be involved in the end-to-end improvement in an organisation.' Indeed, many former consultants expressed the need to expand their operational and functional expertise by moving into a corporate setting. As Susan noted of her desire to move from consulting to another type of organisation, 'I thought it would sharpen my CV, I thought it would deepen it.' These attitudes are expressed in a more extreme form on industry websites and discussion boards, where issues of long working hours, rigid management control and career uncertainty remain a source of criticism.

This movement of consultants into industry – a 'consulting diaspora' – is encouraged by both consultancies and industry (Sturdy and Wright, 2008). For instance, leading management consultancies, especially, have used the high turnover of staff to their advantage through the development of extensive 'alumni' networks of hopefully loyal former consultants who can act as referents back to the consultancy for future work or simply as clients (McKenna, 2006; O'Shea and Madigan, 1997). As management consulting firms have grown in size and scale, so their alumni networks are now significant influencers of managerial employment. For instance, and as noted earlier, McKinsey has an extensive alumni network, characterised as a key way in which former 'consultants make and sustain professional relationships' (www. mckinsey.com/alumni). A number of our respondents commented on the importance of such consultancy alumni networks in sourcing jobs and transitioning from consulting into an organisational role. As Tina recalled, these networks were often crucial in connecting with future employers who may have also worked at the same consultancy:

> I was thinking what do I want to do next? I mentioned this at the alumni meeting and straight away I had a circle of partners who were putting forward potential roles or contacts who I could talk to. That's a really great feeling.

The employment of former external management consultants into managerial roles is considered to be in organisations' interests as well. As we noted in Chapter 2, having been exposed to consultants through promotional/sales activities and consulting interventions and having a more continuous need for change management, corporations have increasingly sought to internalise such skills. In TransCo, for example, this was achieved by directly appointing the external consultants who had previously been contracted by the organisation as head and deputy head of a new ICU. More generally, experience as a management consultant represented an important source of 'reputational capital' in the managerial labour market (Martin, 2005). Indeed, those interviewees who had come from external consulting backgrounds stressed how their former consulting identity was critical to their current activities. Often this background was considered to have symbolic importance in terms of the association between external consultancy, a commitment to enterprise and organisational change and a willingness to question existing operational procedures. As Angela noted:

> I think they do bring you in because you challenge what is known, and your skill in external consulting is trying to get to the root cause of a problem and ask the difficult questions, because you can. Here, they've always done things a certain way. So fresh blood is going to challenge that.

In addition to the ethos attributed to individuals with external consulting experience, organisations were also interested in what they saw as superior knowledge of the *external* commercial environment and their capacity to act as a bridge to 'leading edge' practice. For example, Leah stated, 'I need to tell them what's happening in the market, how we can do it better ... So people are constantly learning things from me and learning about new products and suppliers and ways of doing things.' As we saw in Chapter 5, this external orientation fits well with neo-bureaucratic approaches and was evident elsewhere. In FinCo1, for example, Jeremy reflected on the reasons for his (and other external consultants') recruitment:

> They were looking to get someone to come in with external
> consulting experience to help effectively bring in a different flavour
> to the team, provide an element of external expertise ... what sort of
> good practices could we actually imbue and also what areas of
> thought leadership that we could create or transfer into the business
> here.

In addition to gaining access to new practices and an external orientation, importing consultancy via external experts was also about creating a blend of knowledge within the organisation, as Davina, the
manager of the ICU in FinCo1, explained:

> Over the last two or so years ... we've been hiring people from
> Accenture to bring in another way of looking at things. So now we
> have a mixture of internal people with very sound process-type skills
> [who] ... understand how a bank works, but we also look for those
> Accenture [people] so .... even the way – this sounds really petty,
> but even the way they present data and stuff. We've got some great
> ideas from one of the guys from Accenture.

Although it is hard to establish the precise extent of this movement of former management consultants into industry, we saw in
Chapter 2 how it has been increasingly reported (e.g. Christensen,
et al., 2013) and was certainly evident across our sample. Working in
external consultancy can help individuals' careers by providing exposure to a range of clients, industries and methods. Indeed, the skills and
knowledge acquired in this work are attractive to organisations seeking to develop more consultancy-informed management roles. This
process therefore opens up an alternative career path and creates a
more fluid environment in which former consultants often undertake
movement between different jobs in industry as well as in interim
management and contracting. They also often rely upon informal
personal ties with former colleagues and alumni in this process –
what O'Mahoney and Markham (2013: 368–9) refer to as 'the Merry-
Go-Round'. This fluidity presents challenges to the coherence and

distinctiveness of consultancy as an occupation. Furthermore, the importation of consultancy skills, be it through occupational appropriation, management education or a consulting diaspora, establishes a number of tensions and contradictions for the consultant manager which our data revealed and to which we now turn.

OCCUPATIONAL INSTABILITY AND TENSIONS

As we have seen, the traditional distinction between management and consultancy as occupations appears to be unravelling as different managerial functions appropriate and learn the practices and discourses of consulting and as consultancy and managerial labour markets merge. However, these trends bring with them tensions and pressures which make the role of the 'consultant manager' a problematic one. Here, we focus on two examples of these tensions. We first consider the challenge facing consultant managers operating within often contested occupational domains where the need to establish jurisdictional boundaries is key. In particular, we focus on the case of the HR function and its attempt to appropriate consultancy despite a weak professional status. We then consider the broader challenge of sustaining the novelty of the consultant manager role over a period of time, particularly given the occupational status of management consultancy and the emphasis upon more fluid marketised careers within neo-bureaucracy.

Consultant managers, jurisdictional boundaries and HRM

The appropriation of management consultancy can, in part, be explained through the notion of inter-professional competition for jurisdiction (Abbott, 1988). Here, securing and defending control over certain activities or task domains is seen as central to maintaining and developing occupational status and, even, sustaining a broader 'professional project'. In some contexts, 'jurisdictional boundaries are perpetually in dispute' (1988: 2) such that any attempt to acquire new responsibilities or activities must be done with an understanding of the alternative and competing claims of other professions. Although not all claims are explicitly contested, what can emerge in this process is the ranking or hierarchical ordering of different occupations and the defensive antagonism between them (Ackroyd, 1996; Armstrong, 1986).

Of course, boundaries between occupations are often hard to sustain in practice, especially in the open type of organisational context in which consultant managers operate. For example, Abbott (1988: 6) refers to the 'fuzzy reality' of jurisdictional claims in the workplace where there is a need for all groups to accommodate organisational imperatives (e.g. efficiency and value creation) within their own knowledge base. This has led to the emergence of a set of occupational groups variously described as organisational, knowledge based (Reed, 1996) or corporate. Muzio et al. (2011) regard management consultancy (as well as project management and executive 'headhunting') as a 'corporate profession' that actively rejects some aspects of traditional professionalisation such as the role of the professional association and a single entry point into the occupation. Instead, much greater emphasis is placed upon the commercial application of their technical expertise and ability to 'add value' as part of efforts to sustain their role and relevance to senior management. Indeed, we saw this clearly in the previous chapter with the efforts of consultant managers to justify their role to others. However, as we have also seen, any attempt to establish and protect jurisdictional boundaries and maintain a cohesive occupational identity for consulting is vulnerable given its appropriation by other groups (e.g. HRM) and the general blurring between consultancy and management.

While we have already seen a little of the *external* competition faced by consultant managers, reflected in their boundary spanning roles with external consultants, many also found that they operated in a congested *internal* domain as well. Here, alternative groups with similar skills and claims could challenge their jurisdiction, although the degree to which they faced direct *competition* from other groups varied. In some instances, high credibility and senior management sponsorship ensured that a unit or individuals would secure control over a particular specialism. For example, in HealthCo2, the internal consultancy group was recognised as a specialist organisational development (OD) unit and as the main source of expertise for dealing with interpersonal relationship/team development concerns. In other contexts, consultant managers were able to coexist happily with others in similar, potentially competing roles. In GovServ2, the internal consultancy group contained a number of consultant managers with coaching qualifications, yet there was also a separate dedicated coaching and mentoring team in the organisation. However, as Geoff, the director of the ICU, explained, the two units worked closely together in order to 'avoid eating each other's sandwiches'.

Other consultant managers and units were not as secure. In FinCo1, for example, beyond the internal consultancy group that we studied, there were seven others. There were also numerous re-engineering, project management, quality and strategic planning groups embedded in different business units. As a result, the ICU had to ensure that it actively promoted its work within its own division as well as diversify and expand its knowledge base – something it did partly through the appointment of individuals with external consulting experience. Similarly, in HealthCo1, the ICU had successfully expanded from an OD focus into project management (see Chapter 4). Nevertheless, the organisation had separately appointed a new project manager to establish a Programme Management Office. This was a source of frustration for the existing consultant managers, who felt that their legitimate claim to jurisdiction in this area had been ignored. In GovServ1 as well, the ICU faced direct competition from a smaller continuous improvement team, which had been established around a senior manager who was nearing retirement. By his own admission, this team was specifically created for this manager largely because of the absence of another suitable role. Nevertheless, he achieved some success, which he put down to following work through to implementation, something the original consultancy unit did not do. As a result, he had been able to expand his team, including by seconding some consultant managers from the original unit, thereby depleting its capacity. Hence, the ability of consultant managers to establish their role and jurisdiction over a knowledge or skills domain was always open to challenge from new and alternative groups and individuals who would lay equal (or better) claim to consultancy skills.

These threats also sometimes presented opportunities, whereby consultant managers were able to use shifting occupational boundaries to their advantage. They could challenge the jurisdiction of other management groups, particularly those who actively sought to appropriate consultancy skills. The example of HRM is again particularly illustrative of this issue. Here, the rise of consultant managers is a potentially significant challenge to the HR function because it highlights how 'people management' issues are not the exclusive responsibility of HR professionals. So, among many consultant managers in our study who focused on HRM issues, few acknowledged professional accreditation or specific educational qualifications as important entry ports to their jobs, and while many did have tertiary qualifications in HRM, many others had come from other disciplinary backgrounds such as engineering, science, marketing, law and operations management. Indeed, some of the most successful and senior individuals stressed practical and career experience outside of traditional HR work. Hence, Rick, the Asia-Pacific HR director for one of the world's largest IT companies, highlighted how he had come to HR work relatively late in his career after fifteen years' working in the core sales function of the organisation. Importantly, he argued his years in sales made him a more effective HR manager through his understanding of the business activities of the firm and his ability to speak the language of line management. Similarly, Kaitlin, the HR director of a global investment bank, outlined how she had moved into HR work after ten years as an operational improvement analyst in a large insurance company. At a lower level, Kirk, an internal HR consultant manager in a multidivisional industrial services company, emphasised the advantages of time spent outside of the HR function running a business unit as an operational manager, which gave him a keener appreciation of financial and business drivers:

Understanding the financials of the business, and every HR person that you talk to today will say 'We're all about the numbers, we know the numbers' – it's just bullshit, they don't. Most of them wouldn't even know the back end of a P&L if they saw it. They may be able to look at it and they may be able to say 'Yeah, look that's the loss and that's the profit' but the key skill becomes how do you influence that? What actions actually change those numbers? They can all talk about this, but that's the key.

This emphasis upon a broader business logic in preference to HR-specific skills was also highlighted by senior respondents who outlined their preferences when hiring graduate employees. As Catherine, an HR business partner in a global engineering firm, outlined:

I'm not looking for HR qualifications. I'm looking for business qualifications with an interest in HR ... I mean let's face it, HR is just a number of processes, it's not hard to learn them. I can teach anybody how to do it and hand-hold through that. But I can't teach business acumen.

As we outlined above, it is in this context that the attempted appropriation of consultancy by HR has developed both through the reframing of HR roles as 'business partners' and 'change agents' (Caldwell, 2003, 2008; Francis and Keegan, 2006; Wright, 2008) and also by the appointment of former external management consultants. These individuals appeared to be in particular demand by large organisations for the skills and expertise they could bring to their new host organisations. In particular, consulting skills such as project management and client and change management tools were seen as particularly valuable by many of the more senior HR respondents. For example, Faye, the HR manager of a large insurance company, outlined how, in establishing a new internal OD consulting group, she deliberately recruited former consultants from the change management practices of the major management consultancies. Many of the interviewees were well aware of the desirability of consulting experience.

As Kim noted in describing her move from a leading management consultancy to the HR function in an investment bank:

> they seemed to think that the skills that I'd learnt in [consultancy name] in terms of being able to take a project and turn it into an outcome were valuable. I remember in the interview I had with them, that's what I wanted to do. I wanted to be able to see a project through to its end. So they seemed to like that.

However, opening up HR to consultant managers was not without its problems, too. Indeed, incorporating consulting skills into the HR function did not automatically enhance its standing. For example, for many of these former consultants, their occupational identity remained more closely linked to consulting than their functional focus on HR-related issues (see also Chapter 7). In CommsCo, Belinda, a regional head of HR, was also at pains to stress that 'I'm not a professional HR person, I probably should've said that at the beginning.'

Indeed, in some cases, respondents' roles and structural locations conflicted with mainstream HR work. Where individuals were involved in large-scale organisational change projects (such as the implementation of enterprise IT systems or a corporate culture change initiative), their structural location was sometimes separated from the HR function within a specific cross-functional project team. Here, the potential rivalry with the mainstream HR function could become pronounced as the older established HR 'locals' fought for resources and influence with these new consulting 'cosmopolitans' (Gouldner, 1957). For instance, Betty, who had come to her current organisation after an operations management degree and working for several years with a large consultancy, commented on the tension between her role as head change agent in a process improvement team involving employee training and communications and the company's HR function:

> For example, the Human Resource Department here, there's no interest in dealing with us at all, so there are some people who are

very cold . . . I still can't work it out with HR. It is very common. It happens at all the companies I've been in. Change Management and HR – I've never seen a great working relationship there.

In cases where the HR function had managed to secure overall formal responsibility for internal consultancy, tensions would remain, with some consultant managers rejecting the occupational association. This was starkly demonstrated in ArtsCo, where Pippa, the OD and change director, admitted: 'The fact that I'm from HR is sometimes the thing I have to get over [conceal] more than anything else, so I kind of don't tell people. I say "I'm from an innovation background and I help people change".'

Similarly, in GovServ3, where the ICU had recently been relocated from a more independent structural location to become part of the HR function, Colin, the head of the ICU, acknowledged that there were some concerns among his consultant managers: 'There are certain members of my team who question whether or not HR is the right place for us to be. I'm comfortable with it on the basis of better the devil you know, I suppose.' As Colin went on to explain, his aim was to shift the identity of these individuals – 'we are trying to stretch them out to become *more consultants and less HR people*' (emphasis added).

Former consultants, therefore, represented a new occupational group which were increasingly engaged in HR oriented work and were potential rivals to more traditional HR staff. As noted earlier, their attractiveness to senior managers lay in their 'cosmopolitan' identity and perceived ability to bring with them new, external knowledge and 'cutting-edge' tools and practices. Importantly, their skills in the consulting process also linked neatly to the desired identity of strategic transformational HRM, as opposed to the more traditional image of HR as a transactional, administrative activity (see also Wylie, et al., 2014). The reinvention of HR managers as consultants therefore seemed to favour these newer entrants, whose consulting skills better enabled them to converse with senior managers in the language of business (and of the business school) and apply their HR expertise in this broader context. Consequently, this attempt to establish and extend the jurisdiction of the HR function through the appropriation of consultancy could, paradoxically, increase its occupational uncertainty by opening HR work to other occupational groups who rejected an association with the HR profession (Wright, 2008).

In summary, then, inter-occupational competition presented consultant managers with a paradoxical situation in which their jurisdictional boundaries could be both extended and reduced. On the one hand, open boundaries and shifting occupational dynamics increased the uncertainty of their role because other groups could readily encroach on the jurisdictional domains of consultant managers. However, on the other hand, these shifting dynamics allowed consultant managers to challenge other established management occupations and extend their own jurisdiction, particularly when these occupations actively sought to appropriate consultancy-based skills, as in the case of HRM. Nevertheless, and as we shall see in the following section, such moves within and between occupational spaces could bring further tensions and changes.

The perishability of novelty: losing the status of the 'exotic other' and moving on

Whether consultant managers experienced occupational contestation as an opportunity or a threat, many sought to retain a distinctive – not *just* a manager's – identity around their work skills and knowledge. As we saw in reviewing their activities and relationships in previous chapters, they occupy an uncertain, ill-defined and often vulnerable space in organisations: neither conventional manager nor classic consultant. In part, it is this difference, or hybrid nature, that makes them attractive to more senior management in organisations in the first place. In particular, they often have different skills and orientations from conventional managers (in terms of how to manage organisational change, projects and client relationships) and different loyalties and priorities to those of external consultants.

Our research suggests that maintaining these differences, and thereby sustaining and producing a distinctive occupational identity, was often problematic and sometimes a source of concern to the consultant managers themselves. In particular, for those consultant managers who had been external consultants previously, a key theme in their career narratives was a perception that this identity and its associated prestige was a perishable commodity. Given the importance of *marketised careers* within neo-bureaucracy, such perishability could be problematic to longer-term career development. Hence, Daniel, who had moved into a consultant manager role in an investment bank six years previously, believed he had not only lost some of his 'edge' and become more 'bureaucratic' and 'comfortable' but that perceptions of his expertise had also changed – 'once you become known to people as a person day to day, some of the mystery, the gloss goes. You are not enigmatic to them any longer.' Likewise, in TransCo, Graham, a business consultant, acknowledged that familiarity had changed some of what he held to be key characteristics of his consultancy identity:

> Sometimes I feel I understand this business too well and I have too many preconceived ideas about things. Whereas when I first turned up I just asked all the dumb questions and I didn't care, because I needed to get to the absolute bottom of it. I still like to think I do that, but I don't think ... perhaps we don't do it as much as we used to. And clearly this is a problem for all internal consultancies, over time. If you stay too long ... you go native.

The fragile status of the consultant manager was also stressed by Rosemary, who, as an executive recruiter, had some insight into managerial careers. In particular, she noted that while new entrants into an organisation might enjoy a short-term window of opportunity based on their 'exotic' skills, there was the danger that their market power would diminish over time:

> I have said to some people [former consultants] ... 'Look, you might be learning something now, but keep in mind that this organisation

is draining you. The reason they have picked you up and put you on a two-year contract is you have got some skills and they are draining those skills from you. So who is going to be developing your skills for the next wave? Whereas at [external consultancy] there was always somebody pushing stuff at you, 'are your skills going to be still as sharp in five years' time as they are today?' ... You have either got to make an adjustment to become like them – 'put the spots on' – or you have to find a way yourself of developing those skills that make you new and relevant and bright and shiny again.

The possibility that the status of former external consultants would diminish over time was not just a matter of increasing familiarity, or of losing the initial attractiveness of externally sourced and up-to-date knowledge (see also Menon and Pfeffer, 2003). It was also part of a more general mistrust and suspicion of management consultancy which often sat awkwardly alongside admiration for the occupation – a 'love–hate' position (also Sturdy, 2009). For example, in GovDept1, an internal analysis of the challenges facing the ICU, produced by the unit itself, explicitly argued that, along with the difficulty of securing strategic work, 'the other main barrier is the generally poor perception of management consultants, whether internal or external, which can mean [ICU] is not seen as a useful part of [GovDept1]'. Similarly, in other cases, consultant managers were reluctant to use 'consultancy' in their job title because of a wider stigma of consultancy. According to Mike, a business consultant in CommsCo, the ICU was created by a group of external management consultants who 'brought with them this external consultancy view and model, but they were very clear not to then call it internal consulting. So they set up change delivery units, transformational delivery units or something like that, and avoided the consulting word entirely.'

Even when the 'consultant' title was used, it could create problems for consultant managers, as shown by the exchange which Dan in TransCo relayed:

One of the directors – we had some interesting conversations with him early on, because he reacted quite sharply if we talked about ourselves as consultants. To him consultants were basically people who tried to charge him money and who he was never convinced were great value and he was basically encouraging us to be much more embedded in the business and just think for the business, as opposed to thinking as consultants.

A common response of consultant managers who had previously been externals to the draining away of their prestige and wider resistance to consultancy was for them to move on quickly. This was part of a wider profile of job mobility or marketised career histories of many of our respondents – multiple job changes within short periods of time. For example, after working for five years in a leading global consulting practice, Barry undertook five job changes in six years. While some acknowledged concerns regarding their job mobility, others inter- preted frequent job moves as a strength, in terms of broadening their careers. In doing so, many respondents drew on an enterprise (post- bureaucratic) discourse of market rationality in rejecting the notion of long-term commitment to a single organisation and emphasised a preference for frequent job changes, new challenges and a 'portfolio' career (Brown and Hesketh, 2004; Webb, 2004). As Bronwyn reflected, 'I've never felt part of any one company. I have never felt an attach- ment. I've never had any problem with leaving.' Similarly, Lucinda argued: 'I feel I could always get another job. I'd love to be made redundant ... what is the worst that could happen? Get made redun- dant, get a good pay out and then I just go and get another job.'

Importantly, even for some of those former external consultants who were now well established in their organisations, moving back into external consulting, and hence reinforcing their consulting identity, was seen as an option. For example, Renata's role as a senior consultant manager in a global telecommunications company did not prevent her from acknowledging the possibility of moving on; 'at heart I'm a con- sultant and I suppose my thinking is that I'll go where there's good consulting work to do'. While these comments indicated a possible future course of action rather than a purposive strategy, they nevertheless provided an indication of some individuals' continued identification with consulting alongside or beyond any organisational affiliation. Here and as mentioned earlier, the continued affiliation with consulting 'alumni' and similar networks was also often critical in facilitating future job moves. However, not all former externals felt this way, and certainly not all consultant managers had an explicit or sustained 'consulting' identity. At the same time and as we shall see in the next chapter, so long as consultant managers remained non-standard in management positions, their hybrid status and identity persisted.

CONCLUSION

The emergence of the consultant manager in large corporations and public sector organisations does not only mark a change in the activities and relationships of managerial work. It also has emergent occupational and career implications. As we have seen at both a general level and from our specific data, the appropriation, dissemination and diffusion of consultancy is now a central feature of a number of managerial occupations. This is being achieved through various means, including client use of external consulting and the expansion of a particular – case- and tools-based – form of management education. In addition, and as we have seen in more detail, a 'diaspora' of former external consultants is now emerging, and this development has shed light on different occupational dynamics. For example, it highlights the potential threats and opportunities of jurisdictional competition for both incoming consultants and those seeking to expand work domains into consultancy (e.g. HRM). It also echoes and reinforces wider developments in management such as increasing job turnover (Webb, 2004), an enterprise identity (du Gay, 2004) and the promotion of generic, standardised management skills over specific 'domain' knowledge (Hopper and Hopper, 2009).

However, these occupational and career changes are far from settled and also raise a range of particular and more general tensions for both organisations and consultant managers themselves. So as we have seen in the area of HRM, highlighting the need for 'business partners' and 'internal consultants' opens up the occupational field to outsiders, like former management consultants who better epitomise the skills of change agency, project and client management. While this may benefit the new breed of 'consultant managers' in the short term (perhaps at the partial expense of external consultants), their hybrid identity also poses problems of organisational fit and career permanency. As 'outsiders within' (Meyerson and Scully, 1995: 589), consultant managers trade on their otherness, yet sometimes need to balance this against becoming tied down within an organisational setting which may lack the novelty and change they are accustomed to. So long as the neo-bureaucratic hybrid role continues to represent only a part of management ranks and one tied to discretionary functions, its condition is likely to remain precarious. These tensions therefore raise the broader point of the longevity of the consultant manager as an ongoing role for both individuals and organisations. This has particular implications for the identity of the consultant manager, which we address in the following chapter before returning to some of these broader tensions and challenges in the concluding chapter.

7 The identity boundaries and threats of the consultant manager

INTRODUCTION

Throughout our analysis of consultant managers' activities, relationships and occupational dynamics, we have highlighted a measure of ambiguity and insecurity. In this chapter, we consider the implications of this for how consultant managers make sense of their role(s) within organisations. At the heart of this identity work is their hybrid neobureaucratic status and the adoption of *dual identities* or the need to be both distinctive and integrated within the organisation. For consultant managers, such identities emerged from their often ambivalent or boundary position, as permanent employees operating partly outside of traditional functional and hierarchical structures. They were both within the organisation and also separate from it – as *outsiders within* (Meyerson and Scully, 1995: 589; Stonequist, 1937: 155) – a position which was often a defining characteristic of what it meant to be a consultant manager. Importantly, as we shall argue, this could actually act as a source of strength and differentiation. It set them apart from their operational counterparts and so sometimes enabled them to challenge existing business practices, structures, political hierarchies and power relations.

However, their dual identity was also a source of conflict and confusion to the extent that it could threaten the ongoing viability of their work. In short, consultant managers were acutely sensitive to how they were seen by others (i.e. their social identity) because their discretionary status meant that it was critical to their organisational survival. Again, this is in keeping with a hybrid or neo-bureaucratic identity. It emphasised their status and legitimacy as a specialist, independent from dominant reporting relationships and spanning the internal and external boundaries of the organisation, while at the same time building organisational acceptance as a loyal 'insider', privy to the informal networks through which influence can be enacted. Indeed, and following on from others, our focus on identity also necessarily addresses questions of boundaries (Ellis and Ybema, 2010; Sturdy, et al., 2009). What becomes clear, however, is that tensions arise not only because of ambivalence or ambiguity but also because identity claims depend on the confirmation of others, such as clients and sponsors, and this can never be guaranteed.

The chapter is organised as follows. We begin our discussion by briefly considering how the notion of identity relates to boundary conditions, both in general and in the context of consultant managers. We then draw on our data to examine a series of organisational boundaries – *structural, knowledge, political* and *personal boundaries* – within which consultant managers seek to develop coherent identities, before revealing how a series of challenges faced by the consultant manager work to undermine that coherence.

ORGANISATIONAL MEMBERSHIP, BOUNDARIES AND AMBIVALENCE

Traditional interpretations of organisational actors continue to assume that a primary reference point is the formal organisation and its boundaries. They therefore adopt a simple or, at least, highly dominant distinction between those inside the formal organisation and those outside. However, a considerable body of literature has long emphasised the complex and multifaceted nature of organisational membership. For instance, social identity theorists have shown how individuals' identities as organisational members are combined with 'lower-order' group memberships (job, team, department), as well as 'cross-cutting' associations (cross-functional task forces or informal cliques and networks) and broader occupational and professional identities (Ashforth and Johnson, 2001; Ashforth and Mael, 1989). Rather than exhibiting a singular organisational identity then, individuals are seen as prioritising different identities depending on their subjective

importance to the individual's sense of self, and their situational relevance. Such observations on a multiplicity of identities and of related
boundaries are evident beyond organisational contexts as well. For
example, in the 1970s, Merton (1972: 22) argued that 'individuals
have not a single status but a status set ... [therefore] they typically
confront one another simultaneously as Insiders and Outsiders'. These
views have become slightly more mainstream as *empirical* shifts in the
permeability of organisational boundaries have emerged and as *theoretical* attention to concerns with process and dynamics has increased
(Sturdy, et al., 2009). Indeed, organisational and work identity is a
product of temporal experience and organisational socialisation, in
which individuals encounter different internal boundaries *over time*,
shaping and changing their organisational identification (Schein, 1971;
Van Maanen and Schein, 1979).

Together, these boundaries can be almost tangible features of
an organisation's structure, based on function and hierarchy, or more
intangible 'inclusionary' boundaries based on social and interpersonal processes through which individuals are accepted by other organisational members (Ashforth, et al., 2000; Hernes, 2004; Paulsen and
Hernes, 2003). In particular, newcomers to an organisation (such as
the external consulting diaspora we discussed in Chapter 6) are likely
to start on the periphery of such an inclusionary dimension. As Van
Mannen and Schein (1979: 222) note, 'movement along the inclusionary dimension is analogous to the entrance of a stranger to any
group ... to cross inclusionary boundaries means that one becomes an
insider with all the rights and privileges that go with such a position'
(emphasis in original). These include not only physical boundaries,
which are related to organisational structure, infrastructure and
physical/technological proximity, but also social boundaries, reflecting group norms and social bonding, and mental/knowledge boundaries, linked to ideas and beliefs (Hernes, 2004). These boundaries are
not things, but ordering or social structuring devices acting within
and between organisations (Santos and Eisenhardt, 2005). They ena-
ble and set limits on actions and behaviour, as a source of distinction,

ex-/inclusion and identity for individuals and groups, and act as thresholds through which organisational members may pass. They do this with varying degrees of difficulty via a liminal space from one boundary or stage to another. For example, in a study of knowledge flow between external consultants and clients, Sturdy et al. (2009) identified four interrelated and shifting boundaries – *physical, cultural, knowledge* and *political*. As will be outlined below, we use similar categories here, but not identical ones, given the different research context and focus of our study.

Work and organisational identity then is not simply an expression of one's job role, or functional or hierarchical location. Rather, it is the product of individuals' claims to a certain membership or identity status, which is only achieved through the granting of such claims by, and *in relation to*, other organisational members. As Alvesson and Willmott (2002: 626) argue, managers and employees engage in an ongoing process of 'identity work' involving 'forming, repairing, maintaining, strengthening or revising the constructions that are productive of a precarious sense of coherence and distinctiveness'.

While we are all engaged to varying degrees in boundary spanning as part of everyday life, such work is particularly pronounced in hybrid neo-bureaucratic roles such as that of the consultant manager and, more generally, those seeking to promote change in organisations (Klein, 2004; Meyerson, 2003; Meyerson and Scully, 1995). Meyerson (2003) refers to such individuals as 'tempered radicals' who combine a strong identification with their organisation with a commitment to values and ideologies (e.g. feminism, social equity, racial equality) that may be at odds with the prevailing organisational culture. Meyerson suggests that such 'dual subjectivities' can be a positive source of creativity and transformation, something that resonates with the claims of consultant managers as 'outsiders within'. As we have seen in relation to their activities and relationships, they are members of the formal business organisation but typically act outside of *established* hierarchical structures. They favour new, emergent and more precarious roles and structures such as project teams and stress their

objectivity and independence in advising 'clients' and solving problems (Lacey, 1995; Neal and Lloyd, 1998). Likewise, we saw in the
previous chapter that their occupational identity was often in flux as
well – both undermining others and under threat itself.

Maintaining a coherent balance between different identities,
especially that of the insider and outsider, undoubtedly places consultant managers in a precarious position as they seek to manage and
maintain their relations with clients and other key stakeholders.
For example, in Chapter 5, we demonstrated how, as 'change agents',
consultant managers need to be aware of the complexities of organisational politics and be skilful political players, developing strong client
relationships and using networks of power (Balogun, et al., 2005;
Buchanan and Badham, 1999). However, this is not a simple question
of being identified with the powerful or excluding others. They also
need to avoid the perception of being *too close* to organisational cliques
(Scott, 2000). Likewise, and as we have seen, executive support for the
consultant manager is necessary in providing sufficient legitimacy to
undertake their work, but being seen as the agents of senior management can equally undermine their position. More generally, the expertise of consultant managers is very much a double-edged sword. On the
one hand, their greater familiarity with the organisation and its technical and social idiosyncrasies is often seen as a major advantage over
external consultants (Berthoin Antal and Krebsbach-Gnath, 2001: 463).
However, critics argue this may also result in an insular perspective
which ignores new developments outside of their specific organisational context (Kubr, 1996: 40). Moreover, their legitimacy as experts
may be discounted simply because they are from within the organisation, the problem of being a 'prophet in your own land'.

Consultant managers therefore operate in a highly ambiguous
space, in that they are both within, and also outside the traditional
activities and structures of the business organisation (Kanter, 1979).
While *external* consultants must also bridge organisational boundaries
(Kitay and Wright, 2004; Sturdy, et al., 2004), this process is intensified
for consultant managers. In an early study of internal organisational

development consultants, for example, Ganesh (1978: 13–4) noted the contradiction of adopting an 'expert role' and 'outsider stance' while also requiring a 'high need to belong, to be members of the client systems, to be insiders'. In many ways and as we noted in Chapter 2, this mirrors Gouldner's (1955, 1957) earlier characterisation of the latent identity of the staff expert as a 'cosmopolitan', who can advise but cannot command, who needs to 'sell' ideas to management and who is often outside the promotion track of the 'company men' or 'locals' who are seen as loyal members of the organisation. One practitioner text on internal consultancy summarises this dilemma: 'The internal consultant is constantly working at the edge, disturbing the boundaries, and serving as a bridge between two worlds that have differing values and norms. Finding this balance is difficult and ... can be a source of conflict' (Scott, 2000: 6).

Of course, balancing different identities is not unique to consultant managers, but a recognised feature of social, organisational and managerial activity, including, for example, the role of the middle manager (Harding, et al., 2014). However, our argument is that sustaining balance between dual identities is an especially difficult and often contradictory process for consultant managers, because it requires a constant or periodic process of 'identity work' for differing circumstances and audiences. That said, it is important not to downplay the potential to construct and manage a positive ambivalent identity based upon dimensions of *both* distinction and inclusion and for such ambivalence to be a source of strength (see also Zabusky and Barley, 1997). In the sections that follow, we draw together some of the experiences of consultant managers described in previous chapters to outline four key boundary dimensions within which consultant managers develop their organisational identification and which resonate with the ideal-type neo-bureaucratic manager outlined in Chapter 2. In particular, *structural* boundaries relate to respondents' roles and positions within the formal organisational hierarchy, including reporting relationships, levels of seniority and their degree of operational autonomy. *Knowledge* boundaries refer to individuals' functional and technical expertise, linked to their educational and occupational background, as well as external networking and affiliations. *Political* boundaries reflect respondents' organisational legitimacy and influence, for example, through their access to strategic decision-making and senior organisational stakeholders. Finally, the consultant manager's personal relationships with clients and other managers form a fourth, *interpersonal*, boundary dimension.

CROSSING INTERNAL BOUNDARIES: THE STRUCTURAL AMBIGUITY OF THE CONSULTANT MANAGER

As highlighted in earlier chapters, even when for budgetary or historical reasons, consultant managers were associated with a particular function or division, they tended to operate across the traditional organisational structures, through project and programme working, for example. Indeed, as a quintessential 'boundary spanner' (Sturdy and Wright, 2011; Tushman and Scanlan, 1981), the consultant manager straddles formal functional, product or market divisions and also operates across vertical hierarchical divisions. These lateral and vertical boundaries often serve as barriers to other managers. However, and as noted earlier, they can also represent an important aspect of identity construction, specifying one's formal role and location in a broader entity (Ashforth and Johnson, 2001; Ashforth, et al., 2000; Schein, 1971).

For many of our respondents, operating outside of the traditional reporting relationships was viewed positively. This was pronounced in the imagery of the 'change agent' where individuals talked about their role in diffusing corporate culture and change programmes within their organisations. As Susan, the head of the culture change unit in a large retail bank, outlined, 'Nobody tells me what to do. I essentially run a consulting practice here. I've got thirty people internally ... So essentially we run an outfit which manages the [company] culture but also provides a service.' Characterising one's self as a 'change agent' was often closely aligned with that of 'boundary spanner', working across the divisional and geographic boundaries of the organisation. Hence, several respondents spoke of their 'roving brief' across their organisations underpinned by their 'client' relationships with senior managers and department heads. As Sophie, an organisational development (OD) manager in a global engineering consultancy emphasised, a lot of her time involved travelling within the Asia-Pacific region working with the regional managers in the firm. She had the authority to initiate and develop programmes at will and often floated throughout the organisation in a largely autonomous manner: 'You know I disappear from my office for weeks at a time and then I'll come back and I'll run into someone, "where have you been?" "I was in Japan and Korea", and they're like, "oh wow!" So there's a little bit of a mystery about what I do.' Here then, the structural ambiguity of the consultant manager could promote a strongly positive self-identity, denoting autonomy and an ability to cross internal structural boundaries laterally to a degree other, more bureaucratic managers could not or were not inclined to do. As Nate in LocalGov1 commented, boundary crossing 'suits my personal style. I like dabbling in everybody's business.'

Even when consultant managers were firmly embedded within an organisational function (and so had less explicit structural ambiguity), they still sought to adopt a hybrid neo-bureaucratic identity based on the use of expert power and influence, rather than an authority derived from their formal position within the organisation. As we saw in Chapter 6, these identities were sometimes part of a wider shift in the occupational identity of functions, such as human resources (HR), which sought to appropriate more facilitative consultancy skills. For example, as Della, a senior HR manager in a large industrial services company, argued, her identity hinged upon the use of influence rather than directive authority or a 'policing' identity, as she phrased it: 'Because all people use influence in the organization, but I'm talking about the way that you approach your everyday job is influence first, power second. Most people approach their jobs power first, influence second. And I think it's a fundamental shift as to what your primary approach is.'

Underpinning this distinction from conventional hierarchical relations was the market or professional imagery of being a 'trusted adviser' or 'partner' to their clients. Hence Angela, a change consultant in a major resource company, contrasted this more elite identity with the traditional administrative character of human resources, 'we as a team are being asked to position ourselves as a trusted adviser versus just being their HR person, their "HR go to"'. Here, there was less emphasis upon a bureaucratic managerial identity of enforcing policies and practices because of a hierarchical relationship, and more of a focus on the imagery of 'influence'. As Keira, the 'Best Practice Consultant' in a major automobile manufacturer, also noted, 'I don't like to necessarily be seen as a manager, more as facilitating groups and helping them to do things.' In this sense then, 'non-hierarchical' consulting discourse appeared to help create a relatively safe existential space for those operating on the edges of formal organisational structures.

SPECIALIST EXPERTISE: THE DISTINCTIVE
KNOWLEDGE OF THE CONSULTANT MANAGER

A second dimension of identity formation for consultant managers was the nature of their expertise, in particular the distinctiveness of their disciplinary and functional knowledge in relation to other employees in the organisation. In line with Gouldner's (1957) 'cosmopolitans', many of those we studied highlighted a strong commitment to specialised skills, as well as an external reference group orientation. For instance, in terms of their disciplinary and technical knowledge, group and individual titles such as 'head of cultural transformation', 'leader of culture and capability', 'organisational change' and 'business solutions' clearly demarcated them as specialists. As we saw in the previous chapter, a significant number had developed their skills in their previous careers as external management consultants, often in large global consulting practices. Others had undertaken postgraduate education in areas such as business strategy, operations management, human resource management (HRM) or OD, and maintained their

technical knowledge through reading and external affiliations and networks. The development of consulting skills in client, project and
change management further demarcated them from mainstream
operational managers, and reinforced their 'outsider' status as esoteric
experts and professionals. Indicative of this identity distinction, Leah,
a recently appointed OD consultant manager in a large Australian
retail company, reflected on her own position and expertise:

> I think the key is that for me personally I was brought in for the
> expertise I have to run particular types of projects and so I have a
> certain level of leverage because of that. People are probably going to
> take what I say a little bit more seriously than if I was just an internal
> employee and just doing the same job as other people. So I have a
> unique role and position in the organisation.

In a similar vein, Peter, a consultant manager in a Big Four accounting
firm, highlighted how his distinctive background from outside his firm
allowed him to challenge prevailing norms and behaviour:

> So I'm different enough. I'm not an accountant. I come from the
> military so people expect me to be blunt and straight to the
> point ... It enables me sometimes to ask the hard questions and
> challenge them and say: 'to me, looking at what you do, I
> understand what you do, but it just doesn't make any sense, so you
> explain it to me'. So having that insider knowledge, but outsider
> perspective, and not having been marred and had my brain
> moulded by the system, is a big advantage.

Indeed, distinctive expertise did not have to be associated with external experience, but could be developed by managers who had actively
sought to develop their role around, for example, a specific consultancy
skill. In HealthCo1, Fred had previously held an operational management role in the organisation, but found that 'eight years ago, I had no
management training going on and I heard about this programme on
team development, took myself on it and loved it'. Subsequently, Fred
had developed to become a permanent 'coach', jointly responsible for

running the programme and involved in a range of consultancy activities distinct from his original role in the organisation.

In Fred's and some other cases, a distinctive identity was tied to a specialist (sometimes branded) form of management knowledge. So, for example, we have seen previously that at PhoneCo, the internal 'business solutions' group established its activities around Six Sigma business improvement projects and the training of 'high potential' managers in the group's operational efficiency methodology (see Chapter 4). In this organisation, the approach was accorded significant credibility by the company's CEO and other senior management, and the 'Black Belt' Six Sigma training was seen as a highly desirable career move. The Six Sigma brand was seen as being aligned with the company's project-driven 'can do' culture, as opposed to more generalised change approaches, and also satisfied organisational requirements for easily defined and costed improvements. However, and as we also saw in Chapter 4, branded methodologies such as Six Sigma could become so widely used that they lose their distinctiveness.

Nevertheless, they could also remain powerful symbols of legitimacy and status over long periods (years). Hence, Keira stressed how her promotion of a kaizen methodology of operational improvement represented a core pillar of the firm's broader corporate culture and gave her access to high-status global gatherings of other company experts within the global organisation. In a similar vein at FinCo2, the internal HR consultancy built its identity around the development of a (self-proclaimed) innovative online tool that allowed HR managers to identify and quantify the links between effective people management practices and key business performance indicators. As Stuart, the head of employee engagement, explained, the tool could be used to reinforce the distinctive expertise of the HR function and drive HR issues further up the strategic agenda: 'You sit in an executive board meeting for a retail bank, all of them are looking at tangible, evidence-based measures for how effective they are at sales, at customer service, at financial performance. So why wouldn't they expect to have some tangible measures for looking at the effectiveness of the people?'

However, in other cases, it seemed to be the intangibility of the consultant manager's expertise that justified an individual's structural autonomy in their organisations. For example, Adam, a consultant manager in OD in a global pharmaceutical company, noted how 'OD in its purest sense has no form. People around here used to call me "Manager Stuff". That was my pseudo title. "Who's this?" "Oh this is our Manager Stuff". "What do you mean?" "Well he does stuff, but nobody actually knows what it is".'

Sometimes then, the mystique of a consultant manager's expertise could heighten their claims to a distinctive and elite identity (see also Menon and Pfeffer, 2003). Furthermore, respondents contrasted the novelty and variety of their work – centred on change and the short term – with what they saw as more mundane middle management roles, characterised in a negative sense as just 'business as usual'.

PLAYING THE GAME: THE POLITICAL BOUNDARIES OF THE CONSULTANT MANAGER

While the organisational–structural and knowledge dimensions of the consultant manager identity stressed distinctiveness and difference, the reality of being embedded within an organisation also required that individuals gain a level of organisational acceptance to be effective. As we saw in Chapter 5, managing the political boundaries of the organisation involved a range of issues for consultant managers, including developing senior management support, cultivating strong client relationships through demonstration of 'added value' and mediating relations with external consultancies. Hence, in line with notions of neo-bureaucracy, alongside the 'outsider' identity many individuals emphasised in terms of their structural position and expertise, a contrasting 'insider' identity of inclusion within the power structure of their organisation was required for consultant managers to be effective.

For many, developing such an identity required time spent in the organisation understanding its complexities and culture and gaining the trust of others, that is, crossing the organisation's 'inclusionary boundaries' (Van Maanen and Schein, 1979). While job tenures varied significantly between those we studied, there was clearly a temporal dimension to the development of this aspect of the consultant manager identity. For instance, as Peter characterised his experience after seven years of working in global accounting practice:

> I think I've been around the organisation long enough where people probably now trust me and from that point of view I'm an insider who's known. The other advantage I think that I have is that being around the organisation for that time, I now know the jargon, I now know enough about the business to be able to throw in the right sort of questions, I think I have a good understanding of the issues and I think I understand how *they* think.

The ambivalence of the consultant manager identity as being both 'inside' and also different is clearly evident here, in that while this manager saw himself accepted as an organisational 'insider', he still emphasised his distance from other employees due to his separate expertise and structural location. In other respects, this separateness could place consultant managers in a position mediating or facilitating relationships between different departments or functional groups (see also Chapter 4). Colin, in CommsCo, for example, claimed that it allowed his team to operate outside of a politicised context:

> We are very much a middle man at times. Because we still have the lack of [organisational] baggage and we don't have any agendas on any of the business units; we are there to provide a bit of an impartial view ... So we are using facilitation and even mediation to a certain point, because the internal on-goings and politics of a business like CommsCo is pretty scary and I think we are asked to provide that role sometimes. It is good fun; it is good fun for us.

In a similar manner, Adam characterised himself as the 'organisational conscience', confronting issues that other managers could not because of political sensitivities. Hence, in describing his role in facilitating a recent group development workshop of senior managers, he stated:

> There was a point where I said, 'come on, let's talk about what's really bloody going on because I'll tell you what, I can see it. There is an elephant under the coffee table in this group and no one wants to talk about it. You know what? You're going to have poo in the corner, and it's going to smell eventually, so let's see if we can talk about it.'

In developing this identity, consultant managers still had to be sensitive to the power dynamics operating within the firm. As we saw in Chapter 5, lacking a clear line of authority, most stressed the importance of influencing skills and the ability to 'sell' client managers on the benefits of their proposals. As Faye related of her experience, the success of her initiatives often relied upon a careful consideration of key organisational 'players' and what issues might lead them to support her proposals:

> I mean, it's that whole thing about networking and pulling in favours and about being politically astute. If you want one of the business units to sponsor something, what's in it for them? So, working out what benefits they'll get, and how you're going to support them to get that. Then they get brownie points.

As we have seen, organisational legitimacy as a consultant manager also relied upon senior management patronage or sponsorship regarding the role or unit in general. Respondents provided numerous examples of how senior support allowed them not only to overcome managerial resistance to their initiatives but also to take risks. For example, the stereotypical image of the consultant manager as 'court jester' was raised by several respondents (see also Ganesh, 1978: 15–6; Marsh, 2009). Here, the consultant manager is given licence to challenge organisational taboos and question underlying norms, precisely because they are 'insiders' who are accepted by senior managers and can be trusted. They are seen as non-threatening. As Daniel, a learning and development manager in a global investment bank, outlined:

> I am always conscious that I am designing things to challenge, and I think of it in terms of the jester. He was the only person in the court who was allowed to make fun of the king, and in that, permission was given because the court understood if nobody could challenge the king then we will have corruption. So there is a role for senior HR people and internal consultants and OD people to go and whisper in the ear, to have private meetings with senior executives and say 'you know what, this isn't working, you have got to do something different'. [A role] to stop them, and challenge them and make them think about things differently.

In addition to developing a distinct role and identity in relation to the political context, the consultant manager position provided an opportunity to gain much greater exposure to this context than was possible as an operational manager. This could then give them much clearer insights into organisational relationships and also potentially boost their profile with seniors. As with Colin in CommsCo, a number of organisations saw the consultant manager role as a developmental role in which an individual could build their understanding of the organisation and learn valuable skills in a wide range of managerial roles. In the case of GovServ2, Geoff explained how he had changed the profile of the internal consulting unit (ICU) from one that was

> seen as an end of career job. It attracted old and bold individuals, who did a perfectly good job – don't get me wrong – but they had one eye on their CVs and retirement and the place didn't have the energy that I would associate with a consultancy team. So, we're now getting people volunteering to join the team … I have more people who want to join the team than I have slots. And we now have people who are leaving the team on promotion and going. In my case, I'm going on to [a more senior role]. So I'm getting people now who want to come here, because not only can they see that the skills are hugely relevant to an organisation undergoing change, but they see people getting promoted and posted out of it.

In GovAgency3, the long-standing ICU had recently been decentralised and so had lost some of its influence, yet Diana, the ICU manager, reflected on a period during which 'it was seen as a good breeding ground for employees who were bright and wanted to get promoted – and quite a few of them started off as [consultant managers] and became, years later, became Senior Executives'.

The notion of the consultant manager being a transitory role undertaken for a limited period resonates well with images of the *marketised career* of the neo-bureaucratic manager. However, the fact that its apparent organisational value lay, in part, in its distinctiveness from other managers once again raises the question of its viability as a more generic or widespread management role, an issue we shall return to in the next chapter. Furthermore, consulting roles could themselves become transformed into more established and operational positions. This is evident in proactive efforts from individual consultant managers or units to become more effective 'players' in the political context, such as through expanding responsibilities, including the pursuit of more strategic work (see also Chapter 4). In GovAgency2, for example, the head of the ICU's role had expanded such that he was eventually asked to join the executive management team:

> So I have quite a lot of roles that are outside of just business
> improvement [the ICU], and this is where being the internal
> consultant, you [can] get drawn into the business, the good, the
> bad and the ugly. So it's a double-edge sword. It could be great for
> me, but actually in terms of my team, it's not always been
> helpful because I've been drawn off on other things.

In this case, the consultant manager's and unit's ambivalent identity had once again allowed room for movement or a successful negotiation of the political landscape, but with the result that the unit moved into roles more associated with operational management, thereby making its outsider status and those of its consultant managers harder to sustain.

INTERPERSONAL ASPECTS OF THE CONSULTANT
MANAGER IDENTITY — TARGETING AND USING
CLIENT TRUST AND CREDIBILITY

As we discussed earlier, boundaries can best be seen as ordering or structuring processes concerned with diverse aspects of relationality. They typically operate at multiple levels. So far, we have focused attention on those linked to organisational structures, to forms of knowledge (and occupations) and to relations of power and influence, but relationships cannot be reduced to these or any one of them. In particular, wider social structures are at play, albeit ones we have for the most part not focused on in this book (e.g. gender, race) (see also Whittington, 1992). These shape and are produced by those more formal bases of work relations and are, once again, multiple in form. Overall then, and following Merton's observation earlier, numerous boundary relations and potential sources of (dis)identification are possible and act together. In doing so, their combination can be seen and experienced as unique to the individuals (and contexts) involved, and so, by way of a shorthand, we explore these under the label of interpersonal relations. In particular, and in relation to consultant managers' client relationships, respondents stressed a preferred *inclusive* identity based around being perceived as credible and trusted and this is our focus here (see also Chapter 5).

Credibility is a much used, but often poorly defined term. In our research context, we understand it as the degree of trust placed in actors to address the concerns of senior management or other 'clients' (Armstrong, 1989; Denis, et al., 2007). It is, then, an informal, fluid and localised notion, based on the perceptions of 'client' managers. But, for consultant managers, the identity of 'trusted adviser' discussed above, for example, was often critical to their achieving credibility in individual relationships. As Adam noted in outlining his role as a 'confidant' to the senior managers in his organisation:

> That's all about trust. They will not tell you stuff if they don't trust you. People have to be able to know that it isn't going to go any

further. You're working with succession plans and discussions
about people at all levels of the business and with the directors, and if
they don't think that they can trust saying what they think about
people in front of me, then I'm stuffed. Without that, I can't do my job.

Credibility or trust expressed in this way could have a highly emotive
element to it. For example, Susan, who had, over five years, taken on a
strong *organisational* identity, linked her *personal* credibility to the
impact of a significant change programme in which she had been
involved – 'So we are very credible in the internal market and seen to
be trusted advisers ... I mean when you've touched people's lives as
deeply as the [X] programme you have a very privileged position.' Here,
the object of credibility slips from the individual to the unit and, in
either case, it could have significant implications.

Of course, trust and credibility are important in many work contexts, but its significance here derived in part from some of the political
sensitivities associated with, or drawn out by, change programmes. For
example, Diana in GovAgency3 explained how senior managers would
continue to call on her unit's services, saying to her:

'When I was in that department over there, you came and did
it for me there, can you come and do it for me here?' So there
was a lot of repeat business because we knew the organisation
well; they asked us to do things which they wouldn't get
external consultants in to do for all sorts of reasons, whether it
was security, whether it was washing dirty linen, whether it
was, you know, sensitive stuff that they really didn't want
publicised or whatever.

In some cases, work-based trust was associated with more informal
relations. For instance, Daniel, working as a consultant manager in
learning and development in a global investment bank, outlined how
his personal friendship with the chief operating officer (COO) of the
company allowed him to take risks in designing organisational
interventions:

we designed a programme around partnership and creativity and innovation. And we used a jazz band to demonstrate that in real time and as an experiential activity, that people could draw from. And he [the COO] was up to his neck in that with me; he was delighted with that idea and he encouraged me with that idea and I encouraged him. So we got together and we were partnering; we were egging one another on to see how outrageous we could get without going over the line. So that is how that relationship works ... If I didn't have him, I would have been out there on a limb on my own and it probably wouldn't have happened.

The sense of reliance by the consultant manager on an individual with greater hierarchical power expressed here is a reminder that, however seemingly 'interpersonal' relations were, features of the *bureaucratic* organisation remained important. However, in some cases, by formally operating at a distance from hierarchical structures, social capital derived from informal social networks could be reinforced. For example, GovServ1 was a deeply hierarchical organisation, yet Alan, a principal consultant, had the opportunity to secure work intended for external consultants by taking advantage of a long-standing relationship with a senior executive: 'He knew me and I'd worked with him in the past, and he gave us important work, which elsewhere might have gone to external consultants.'

As we saw in Chapter 5, the discretionary status of much of the work of consultant managers meant that they had to actively seek to achieve credibility, rather than wait for it to emerge over time or through informal networks. Indeed, building individual client relationships involved a strong awareness of self-image and the need to manage impressions. As Sophie noted: 'as much as I hate to admit it I use my looks, I use my personality to find a connection ... Sometimes I'll play the blonde klutz and, you know, "I don't know what I was thinking!" But each of them [client relationships] are different and each of them works.'

This need to be flexible in managing one's self-image in order to build a connection with different clients operated in different ways. For instance, the same manager also highlighted how many of her clients had distinctive social and educational backgrounds which she focused on in the development of each relationship, pointing to areas of shared leisure interests, for example. This formal use of informality or relationship management is quite institutionalised in external consulting and is, perhaps, an area of neo-bureaucracy that requires further research (see, e.g., Sturdy, et al., 2006).

An alternative to seeking to exploit work–non-work boundaries to secure trust was for consultant managers to seek to demonstrate understanding of the *business* concerns of operational managers, either by highlighting a shared organisational (insider) identity or by targeting specific functional or occupational issues. For instance, Angela, a consultant manager who worked in an energy company, noted how she had spent significant time educating herself about the company's products and processes 'because I want to talk credibly to my clients'. In a similar manner, Sophie sought to develop interpersonal connections with managers and employees through getting involved in client site visits and making it apparent that she was interested in the core business of her firm:

> But then I think they appreciate the fact that I try and
> understand. You know, so I go to the sites. I've got my little steel-
> capped boots, my RM shirt and I'll head out to some of the sites
> for a couple of days every now and then and visit them and help
> them do soil samples and all that kind of stuff. So I think they see
> in me that I'm trying to learn their business and, you know, get a
> better picture and a feel for them.

In short, then, in seeking to shape individual relations with clients, consultant managers would seek to reduce boundaries of difference. However, and as we have seen earlier, at other times it was important to emphasise their difference and independence.

FROM STABLE AMBIVALENCE TO REJECTION – THE
CONTRADICTIONS OF BEING AN 'OUTSIDER WITHIN'
While ambivalent identities have often been viewed as either temporary
or problematic states resulting in uncertainty and confusion (Merton,
1976), our research suggests that ambivalence as both outsiders *and*
insiders could be a personal source of strength and distinctiveness (see
also Meyerson, 2003; Zabusky and Barley, 1997). In particular, we have
seen how consultant managers constructed their work identities around
their role and position in the organisational hierarchy (structural boundaries), their expertise and functional activities (knowledge boundaries),
their organisational legitimacy and power (political boundaries) and
their personal relationships with clients and other stakeholders (interpersonal boundaries). Here, individuals and consulting groups sought to
claim preferred dual (neo-bureaucratic) identities which employed
combinations of differentiation and inclusion around these four dimensions. In broad terms and as outlined in Table 7.1, the key imagery
employed in such claims involved the promotion of distinctiveness

Table 7.1 *Preferred identities and boundary dimensions
of the consultant manager*

Preferred vision	Boundary dimensions	Ambivalent identity – key imagery
Outsider status	*Structure*: role and position in organisational structure	Change agent/boundary spanner/ trusted adviser/partner
	Knowledge: technical expertise	Cosmopolitan/specialist/esoteric expert/professional
Insider status	*Political*: legitimacy and power	Mediator/facilitator/ organisation's conscience/ court jester/players/
	Interpersonal: personal relationships	Colleague/confidant/trusted adviser

(as an 'outsider') in relation to both the structural and knowledge dimensions of organisational interaction, while at the same time emphasising inclusionary imagery (as an 'insider') at the political and interpersonal levels.

We have seen how, structurally, consultant managers could operate outside of conventional or fixed reporting lines and authority structures, with sometimes significant autonomy over their activities. Here the imagery of being a 'change agent' and 'boundary spanner' expressed the preferred vision of the freedom of being able to cross the divisional, hierarchical and geographic boundaries which constrained other managers. Similarly, the imagery of being a 'trusted adviser' emphasised the consultant manager's elite status in the organisation and an ability to influence senior and operational managers outside of traditional authority relations. Such 'otherness' was further emphasised in terms of an externally oriented knowledge base, which included not only an individual's or group's technical or specialist expertise but also, as we saw in Chapters 5 and 6, external affiliations and peer networks. Here, the imagery of the 'esoteric expert' and 'professional' underpinned a preferred identity of exclusive knowledge and skills beyond the grasp of 'normal' managers.

At the same time, consultant managers emphasised a contrasting imagery of inclusion. In terms of the political dimensions of their role, respondents stressed a preferred identity which emphasised their access to the centre of organisational power, specifically senior managers, whom they could interact with, not only as 'trusted advisers' but, in cases where they had developed significant trust, also as the 'jester' or 'organisational conscience' – that is, challenging accepted wisdoms and raising taboos. The preferred identity at this level also stressed the imagery of respondents as accepted 'players' within the process of organisational politics: knowing the key people with influence and being able to call in favours. Interpersonally, the preferred identity focused on the imagery of 'colleague' and 'confidant'; the consultant manager was someone who enjoyed close relationships with a broad range of organisational 'clients' and through the development of trust and friendship was able to engage in activities that, as one respondent termed it, 'pushed the boundaries' of accepted behaviour.

This imagery, employed by consultant managers, helped to sustain an identity that was both seemingly coherent and ambivalent. It is one that is strikingly similar to the hybrid profile of the neo-bureaucratic manager outlined in Chapter 2. For example, the outsider imagery used by consultant managers to describe their position within organisational structures emphasises a horizontal (i.e. cross-functional) focus common in models of post-bureaucracy, yet they remained reliant on the vertical (i.e. hierarchical) focus most redolent of bureaucracy. Likewise, the identity of the consultant manager as 'cosmopolitan' or even 'court jester' engaged in informal political relationships resonates with the emphasis placed on enterprise and change (innovation) within post-bureaucracy, while the distinctiveness of their expertise reflects the specialisation associated with the bureaucratic organisation.

However, a key theme in our analysis of consultant managers' activities, relationships and occupational associations is that such hybrid neo-bureaucratic roles generate and comprise considerable tensions and insecurities. This does not simply derive from ambivalence, contradiction and hybridity but also from the *interdependent* nature of social identity. In short, consultant managers' claims to a preferred identity did not mean they were accepted by others in their organisations; 'identity work' is after all a reciprocal process between the self and others (Bartel and Dutton, 2001). Indeed, even though ambivalent identities could be a source of strength and differentiation, negative or 'spoiled' identities also often emerged which could undermine any positive outcomes of their identity work.

Spoiled identities – homelessness, client resistance,
perishable knowledge and exclusion
In terms of structural boundaries, while consultant managers might claim the preferred 'outsider' identity of 'change agent' or 'boundary

spanner', rejection of these claims by others could leave individuals on the periphery of the organisation or relegated to more mundane administrative activities. Furthermore, and as we have noted before, in some organisations, the term 'consultant' was a 'dirty word', and individuals avoided using such terminology in their interactions with managers. Also, its meaning varied according to a diversity of roles. For example, having worked in a number of consultant manager roles in different companies, Della noted: 'It depends what role the organization wants you to play. If they want you to be "hand maiden" or "doormat" or "fix-it person" or "fire-fighter" then it's very hard'. Rather than a strategic, autonomous agent, the consultant manager here became a more familiar bureaucratic functionary with limited autonomy – such as the case with the use of the ICU in CommsCo as a 'body shop' (see Chapter 5).

These uncertainties were exacerbated by the difficulty many consultant managers had in establishing a stable location within the organisation. As we outlined in Chapter 3, in some instances, they were *centralised* – moved from an operational department to a support function for the CEO. In others, they were *decentralised* and experienced a contraction of their remit. In a similar fashion, consultant managers who had previously operated with some independence were relocated into service functions such as HRM or IT which could be done regardless of occupational fit. Indeed, some consultant managers operated in an almost permanent state of insecurity about whether their role would be sustained over the short and long term. Once again, the key issue here was the discretionary nature of consultant managers' work, which placed it outside of a 'traditional' structural identity and made costs highly visible. Shaun in FinCo3 and Colin in GovServ3 both reflected on this issue in a similar fashion:

> Organisationally there's a lot of pressure to cut costs. Now if you look at an organisation, and you say, 'Right, who do we make redundant next?' Or, 'What do they do?' Or you're saying, 'No we don't need that, that's not doing anything, cross it off, get rid of it.' So [internal consultancy] is an easy target. *(Shaun)*

> We're an easy hit, we're an easy target, an easy saving. We don't
> actually have proper jobs, if they abolished us tomorrow, what
> would change? *(Colin)*

Colin's somewhat pessimistic view was based on his experience of the
ICU he led having gone through two stages of cost and manpower
reductions, seeing the unit amalgamated with others, headcount
reduced from a high of eighty to thirty and the unit relocated to become
part of the HR function (see also Chapter 6). In LocalGov1 too, the ICU
were so nervous of being disbanded that they took an unconventional
approach to protecting themselves after a local election led to them
working with a new set of councillors. As Nate explained:

> We're an easy target potentially for service cuts. When the new
> administration came in we all had our names on our doors or in our
> office with 'performance manager' and we had to take them all off
> because the view was that the new [elected] members may think
> there's too many people working in performance, or too many
> people working in policy. So for several months, literally, we had our
> names off the doors so that we were well hidden. We called ourselves
> the Anne Frank Team!

In a number of organisations, such insecurity was not without founda-
tion as some units were disbanded altogether. In TransCo, for example,
changes to the senior management team led to the internal consulting
group being decentralised into a service function where it was no
longer able to justify its existence under different organisational
imperatives. In this case, the shift from being a high-profile and high-
credibility group to one deemed surplus to organisational requirements occurred in a matter of months. It also came as a surprise to
the consultant managers, who considered their structural location to
be a matter of budgetary allocation rather than critical to their identity
as consultant managers.

The status of individual consultant managers and their units
depended upon client and sponsor perceptions of their expertise. This

too was vulnerable to variation and change. Thus, rather than the 'esoteric expert', 'professional' or purveyor of new external knowledge, the 'spoiled' identity of the consultant manager often focused on the rejection of their knowledge as 'impractical', alien or irrelevant to organisational concerns. Hence, several respondents recounted examples of managerial resistance and rejection of their change programmes on the grounds that their advice was too far removed from the core business or culture of the organisation. As Karli, the head of a consultant manager OD team in a global software company, related:

> so there is some tension at times between our team being perceived as being realistic, and trying to push the boundaries … They [client managers] can think that we're airy-fairy, 'oh, they're training people, they're different, sensitive, you know, a bit more volatile' and all this stuff. You know, these perceptions are made.

Similarly, as we explored in Chapter 4, where consultant managers were associated with branded methodologies and products, there was also the potential for rejection of their expert claims based on perceptions of these methods being outdated, overly standardised or otherwise stigmatised – the 'secret Six Sigma Society' at CommsCo, for example. In GovAgency1, this association with a specific, seemingly redundant, expertise continued to stigmatise the consultant managers even after they were no longer involved in work of this nature. Dan, the ICU manager, explained that 'some of the team actually were in an old efficiency and services group. They're still seen as the hatchet boys, the pad and stopwatch guys, so we're trying to get away from that'.

The spoiled identity of consultant managers based on their expertise could occur almost instantly, with a change in client/sponsors with different preferences or as ideas lost fashionable status in the wider business/sector community. In addition, the spoiled identity could emerge over time as consultant managers gradually lost their outsider status and with it the association with external or new expertise. In short, the expert became just a 'service provider' at the beck and call of operational managers to solve routine operational problems. In this sense, becoming an organisational 'insider', or a known quantity, could serve to undercut claims to expert knowledge that is valued. Hence, as we noted in Chapter 6, Daniel, a regional OD consultant manager in a global investment bank, recounted, 'Your expertise becomes devalued; your technical expertise, your knowledge as a theoretician and expert is presumed to be not as strong.'

In these cases, managers were sometimes found bypassing consultant managers and seeking out external providers, who were seen as having a more legitimate (outside) expertise (see also Menon and Pfeffer, 2003). For example, Colin in GovServ3 spoke of how his group was viewed in relation to external consultants:

> I tell the anecdote of my own boss who said, 'Oh [Manager X] wants this piece of work doing. It's certainly not a McKinsey's job, we might call on the externals on our [preferred supplier] framework, the second league ... or we could *even* let the internals have a go at it.'

Losing the status of being a newcomer or a purveyor of modern external knowledge could bring consultant managers some benefits from losing something of their outsider status or what Kipping and Armbrüster (2002: 204) called the 'burden of otherness'. However, this was by no means guaranteed. In terms of the political and interpersonal dimensions of identity construction, for example, 'insider' claims could still be rejected. Rather than being accepted as political 'players', 'confidants' or 'trusted advisers', they had yet to bridge the organisation's 'inclusionary' boundaries (Schein, 1971; Van Maanen and Schein, 1979). This was particularly pronounced among some respondents who were new recruits and who expressed disillusionment with the prevailing organisational culture. Hence, Leah, who had been recently hired from overseas as a consultant manager in OD in a large retailer, noted how she had yet to be accepted within the organisational politics of her company:

> So they bring in external consultants or external professionals, but you are really not going to be seen as an insider probably for a good

two to three years, because you haven't adapted to the culture, you haven't learnt all the ways ... So there's the sense that I'm still sort of there [externally] consulting and giving them information about what I already know, what I've brought to them, but that I don't have deep enough knowledge of their business. So that's really why it still feels like I'm an outsider.

Similarly, Betty emphasised how the male, blue-collar culture of her current employer, an equipment hire company, contrasted markedly with the professional services environment she was familiar with: 'the culture here is very much the old boys club ... I've been in a couple of meetings with the CEO and it's just all swearing and you know, "these GMs [general managers] have got to get their cocks on the block" type stuff! ... So you're sitting there going, "okay?"'

Of course, all organisational newcomers, managers or otherwise, have to face challenges of transition and acceptance, but for consultant managers, the fact that they seek to maintain an 'outsider within' status presents particular challenges of adaptation. Likewise, while all employees need to secure political favour in some ways from colleagues, for consultant managers, their discretionary role renders this a particularly fragile process. In particular and as we saw in Chapter 5, securing acceptance and a close relationship with some clients could lead to exclusion from others, especially if consultant managers were seen as too close to senior sponsors who posed a potential hierarchical threat. In such ways, consultant managers became firmly (if informally) enmeshed in the organisation's hierarchy, rather than independent from it. This was problematic in various ways, not least in maintaining an identity as independent or professional with clients, but, as we have seen, this was especially threatening if the senior sponsor left or fell out of favour.

Political and social exclusion was not always an all-or-nothing matter, resulting in resignations or unit closures, for example. Rather, consultant managers highlighted how their organisational and 'client' relationships often involved a spectrum of interactions, varying from close friendships and collaboration at one end, to more intermittent, transactional exchanges or full exclusion at the other. Commenting on such variability, Peter, a consultant manager who worked in a large accounting practice, noted: 'We actually rate our relationships with various people in the organization, and some we have excellent, what I would rate as ally relationships. Others we have, what I would call, tradesmen relationships, and with others we have no relationship at all.' Other respondents concurred, noting examples of managers whom they interacted with infrequently, or who had rejected their advances. Colin in GovServ3 summed up the tensions and insecurity of the interpersonal identity and the need for relationships to be continually renewed – 'I said to my people, "Reputation, reputation, reputation". We're only as good as our worst piece of consultancy.'

While problems of exclusion were often acute for those relatively new to their consultant manager role (perhaps also because they were sometimes separating from a prior identity themselves), the process of identity work was an ongoing one. In particular, many respondents who had spent a number of years in their organisations as consultant managers commented on the problem of maintaining their distinctiveness and novelty and not being seen as just 'part of the furniture'. A key issue for these individuals was that as their claims to distinctive expertise weakened, operating outside the traditional hierarchical structures limited their options for career progression, especially while retaining a consultant role. They acknowledged that, at some point, they would have to decide between opting for full induction in a senior managerial position ('putting the spots on') and leaving the organisation in search of a similar role elsewhere ('starting again'). Hence, even as a preferred identity, the consultant manager, as currently organised, could well have a limited organisational lifespan. Although we did not explore the precise longevity of consultant manager roles, the propensity to maintain such an identity is likely to be shaped by the strength and nature of the prevailing organisational culture, and the degree to which such organisational roles remain atypical and are tolerated or, indeed, encouraged.

CONCLUSION

A key feature of the emergent role of the consultant manager in business organisations is the complex and ambivalent nature of the work identity these roles call forth. While the issue of ambiguous organisational membership is well recognised among employees in marginal job settings such as volunteers, contractors and other 'atypical' employees (Barley and Kunda, 2004; Garsten, 1999; Padavic, 2005), it is clear that a growing range of middle and senior managers now also exist in such non-traditional, boundary-spanning roles. Reduced job security, technological change and a popular business discourse that stresses the need for managers to be increasingly change focused, project oriented, flexible, innovative, integrative and value adding highlight that a growing range of managerial employees view organisational membership as an increasingly ambiguous or conditional affair (Morris, et al., 2008). As we have argued throughout, consultant managers are at the front line of this neo-bureaucratic form of organising and, as demonstrated in this chapter, actively seek to construct their identities as both organisationally distinctive and inclusive – as 'outsiders within'.

In particular, we explored identity claims in a relational sense, through the concept of boundaries. Here, consultant managers felt freed from traditional organisational structural constraints and as distinctive or cosmopolitan in terms of their expertise. At the same time they pursued, sometimes quite tactically, an insider status politically and interpersonally, which sometimes allowed them innovative roles and the ability to overcome political sensitivities which other managers might have been more constrained by. What may seem surprising is that many of our respondents achieved some success in creating this preferred identity of ambivalence. The result was an increased sense of self-worth, status and legitimacy. However, others alluded to the rejection of their identity claims and all experienced difficulties in identity work.

In the second part of the chapter, we explored some of the reported threats to a coherent sense of ambivalence. Here, it would be easy to assume that these arose primarily from the hybrid or contradictory nature of claims, which contrast from those by managers in more secure, established and coherent contexts. The image here would be one of bureaucratic managers with, for example, designated positions within a fixed job hierarchy and aligned to the local expertise of their organisation. While such positions are by no means immune from contradiction and insecurity (Harding, et al., 2014; Jackall, 1988), they might be seen as less so than that of consultant managers. The latter exist in a far more liminal space, regularly crossing structural, knowledge, political and interpersonal boundaries and subject to the uncertainty and ambiguity of a more fluid organisational existence – a 'dual identity'. Although this was evident in terms of the sense of structural 'homelessness' that was experienced and political exclusion that derived from a discretionary status, their preferred identity was often spoiled by others in the form of resistance or the perishability of knowledge value. In short, it was the interdependence of identity that undermined it as much as any sense of contradiction.

8   Conclusion

We started this book by posing the question: if management was becoming neo-bureaucratic, what would it look like, how would it happen and what issues/tensions would emerge? We approached these questions by focusing on a particular case which was both a mechanism and an outcome of change – the *consultant manager*. Our basic argument has been that management is not post-bureaucratic, but is often assuming a hybrid form, one that in many respects mirrors the work of management consultants – what we have termed *management as consultancy*. This is evident in terms of activities, relationships, occupational dynamics and identities and is achieved through various means of importing consulting practices into organisations. We have also been concerned with outcomes and, in particular, assessing the degree to which tensions of management and organisation are resolved, reproduced and/or transformed through this hybrid form of management. Thus, the book has been about management *and* consultancy, and our findings have implications for understanding them both as well as for the further research that is needed. These form the focus of this concluding chapter.

MANAGEMENT AS CONSULTANCY – AN OVERVIEW
There is considerable agreement in the literature, even among the sceptics, that management has changed. This is linked to wider organisational changes, and, although terms differ, various hybrid neo-bureaucratic forms have been identified. However, few studies set out in detail what neo-bureaucracy comprises, nor do they link this

to management work empirically. Much of the recent research on the job of the manager has been associated with *post*-bureaucracy. It is also sometimes limited in its focus on management as practice at the expense of wider control dynamics ('causal powers'), occupational competition and the processes through which any change has occurred. We have sought to address these limitations by outlining an ideal type of neo-bureaucratic organisation and then focusing on the case of management as consultancy, where many of the characteristics of neo-bureaucracy are pronounced: change and project orientations and methods and a focus on market, external, lateral and 'non-hierarchical' relationships as well as more bureaucratic elements. Furthermore, we have explored some of the processes through which such practices are introduced into management: managers recruiting former external consultants; partnering existing ones; appropriating consulting into their occupational specialisms; and organising change projects and programmes through internal consulting units.

Our analysis of management as consultancy has been structured around a consideration of the activities, relationships and occupational and identity implications of this neo-bureaucratic hybrid (see Table 8.1). This began in Chapter 4, where we explored what consultant managers do – that is, the purpose and content of their activities and how they organise and structure their work. Here, we found that consultant managers were strongly focused on the idea and practice of organisational change and saw themselves as key 'change agents', often emphasising their coordinating and integrative role in the process of managing change. Consultant managers stressed their need to be free from traditional organisational constraints in order to deliver change and often framed their work around a seemingly neutral discourse of cost reduction and efficiency improvement. Their work methods were often highly structured and presented in systematic terms, specifically around project and programme management and techniques such as Six Sigma and lean management. Not surprisingly, this agenda was often subject to challenge and resistance and, as we note below, was underpinned by multiple contradictions and tensions.

Table 8.1 *Management as consultancy – key features*

Key features	Themes and examples
Activities (Chapter 4) What do consultant managers do? What are the purpose and content of their work? How is their work structured?	Change agency – coordinating and integrating organisational change Focus on cost reduction, efficiency and culture change Highly structured and systematic work methods (e.g. project and programme management, Six Sigma, lean)
Relationships (Chapter 5) With whom do consultant managers work? What is the nature of their work relationships?	Greater concern with lateral and external relations (e.g. organisational boundary spanners) Focus on 'client relationships' and 'client management' with operational peers and senior sponsors Emphasis on 'adding value', while also maintaining autonomy (e.g. saying 'no') Acting as 'gatekeepers', 'brokers' and 'partners' to external consultants
Occupations and careers (Chapter 6) What does the emergence of the consultant manager mean for managerial careers and the future of management as an occupation?	Growing appropriation of consultancy activities and discourse by different managerial occupations (e.g. accounting, IT and HRM) Adoption of consultancy tools and thinking in management education (e.g. MBA case method, consultancy as preferred graduate career) Career dispersion of former management consultants into organisational roles (the 'consulting diaspora')
Identity (Chapter 7) How do consultant managers make sense of their hybrid role in organisations? How can we better understand ambivalent neo-bureaucratic managerial identities?	Different intra-organisational boundaries which shape managerial identity (e.g. structural, knowledge, political and interpersonal) Ambivalent identity as both a core part of the organisation but also separate from it (consultant managers as 'outsiders within') Preferred and 'spoiled' identities

In Chapter 5 we extended the analysis of the work activities of consultant managers to a consideration of whom they worked with and the nature of these relationships. Here, traditional hierarchical concerns were not wholly absent, but rather supplemented by a greater concern about lateral and external relations with internal 'clients' and outside providers. Indeed, the focus upon organisational relations in terms of 'client relationships' was another defining feature of the work of consultant managers. Rather than characterising their work in terms of positions in a hierarchical chain of command, consultant managers characterised it in terms of being advisers and service providers to their 'clients' and senior sponsors in the organisation. This required various relationship management strategies in seeking to win work and maintain legitimacy. Some stressed the use of more formal contracting and networking approaches, while others emphasised their ability to 'add value' to operational activities and organisational outcomes in selling their expertise and skills. Importantly, this also required the need to maintain autonomy and being able to say 'no' to other managers. This contested and ambiguous role became most apparent when consultant managers were in competition with rival external consultants. Here, consultant managers could act as 'gatekeepers', 'brokers' and even 'partners' with their external counterparts, highlighting the ambivalent and changing role of these organisational boundary spanners and the concern to engage in external relationships alongside internal ones.

The emergence of management as consultancy also has significant occupational implications for both management and management consultancy. As we saw in Chapter 6, one interesting development has been the blurring of managerial and consultancy career paths and occupational boundaries. As we noted, this has involved the growing appropriation of consultancy activities and discourse by consultant managers located within different managerial occupations such as accounting, IT and more recently HRM. More generally, management education has also become increasingly influenced by consultancy thinking, evident in curricula (e.g. the case method and consultancy projects) and career and job destinations (the increasing number of graduates going into management consultancy as part of their management careers). Indeed, this was particularly evident in what we termed the 'consulting diaspora': the career dispersion of former external management consultants into organisational roles. Once again, while these developments offer up new contradictions and tensions (which we explore shortly), they also provided evidence of an increased blurring of the occupational distinction between managers and consultants.

This led on to our final empirical section (Chapter 7), where we explored what these developments meant for managerial identity and how consultant managers made sense of their hybrid role in organisations. Here we distinguished between different intra-organisational boundaries which informed such identity work. In particular, we explored the way in which consultant managers presented different identities in relation to organisations' structural, knowledge, political and personal boundaries. Here they stressed preferred images as 'change agents', 'trusted advisers', 'cosmopolitans', 'esoteric experts', 'court jesters', 'political players' and 'confidants'. The key theme that emerged in our analysis was of individuals and groups expressing an ambivalent identity as both a core part of their organisations and also separate from it: as *outsiders within*. This dual identity could serve as a source of strength and differentiation in setting them apart from their more operational peers and also enabling them to challenge existing practices, thinking and power relations. However, such identity work was also subject to contestation, challenge and internal contradiction.

As indicated, a central theme of our analysis has been to locate the experiences of consultant managers around an ideal type of neo-bureaucracy set out in Chapters 1 and 2. In keeping with ideal types in general, there is not likely to be a precise match with practices observed in the field. Nevertheless, many of the points outlined above (and in Table 8.1) support the relevance of our framework as a means of evaluating management roles where bureaucratic and post-bureaucratic discourses are combined (see also Table 2.1 in Chapter 2).

For example, the neo-bureaucratic characterisation of *long-term/ strategic and short-term operational* concerns and the use of highly structured methods to deliver innovation projects (*managed improvisation*) were evident in the content of consultant managers' work. Additionally, the less direct emphasis on hierarchy (*delegated autonomy*) and specialisation (*functional integration*) within neo-bureaucracy was evident in the organisation and structure of the work of consultant managers. Similarly, the nature of consultant manager relationships included both an *internal* and *external orientation*, the use of relationship management techniques (*structured organisational politics*) and a blend of market- and network-based measures of value and credibility (*networked meritocracy*). Finally, we showed how the development of *marketised careers* and *dual identities* within neo-bureaucracy applied to consultant managers in their shifting and ambivalent identities as 'outsiders within'.

This analysis of neo-bureaucracy, developed through the case of consultant managers, contributes to an understanding of managerial work in two key areas. First, our ideal type draws attention to the need for a debate around managerial work that avoids polarised positions between continuity and change. Neo-bureaucracy, at least in terms of the characteristics we have set out, acknowledges that management has incorporated new ways of working, yet retains many features consistent with managerial work as understood over many decades, as operational and bureaucratic. Such a view reflects the emphasis we have placed on hybridity in our model. At the same time, we have been concerned to see management as *both* a set of tasks and functions *and* a social activity with more fundamental (and therefore persistent) 'causal powers' focused on control and contradiction (Tsoukas, 1994). This position also relates to the second observation as to the value of our ideal type, namely that it incorporates characteristics of management that extend beyond those used in the 'work activity' school. More specifically, by incorporating identity work and the broader occupational context (alongside the more familiar focus on activities and relationships) within an idealised depiction of neo-bureaucracy, we are able to draw out elements of management that are sometimes neglected in attempts to trace the extent of change from bureaucracy to post-bureaucracy or hybrid forms. Furthermore, one of the central themes of this book has been the tensions of neo-bureaucratic work, represented in the ambiguities and insecurity of the consultant manager role. In the following section, we explore the nature of these tensions and their implications for the notion of neo-bureaucracy as a solution to managerial dilemmas.

NEW AND OLD TENSIONS

As we outlined in Chapter 1, even if the outcomes of changes in management were not *post*-bureaucratic (in the sense of lacking bureaucratic qualities), they were often linked to a prevailing ideological critique of bureaucracy. For example, we cited Boltanski and Chiapello's (2005a) account of the perceived problems of management as being bureaucratic: static, hierarchical, internally focused, tactical, 'excessively technical', limiting of autonomy and authenticity, open-ended (ongoing) and lacking in commerciality or market discipline. These echo some of the classic organisational tensions of the ideal type of bureaucratic organisation we mentioned, such as those around specialisation, hierarchy, formalisation, standardisation and stability. These sets of problems can be linked to some of the characteristics of management as consultancy we have outlined as a potential alternative, such as a focus on external relations, enterprise, 'non-hierarchical' styles of interaction and integrative project/change management and methods. In other words, management as consultancy can be seen as an attempt to resolve some of the problems of bureaucratic organising (see Table 8.2, columns 1–3). For example, the consultant manager's external orientation was seen by proponents as a way of bringing in enterprise, change and new knowledge, while the strategic/enterprise focus made added value and an internal market more visible and important. Similarly, an emphasis on advisory or partnership relations downplayed hierarchy and reinforced market–client relations. Finally, integrative project/change management and methods countered the problems of lateral communication between functions and the idea of management as open ended and static. These connections serve to reinforce the suitability of management as consultancy as a site to explore changes in management and bureaucracy.

However, as we have emphasised throughout, despite the hype, bureaucracy is not replaced or even necessarily reduced through such changes. This means that its tensions are not likely to be fully removed. Rather, it is transformed into the hybrid of neo-bureaucracy. Here, as we outlined in Chapter 2, some cautiously suggested a potential to resolve tensions such as those between rational and post-bureaucratic ideal types – between hierarchy and market or, as Reed (2011: 245) puts it, between the control of the 'cage' and the 'gaze'. Indeed, we have seen indications of this potential, such as some consultant managers' ability to combine insider and outsider identities, their sometimes successful role in functional integration and change management and the discipline of their quasi-internal market status. At its most positive then, consultant managers can combine the outsider status, change orientation and integrating role of external consultants with the longer-term commitment, responsibility and organisational/sector expertise of conventional internal managers.

However, overall, our findings have pointed to a wide range of tensions and conflicts within the hybrid role of the consultant manager. These can be understood in three ways: as part of the specific neo-bureaucratic regime of management as consultancy; as classic dilemmas of bureaucratic organisations; and, to a lesser extent, as reflecting the value of both internal and external knowledge (see Table 8.2, columns 4–5). In terms of the examples listed above, then, partnering with external consultants could bring client resistance to any claim of increased status among consultant managers, who were also placed under a potential occupational/jurisdictional threat of being substituted. In short, their distinctive position meant that the problems of specialisation persisted, exacerbated by client scepticism of the external knowledge they purveyed. Likewise, with a strategic/enterprise focus, consultant managers often pursued sectional or

Table 8.2 *Management as consultancy – 'solutions' and tensions of neo-bureaucracy*

1. Management as consultancy	2. Anti-bureaucratic characteristics	3. Principal critiques of bureaucratic management targeted (Boltanski and Chiapello, 2005a)	4. Specific tensions of neo-bureaucratic regimes	5. Persistent tensions of organisation	6. Potentially emergent tensions
External orientation (draw from and partner external consultants)	Instil enterprise/change; adopt external knowledge	Bureaucracy as internally focused and static (see also below)	Client resistance to acquired status of consultant managers; risk of substitution and blame attribution	Specialisation and conflict within capital; scepticism of external knowledge and actors	Excessive change resisted, devaluing internal expertise
Strategic/ enterprise focus	Enhance commercial role, demonstrate 'added value'	Management functions as tactical, 'excessively technical' and lacking in commerciality	Failure to discard traditional roles/ status; strategic role pursued for own sectional gain; internal market brings risks of being disbanded	Specialisation – pursue sectional interests	Focus on added value over development ('Theory E' over 'Theory O')

Table 8.2 (*cont.*)

1. Management as consultancy	2. Anti-bureaucratic characteristics	3. Principal critiques of bureaucratic management targeted (Boltanski and Chiapello, 2005a)	4. Specific tensions of neo-bureaucratic regimes	5. Persistent tensions of organisation	6. Potentially emergent tensions
'Non-hierarchical' style (adviser/ partner relationship)	Reinforce market/ client-based relations; reduce hierarchical control; achieve 'buy-in'	Hierarchy as limit to authenticity and autonomy	Hierarchy remains visible; internal market serves as substitute for control and is contested and variable	Hierarchy and formalisation of social relations	Loss of ethics of rationality through informality; over-commitment
Integrative project/change management and methods	Ensure systematic approach to change; overcome political and lateral communication barriers from structural/ functional divisions	Work as open ended/ ongoing; emphasis on vertical relations; management as static	Reputational risk of reliance on specific methods; client resistance to standardised tools	Formalisation and standardisation; hierarchy; loss of specialisation through integration	Short-term (project/ programme) focus over organisation development ('Theory O')

functional interests – leading to conflict *within* management as much as *between* management and other stakeholders. At the same time, the market discipline of neo-bureaucracy brought with it a constant threat of being disbanded or absorbed, and those who aspired to become consultant managers could often not lose their prior administrative status (e.g. as HRM managers). In terms of 'non-hierarchical' practices, this was always most problematic in that hierarchy persisted within or alongside management as consultancy, by acting with sponsor support or as change programme controllers. There was sometimes greater ambiguity as to who had formal power, but this could merely add to contestation. Furthermore, through relationship management practices, client relations were subject to the problem of formalisation. This was particularly evident in terms of project/change management methods, where formal and standardised tools were the norm. This activity did, however, temper specialisation, but this too could bring potential problems if expertise was lost. A more specific issue here was the use of branded methods (e.g. Six Sigma) which were sometimes highly perishable and could also be resisted by clients on the basis of their standardised form.

Of course, the above account (and Table 8.2) is only illustrative of the tensions we identified in the earlier chapters. However, it clearly shows that, in the form of management as consultancy at least, neo-bureaucracy retains many of the classic general tensions of organising and brings with it specific new ones. It does not then resolve the tensions between bureaucracy and post-bureaucracy as has been suggested. This is perhaps most visible when considering the experiences and identities of consultant managers as 'outsiders within'. Furthermore, doing so draws attention to a more dynamic quality to organisation and to its tensions in that a seemingly stable sense of ambivalence, such as that of the 'court jester' role or 'trusted adviser', could quickly fade. We saw, for example, how consultant managers' boundary work was evident in relation to the organisation structure and knowledge claims, where an outsider status was pursued while simultaneously seeking to be politically and interpersonally accepted.

However, in each case the identity was fragile and vulnerable to being 'spoiled' over time through client resistance and rejection.

It would be easy then, given the focus of our analysis, to attribute this (along with other tensions in the work of consultant managers) entirely to the hybridity of neo-bureaucracy. However, we have already outlined how such hybridity can itself often be linked to more generic tensions of organising. Included in this would be contradictions arising specifically from the capitalist form of control, reflected, in part, in client resistance to rationalisation. To these general phenomena, we might add that consultant managers appeared to be especially vulnerable to experiencing the consequences of tensions by virtue of their dependence on others in the organisation. We all rely on others to have our identity claims confirmed or rejected (Bartel and Dutton, 2001; Knights and Willmott, 1989), but consultant managers' structural position, where their services were discretionary, rendered them both materially and existentially dependent on other managers and functions. In a stronger structural position within the organisation, tensions might be less damaging. Finally and relatedly, the tensions they experienced may well have partly arisen by virtue of their status, identity and structural position as *different* from many other managers in their organisation, a point to which we shall return shortly.

In addition to the tensions we identified in our data analysis, we can speculate over other potential tensions that could emerge (see Table 8.2, column 6), as well as wider implications for management. For instance, we can see how bringing in a change orientation and new knowledge from the outside could lead to an overemphasis on change and a devaluing of internal knowledge. Likewise, a focus on enterprise, the market and on projects shifts attention away from longer-term organisational development in favour of short-term economic concerns such as 'added value' ('Theory E' over 'Theory O'). Indeed, such shifts have been documented elsewhere as part of a wider move to financialisation (Morris, et al., 2008). More speculatively, the focus on 'non-hierarchical' styles of relating, such as through advisory or partnership roles outside of a formal structure, and a focus on the interpersonal bring an element of informality, which can generate over-commitment and undermine the ethics of impersonality inherent in more bureaucratic organising (see also du Gay, 2000).

Given the productive potential of tensions and contradictions, we can expect further, unanticipated changes to emerge. Similarly, we can outline some wider, more speculative implications of our analysis if management continues to become like consultancy. For instance:

- Different management occupations (e.g. HRM) may risk losing their distinctive role and occupational jurisdiction in pursuit of consultancy's currently high status. In this sense, they risk being colonised by other occupations.

- Acquiring the professional trappings and aspirations of external consultancy combined with its abstract and standardised methods could support the long-standing professionalisation project for management, as a *corporate profession* at least.

- Although rarely transparent in practice, patterns of managerial accountability may be further blurred. On one hand, project management methods seek to clarify responsibilities, while on the other hand diffuse structural boundaries and multifunctional teams could undermine traditional hierarchical lines of accountability.

- As claims to consultancy practices become more widespread, the currently aspirational and exclusive status of external consultancy will decline among managers. It will be less special (see also below).

- The use of internal market mechanisms of discipline, whereby managers compete for resources, is likely to further intensify the job insecurity and enterprise of managers.

- By appropriating particular methods- and project-based practices into management, other less masculine and structured and more participative forms are marginalised or silenced (see also Buchanan, et al., 2007; Marsh, 2009). This echoes a broader argument about the spread of management more generally, which 'closes off alternative conceptions of coordination, most notably those of community' (Grey, 1999: 579).

CONSULTANCY AS MANAGEMENT – THE EXTERNAL CONSULTANT IS DEAD; LONG LIVE THE CONSULTANT MANAGER?

While focused on management in its neo-bureaucratic form, this book has also been about consultancy. As we set out in Chapters 2 and 3, we sought to reveal neglected dimensions of consultancy that challenged the conventional assumptions that consulting organisation is about professional service firms; that internal consulting is about individuals in relation to their external counterparts; that consulting is a distinct profession or professional project; and that consulting is an elite, successful activity shrouded in mystery. Rather, we have shown how consulting can be organised in internal units or departments and within 'non-consulting' occupations; how consultants can be understood in relation to managers and specialist management occupations as much as, or even more than, in relation to the professions; and how consulting can be looked down upon, struggle for its organisational and occupational existence and be highly standardised in its approach. In short, we have sought to *de*-differentiate management and consulting. Of course, our focus has been on a particular form of consulting, but some of these characteristics such as stigma, standardisation and organisational insecurity are shared more widely in consulting (Sturdy, et al., 2009, 2013) and need to be explored further. Moreover, if the use of consultant managers in organisations continues to develop, there are implications for all forms of consulting and for the management of change.

The most obvious implication of the development of consultant managers is a substitution for external management consultancy. Until recently, management consultancy has largely been appropriated by a limited range of occupational groups and those which typically act as organisational outsiders with relatively high status (e.g. accounting, IT). This largely preserved a distinctive role and cosmopolitan identity for the consulting occupation, a mystique even (see also Kitay and Wright, 2007), and one typically reproduced in much of the academic literature. But as change management methodologies become more commonplace and commodified among management ranks and as internal advisory services extend, external consultants are unlikely to constitute a sufficiently attractive/distinctive service for clients. They will be demystified, much as has happened in auditing, for example. Indeed, industry commentators have already made similar observations about a wider disruption and threat to the (external) consulting industry (Christensen, et al., 2013; Czerniawska, 2011). Of course, such a change might also lead to a lessening of the stigma attached to consulting as this often comes with power and privilege, as with lawyers, for example (Sturdy, 2009). Here, the decline in status could paradoxically be seen as an indication of the broader *success* of consultancy. Much as the dominance of *managerialism* brought a decline in the status of *management* (Grey, 1999), we might be witnessing *the demise of the consultant with the dominance of consultancy*, albeit a particular, methods-based form of consultancy.

However, such a claim is perhaps premature. Similar predictions of the demise of consulting have been made before (see, e.g., Trinca, 2002), and yet the external consulting sector continued to grow dramatically. This is largely because external consultancy cannot just be understood as a provider of expertise. Rather, its external quality adds value to its knowledge compared to that produced internally and offers the prospect of legitimating managerial decisions which cannot be done so easily internally. Furthermore, external consultancy has always responded to threats and criticisms (Kipping, 2002). In this case, for example, we could suggest that the growth of the consultant manager might lead to external consultants making even more of their outsider status and legitimating role and marketing themselves as offering more esoteric or novel expertise – de-commodification. At the same time, an alternative approach would be to standardise further, through outsourcing, for example, and challenge the cost efficiency of internal options of managing change. In short, the rise of the consultant manager could lead to a polarisation of the external consulting sector.

FUTURE RESEARCH

While our research is one of the largest ever studies of management consultancy and is even significant in scale in terms of academic research on management, it is clearly limited in various respects. We identified some limitations in Chapter 3 and how these might impact on our findings and analysis. For example, our reliance on interviews of consultant managers meant that other voices were relatively silent, notably those of labour and other non-consultant managers. Similarly, the contexts of our research were quite specific, rather than generalisable. Here, we shall briefly draw out those limitations which became apparent in the analysis and which prompt the need for further research. Two areas in particular should be highlighted.

First, and as intimated above and in earlier chapters, the consultant managers in our study were not typical of managers in their organisations, but a minority and often change specialists. This echoes other research findings where contrasting organisation structures (bureaucratic and post-bureaucratic) were found existing alongside each other, in the same workplaces (Bolin and Härenstam, 2008). But it raises a number of questions such as under what conditions is it possible to have all, or the majority of, managers in an organisation assuming a neo-bureaucratic role, with quasi-market and ambiguous hierarchical relations, for example. Alternatively, is neo-bureaucracy, in part, only sustained by its other? Similarly, how does our case of consultant managers compare to management in organisations which seek to embed modern management practices throughout, in companies like Google, for example (Garvin, 2013)?

The second significant area of new research questions emerges from the fact that although we have demonstrated strong parallels between neo-bureaucracy and consultancy, an 'elective affinity' even, they are not synonymous. Thus, there are dimensions of neo-bureaucratic management that have not been explored and features of consultancy examined that do not neatly fit models of neo-bureaucracy or, at least, are not central to them. Thus, for example, in Reed's (2011) model of neo-bureaucracy, continuous self-surveillance in project teams is an important element along with 'managed democracy', neither of which has been central to our research. Furthermore, Reed sets out how dimensions might work together. Likewise, we have highlighted 'non-hierarchical' relations such as through providing advice to clients, and yet this is not specific to neo-bureaucracy. Rather, it is associated with new management more generally and *post*-bureaucratic discourses in particular. Thus, there remains a necessary mismatch between ideal types and empirical studies such as ours, which points to various new avenues for research. To these we could add a call for a more dynamic approach to neo-bureaucracy and other hybrid forms and their tensions. For example, our cross-sectional approach did not lend itself to considering how actors might deal with tensions such as role conflicts by alternating positions over time. We saw something of this when considering identity, but given the everyday nature of tensions, it is possible that their problematic nature can be overstated.

Finally, there remain areas of further research needed on management and its continuities and changes at a more general level. In this book, we have consistently avoided making claims over the precise extent of change in management for various methodological and theoretical reasons. However, we have drawn attention to some of the mechanisms of change. Indeed, our focus on consultancy was justified on the basis of being both an outcome and a mechanism of new forms of management. Here, some attention was given to education and training as means through which managers can acquire new practices, but there is still very little large-scale research which assesses the extent to which knowledge is learned and applied in management. More importantly, there are potentially many other routes to becoming neo-bureaucratic other than through education which need to be explored and compared. How, for example, do the processes of becoming consultant managers and project managers compare? And at a societal or sectoral level, what are the wider institutional and economic conditions for the emergence of neo-bureaucracy and of management and what different forms do they take in these contexts? At an even broader level, we need to explore further the generative power and pervasiveness of tensions. Our focus on tensions was mostly directed at revealing them to be problematic, as a counter to those seeking resolution in the form of perfect management control, for example. While this is important theoretically, practically and politically, there remains a danger of seeing them as outcomes of change rather than also as a generator of change, and of obscuring the inevitability of tensions within organising. Such questions remain open here, but we hope to have contributed to a critical account of contemporary management that simultaneously reveals consulting in a different and emergent light – in short, as management.

CLOSING THOUGHTS

We began this book by drawing attention to the largely unacknowledged parallels between images of new managers and the practices of management consultants. Through the particular case of *consultant managers*, we have explored neglected and important features of both management and consultancy. We have also developed an account which challenges existing understandings of each domain and their interrelationship – *management as consultancy*. At the same time, we have followed those who have emphasised the persistence of bureaucratic organising in the face of popular and persistent claims of its demise. But we have added to these debates by developing an ideal type of neo-bureaucracy as an explicit hybrid of bureaucracy and post-bureaucracy. This was then examined in relation to the activities, relationships, occupational dynamics and identities of managers in consulting roles. This not only is of analytical value but also continues a long tradition of understanding management and organisation through a focus on tensions and ambiguities. Our analysis has also revealed some of the processes through which change and continuity occur, as well as a number of significant practical implications for the future of both consulting and management, as the boundaries between them become more diffuse.

Appendix 1 Details of UK interview respondents

Pseudonym	Title	Organisation (pseudonym)	Job tenure (years)	External consulting experience
Alan	Principal Consultant	Government Service (GovServ1)	1–5	No
Joan	Senior Analyst	Government Service (GovServ1)	1–5	No
James	Consultant	Government Service (GovServ1)	5–10	No
Ray	Assistant Director of Continuous Improvement	Government Service (GovServ1)	<1	No
Anthony	Business Process Re-engineer	Government Service (GovServ1)	1–5	No
Geoff	Principal Consultant	Government Service (GovServ2)	1–5	No
Colin	Principal Consultant	Government Service (GovServ3)	1–5	No
Celia	Principal Consultant	Government Service (GovServ3)	1–5	No
Christine	Director Man. Consultancy Services	Central Government Dept. (GovDept1)	1–5	No
Mark	Head of Business Improvement	Central Government Dept. (GovDept1)	<1	No
Dan	Corporate Assurance Practice Manager	Central Government Agency (GovAgency1)	1–5	Yes
Pete	Corporate Assurance Resourcing and Development Manager	Central Government Agency (GovAgency1)	1–5	Yes
Matt	Marketing Manager	Central Government Agency (GovAgency1)	1–5	Yes
Isaac	Head of Business Improvement	Central Government Agency (GovAgency2)	1–5	Yes
Diana	Head of Performance Improvement Unit	Central Government Agency (GovAgency3)	5–10	No
Bruce	Head of Performance Management and Consultancy	Central Government Agency (GovAgency4)	1–5	No

Pseudonym	Title	Organisation (pseudonym)	Job tenure (years)	External consulting experience	Client Manager
Natalie	Head of HR Operations Office	Business Support (BusServ)	5–10	No	
Jan	Head of HR Operations Global Services	Business Support (BusServ)	1–5	No	
Belinda	Director – Head of Consulting and PMO	Global Financial Services (FinCo1)	1–5	No	
Davina	Managing Director – Client Delivery	Global Financial Services (FinCo1)	1–5	Yes	
Rachel	Senior Vice-President – Head of Consulting	Global Financial Services (FinCo1)	1–5	No	
Daniel	Vice-President – Senior Project Manager	Global Financial Services (FinCo1)	1–5	Yes	
Jeremy	Project Manager	Global Financial Services (FinCo1)	1–5	Yes	
Steve	Project Manager	Global Financial Services (FinCo1)	1–5	No	
Andrew	Senior Business Analyst	Global Financial Services (FinCo1)	1–5	No	
Maurice	Senior Business Analyst	Global Financial Services (FinCo1)	1–5	No	
Debbie	Project Manager	Global Financial Services (FinCo1)	1–5	No	
Gary	Associate	Global Financial Services (FinCo1)	1–5	No	
Rick	Project Manager	Global Financial Services (FinCo1)	1–5	Yes	
Simon	MD Product Management	Global Financial Services (FinCo1)	1–5	Yes	
			Not available (n/a)		Client Manager
Fabio	MD Ops. Region Head	Global Financial Services (FinCo1)	n/a		Client Manager
Ryan	MD Ops. Region Head	Global Financial Services (FinCo1)	n/a		Client Manager
Pete	MD Relationship Management	Global Financial Services (FinCo1)	n/a		Client Manager
Frank	Cash Management Services	Global Financial Services (FinCo1)	n/a		Client Manager
Nathan	Head of Global Transaction Division	Global Financial Services (FinCo1)	n/a		Client Manager
Jamie	Head of Business Development	Global Financial Services (FinCo1)	n/a		Client Manager
Sam	MD Region Head Global Transaction Division	Global Financial Services (FinCo1)	n/a		Client Manager
Anthony	Head of Product	Global Financial Services (FinCo1)	n/a		Client Manager

Pseudonym	Title	Organisation (pseudonym)	Job tenure (years)	External consulting experience
Jack	Head of Employee Engagement	UK Bank (FinCo2)	5–10	No
Tina	Employee Engagement Manager	UK Bank (FinCo2)	5–10	No
Kate	Resourcing Manager, Organisational Effectiveness	UK Bank (FinCo2)	1–5	No
Dale	Employee Engagement Manager	UK Bank (FinCo2)	1–5	No
Shaun	Infrastructure Design Consultant	Insurance Company (FinCo3)	5–10	No
Dean	Infrastructure Design Consultant	Insurance Company (FinCo3)	5–10	No
Ian	Head of Department	UK Building Society (FinCo4)	5–10	No
Rhianna	Patient Services Manager – Team Coach	Hospital (HealthCo1)	<1	No
Lorrain	Consultant Anaesthetist – Team Coach	Hospital (HealthCo1)	1–5	No
Jonah	Project Manager, Patient Services	Hospital (HealthCo1)	1–5	No
Austin	Programme Director	Hospital (HealthCo1)	1–5	No
Fred	Coach	Hospital (HealthCo1)	1–5	No
Sue	Team Coach	Hospital (HealthCo1)	1–5	No
Simone	Team Coach	Hospital (HealthCo1)	1–5	No
Isabel	Team Coach	Hospital (HealthCo1)	1–5	No
Catherine	Director Performance & Development	Hospital (HealthCo1)	5–10	No
Hugh	Consultant Paediatrician – Team Coach	Hospital (HealthCo1)	5–10	No
Tamsin	Paediatric Nursing Sister – Team Coach	Hospital (HealthCo1)	1–5	No
Emma	Consultant Anaesthetist – Team Coach	Hospital (HealthCo1)	<1	No
Bryony	Ward Manager	Hospital (HealthCo1)	1–5	Client Manager
Barry	Head of Learning Disabilities	Hospital (HealthCo1)	1–5	Client Manager
Nina	Director Human Resources	Hospital (HealthCo1)	5–10	No

Pseudonym	Title	Organisation (pseudonym)	Job tenure (years)	External consulting experience
Steve	Deputy CEO	Hospital (HealthCo1)	1–5	No
Ursula	Customer Services Manager – Team Coach	Hospital (HealthCo1)	1–5	No
Celia	Director of SLAM Partners	Health Care Trust (HealthCo2)	1–5	No
Neil	CEO	Health Institute (HealthCo3)	1–5	Yes
Aiden	Business Consultant	Private Health Care Provider (HealthCo4)	1–5	Yes
Nate	Head of Performance Management Team	Local Government (LocalGov1)	5–10	No
Fern	Improvement Manager	Local Government (LocalGov1)	5–10	No
Tom	HR Consultant	Local Government (LocalGov1)	5–10	No
Johnny	Performance Review Team Manager	Local Government (LocalGov2)	1–5	No
Brian	Business Service Manager	Local Government (LocalGov2)	1–5	No
Dennis	Customer Strategy Manager	Local Government (LocalGov3)	<1	No
Robin	Performance Improvement Manager	Local Government (LocalGov4)	1–5	Yes
Pippa	OD and Change Director	Media Company (ArtsCo)	1–5	Yes
Celia	Consultant OD and Change	Media Company (ArtsCo)	1–5	No
Jean	Consultant OD and Change	Media Company (ArtsCo)	1–5	No
Rob	Procurement Manager	Telecoms Company (CommsCo)	5–10	No
Mike	Business consultant	Telecoms Company (CommsCo)	1–5	Yes
Belinda	Head of HR (Regional)	Telecoms Company (CommsCo)	1–5	Yes
Joan	Managing Director	Telecoms Company (CommsCo)	1–5	Yes
James	Programme Director	Telecoms Company (CommsCo)	1–5	No
Ray	Continuous Service Improvement Manager	Telecoms Company (CommsCo)	5–10	No
Anthony	Continuous Service Improvement Manager	Telecoms Company (CommsCo)	1–5	No
Christine	Continuous Service Improvement Manager nt	Telecoms Company (CommsCo)	1–5	No

Pseudonym	Title	Organisation (pseudonym)	Job tenure (years)	External consulting experience
Colin	Continuous Service Improvement Manager	Telecoms Company (CommsCo)	1–5	No
Piers	Programme Director	Telecoms Company (CommsCo)	1–5	No
Matt	Programme Director	Telecoms Company (CommsCo)	1–5	Yes
Diana	Programme Director	Telecoms Company (CommsCo)	1–5	No
Mark	Director	Telecoms Company (CommsCo)	n/a	Client Manager
Pete	Change Partner	Telecoms Company (CommsCo)	n/a	Client Manager
Steve	Head of Governance	Telecoms Company (CommsCo)	n/a	Client Manager
Valerie	Divisional Director	Telecoms Company (CommsCo)	n/a	Client Manager
Dan	Head of Strategic Analysis	Rail Firm (TransCo)	1–5	Yes
Graham	Business Consultant	Rail Firm (TransCo)	1–5	Yes

Appendix 2 Details of Australian interview respondents

Pseudonym	Title	Organisation	Job tenure (years)	External consulting experience
Adam	OD Manager	Pharmaceutical company (European MNC)	4–5	No
Andy	Head of Innovation & Strategy	Retail bank (Australian MNC)	<1	Yes
Angela	Learning & Development Consultant	Resources company (Australian MNC)	<1	Yes
Arnie	Director, People & Performance	Accounting and consulting firm (global partnership)	<1	No
Barry	Group Manager, Human Resources	Resources company (Australian MNC)	1–2	Yes
Betty	Business Improvement Consultant	Equipment hire company (local)	1–2	Yes
Bronwyn	Change Consultant	Retail bank (Australian MNC)	<1	Yes
Catherine	HR Business Partner	Engineering company (US MNC)	<1	Yes
Celine	Leader, Business Improvement	Telecommunications company (Euro. MNC)	5–6	Yes
Cherie	Manager, Learning & Development	University (local)	<1	Yes
Daniel	Director, Learning & Development Asia-Pacific	Investment bank (European MNC)	6–7	Yes
Della	National Human Resource Director	Industrial services company (Australian MNC)	4–5	No
Faye	Human Resource Manager	Insurance company (local)	4–5	No
Frances	OD Manager, People & Culture	Accounting and consulting firm (global partnership)	<1	No
Garry	General Manager Supply Chain	Metals manufacturing (Australian)	<1	Yes
Hannah	Group HR Manager, Australia/NZ	IT company (US MNC)	1–2	Yes
Ingrid	Customer Retention Manager	Insurance company (local)	<1	Yes
Jean	General Manager Solutions Delivery	Telecommunications company (European MNC)	8	Yes

Pseudonym	Title	Organisation	Job tenure (years)	External consulting experience
Jerry	Business Solutions Manager	Food manufacturer (Australian)	7	No
Kaitlin	HR Manager Asia-Pacific	Investment bank (European MNC)	12	No
Karli	Global Head of OD	IT software company (US MNC)	7–8	No
Keira	Best Practice Consultant	Automotive manufacturer (Asian MNC)	1–2	No
Kelley	HR Director	IT company (US MNC)	2–3	No
Keith	Employee Relations Manager	Food manufacturer (Australian)	2–3	Yes
Kim	Consultant, People & Performance	Investment bank (Australian MNC)	1–2	Yes
Kirk	HR Manager	Industrial services company (European MNC)	1–2	No
Kristen	Manager, People & Performance	Retail bank (Australian MNC)	3–4	No
Lauren	Organisational Change Consultant	Insurance company (local)	2–3	Yes
Leah	HR Manager – Organisation & Development	Retailer (local)	<1	Yes
Lucinda	Change Manager	Airline company (local)	1–2	Yes
Natalie	Learning & Development Manager	Law firm (local)	4–5	Yes
Nell	HR Director, Organisation & Development	University (local)	1–2	No
Patrick	Divisional Manager, HR & Strategic Management	Local government (local)	5–6	Yes
Peter	Director, Professional Education	Accounting and consulting firm (global partnership)	4–5	No
Quincy	Strategic Planner	Transport company (Australian MNC)	1–2	Yes
Ralph	General Manager Supply Chain	Food manufacturer (US MNC)	<1	Yes
Renata	Leader, Culture & Capability	Telecommunications company (European MNC)	4–5	Yes

Pseudonym	Title	Organisation	Job tenure (years)	External consulting experience
Ric	Director, Human Resources	IT company (US MNC)	5–6	No
Rosemary	Manager	Recruitment consultancy	7–8	Yes
Roy	Quality Director	Telecommunications company (European MNC)	6	No
Sandy	Human Resource Partner	IT company (US MNC)	4–5	No
Sophie	OD Director, Asia-Pacific	Engineering consultancy (Australian MNC)	1–2	Yes
Susan	Head of Cultural Transformation	Retail bank (Australian MNC)	4–5	Yes
Teresa	Human Resource Manager	Consumer products firm (US MNC)	4–5	No
Tina	Competition Lawyer	Law firm (global)	<1	Yes

Appendix 3 Key features of UK internal consultancy units (ICUs)

Sector/industry	Structural location/consultancy tradition	Size (full-time equivalent, FTE)	Evaluation of uncertainty/credibility	Other sources of change agency (CA) in organisation
Central government service (GovServ1)	Centralised and independent/operational efficiency	10–20	Concerns with credibility	Multiple and competing sources of CA
Central government service (GovServ2)	Centralised and independent/operational efficiency and organisational development (OD)	20–50	High credibility associated with ICU manager	Multiple but not competing sources of CA
Central government service (GovServ3)	Centralised service function (human resources [HR])/operational efficiency and OD	20–50	Concerns with sustaining credibility	Unit single source of CA
Central government dept (GovDept1)	Centralised and independent/operational efficiency	20–50	Concerns with credibility – unit disbanded	Unit single source of CA
Government agency (GovAgency1)	Centralised service function (audit]/ operational efficiency	10–20	Concerns with credibility – unit disbanded	Multiple and competing sources of CA
Government agency (GovAgency2)	Centralised and independent/operational efficiency	<10	High credibility	Single source of CA
Government agency (GovAgency3)	Divisional operational efficiency/OD and project management	<10	Concerns with credibility	Multiple non-competing sources of CA
Government agency (GovAgency4)	Centralised service function (HR/finance]/ operational efficiency and OD	20–50	Concerns with credibility	Multiple non-competitive sources of CA
Business services (BusServ)	Centralised service function (HR]/OD	20–50	Occasional concerns with credibility	Multiple and competing sources of CA

Sector/industry	Structural location/consultancy tradition	Size (full-time equivalent, FTE)	Evaluation of uncertainty/credibility	Other sources of change agency (CA) in organisation
Financial services (FinCo1)	Divisional operational efficiency and project management	10–20	Concerns with credibility	Multiple and competing sources of CA
Financial services (FinCo2)	Centralised service function (HR)/OD	50+	No concerns with credibility	Multiple and competing sources of CA
Financial services (FinCo3)	Centralised service function [IT]/operational efficiency and project management	<10	Concerns with credibility	Multiple and competing sources of CA
Financial services (FinCo4)	Centralised and independent/operational efficiency	20–50	Occasional concerns with credibility – unit disbanded	Multiple and competing locations for CA
Local health care provider (HealthCo1)	Centralised service function (HR)/OD and project management	<10	No concerns with credibility	Multiple and competing sources of CA
Local health care provider (HealthCo2)	Centralised and independent/OD	<10	High credibility	Multiple and non-competing sources of CA
National health care agency (HealthCo3)	Centralised and independent/operational efficiency and OD	50+	Concerns with credibility	Single source of CA
National health care provider (HealthCo4)	Centralised service function [IT]/operational efficiency and strategy and project management	<10	Concerns with credibility	Single source of CA
Local government (LocalGov1)	Centralised and independent/operational efficiency and strategy and project management	10–20	Occasional concerns with credibility	Multiple but non-competing sources of CA
Local government (LocalGov2)	Centralised and independent/operational efficiency	10–20	No concerns with credibility	Single source of CA

Sector/industry	Structural location/consultancy tradition	Size (full-time equivalent, FTE)	Evaluation of uncertainty/credibility	Other sources of change agency (CA) in organisation
Local government (LocalGov3)	Divisional/operational efficiency	<10	No concerns with credibility	Single source of CA
Local government (LocalGov4)	Centralised service function (HR)/operational efficiency	<10	Occasional concerns with credibility	Multiple and competing sources of CA
Media and arts (ArtsCo)	Centralised service function (HR)/OD	<10	Occasional concerns with credibility	Multiple but non-competing sources of CA
Communications (CommsCo)	Divisional/operational efficiency and OD and strategy	50+	Occasional concerns with credibility	Multiple and competing sources of CA
Transport (TransCo)	Centralised service function (legal)/strategy	20–50	Occasional concerns with credibility – unit disbanded	Multiple but non-competing sources of CA

Appendix 4 Data analysis on standardisation in UK and Australian case studies

Organisation	Context	Interview respondents	Forms of standardisation
BankCo	Global financial institution (UK operations). Internal consultancy part of HR centre of excellence responsible for delivering variety of OD projects	Head of Employee Engagement; Employee Engagement; Resourcing Manager, Organisational Effectiveness; Employee Engagement Manager	Standardising agenda aimed at achieving greater consistency across all divisions in the approach to leadership, development, learning and employee engagement. Evidence of negotiation with and resistance from divisional human resources (HR) specialists around implementation of projects
CarCo	Global automotive manufacturer and retailer (Australian operations). Internal consultancy responsible for distributor and dealer sales training and efficiency improvement	Best Practice Manager; HR Manager; Divisional Sales Manager; Operations Development Manager	Use of a standardised method of process improvement based on quality management principles. Evidence of process innovation and internal diffusion of changed practice via standardised methods
CommsCo	Global telecommunications company (UK operations). Internal consultancy responsible for large-scale transformation project of major business division	Procurement Manager; Business Consultant; Head of HR; Managing Director; Programme Director; Continuous Service Improvement; Change Partner; Head of Governance	Standardising agenda aimed at delivering substantial cost savings across division. Also a focus on standardised change management methods and continuous improvement activity. Evidence of resistance to standardised programme management reporting process and extensive negotiation with individual business units around project scope

Organisation	Context	Interview respondents	Forms of standardisation
FinCo	Australian financial services business. Internal consulting group of 30+ consultants charged with the design and roll-out of a 'branded' culture change process throughout the bank's 30,000 employees. Process initiated by an external consultancy and then taken over by the internal consulting group	Head of Cultural Transformation; Change Consultant; Manager, People & Performance; Organisational Change Consultant.	Standardising agenda of promoting corporate values and changing employee behaviour to fit with these values. Standardised methods of change and project management. Evidence of employee resistance, but limited customisation across business units
FoodCo	Australian food manufacturer employing over 1,200 employees across a range of geographically dispersed production and distribution sites. Joint internal-external consulting project team charged with the implementation of a SAP enterprise information system	QA Manager; Logistics Manager; Site Procurement Officer; Business Solutions Manager; Stores Supervisor; Change Manager; Production Supervisor; Production Planner	Standardising agenda associated with the implementation of an enterprise resource planning software. Focus on standardising business processes in line with the software requirements ('vanilla' implementation). Use of standardised methods of change and project management. Some evidence of local resistance and customisation
MediCo	Local UK health care organisation employing over 3,500. Internal consultancy of four full-time and approximately thirty part-time consultants (coaches) established after organisation-wide team working skills programme	Deputy CEO; Project Manager; Team Based Working Coach; Director Performance & Development; Director HR, Team Coach	No evidence of a standardising agenda of change, but use of standardised methods of group facilitation. Internal consultancy became synonymous with these methods with some evidence of resistance to their use across the organisation, particularly amongst senior management team

Organisation	Context	Interview respondents	Forms of standardisation
PhoneCo	Leading global telecomm-unications company (UK and Australian operations). Establishment of a Six Sigma business improvement group globally and within regional business units	Leader, Business Improvement, Six Sigma Black Belt; Manager Solutions Delivery, Six Sigma Black Belt; Leader, Culture & Capability; Quality Director	Focus on standardised methods process improvement via Six Sigma methodology (DMAIC) and internal accreditation of 'Black Belts' and 'Red Belts'. Evidence of internal process innovation leading to further standardisation

Source: Wright, et al., 2012.

References

Abbott, A. (1988) *The System of Professions: An Essay on the Division of Expert Labor*. Chicago: University of Chicago Press.

Ackroyd, S. (1996) 'Organization Contra Organizations: Professions and Organizational Change in the United Kingdom', *Organization Studies* 17(4): 599–621.

Adler, P. S. and Borys, B. (1996) 'Two Types of Bureaucracy: Enabling and Coercive', *Administrative Science Quarterly* 41(1): 61–89.

Alvesson, M. and Thompson, P. (2005) 'Post-Bureaucracy?', in S. Ackroyd, R. Batt, P. Thompson and P. S. Tolbert (eds) *The Oxford Handbook of Work & Organization*, pp. 485–507. Oxford: Oxford University Press.

Alvesson, M. and Willmott, H. (2002) 'Producing the Appropriate Individual: Identity Regulation as Organizational Control', *Journal of Management Studies* 39(5): 619–44.

Alvesson, M. and Willmott, H. (2012) *Making Sense of Management: A Critical Introduction*. London: Sage.

Anderson-Gough, F., Grey, C. and Robson, K. (2000) 'In the Name of the Client: The Service Ethic in Two Professional Services Firms', *Human Relations* 53(9): 1151–74.

Armbrüster, T. (2004) 'Rationality and Its Symbols: Signalling Effects and Subjectification in Management Consulting', *Journal of Management Studies* 41(8): 1247–69.

Armbrüster, T. (2006) *The Economics and Sociology of Management Consulting*. Cambridge: Cambridge University Press.

Armbrüster, T. and Kipping, M. (2002) 'Types of Knowledge and the Client–Consultant Interaction', in K. Sahlin-Andersson and L. Engwall (eds) *The Expansion of Management Knowledge: Carriers, Flows and Sources*, pp. 96–110. Stanford, CA: Stanford University Press.

Armstrong, P. (1986) 'Management Control Strategies and Inter-Professional Competition: The Cases of Accountancy and Personnel Management', in D. Knights and H. Willmott (eds) *Managing the Labour Process*, pp. 19–43. London: Gower.

Armstrong, P. (1989) 'Human Resource Management in an Age of Management Accountancy', in J. Storey (ed) *New Perspectives on Human Resource Management*, pp. 154–66. London: Routledge.

Ashcraft, K. L. (2001) 'Organized Dissonance: Feminist Bureaucracy as Hybrid Form', *Academy of Management Journal* 44(6): 1301–22.

Ashforth, B. E. and Johnson, S. A. (2001) 'Which Hat to Wear? The Relative Salience of Multiple Identities in Organizational Contexts', in M. A. Hogg and D. J. Terry (eds) *Social Identity Processes in Organizational Contexts*, pp. 31–48. Philadelphia, PA: Psychology Press.

Ashforth, B. E., Kreiner, G. E. and Fugate, M. (2000) 'All in a Day's Work: Boundaries and Micro Role Transitions', *Academy of Management Review* 25(3): 472–91.

Ashforth, B. E. and Mael, F. (1989) 'Social Identity Theory and the Organization', *Academy of Management Review* 14(1): 20–39.

Balogun, J., Gleadle, P., Hope-Hailey, V. and Willmott, H. (2005) 'Managing Change across Boundaries: Boundary-Shaking Practices', *British Journal of Management* 16(4): 261–78.

Barley, S. R. and Kunda, G. (2004) *Gurus, Hired Guns and Warm Bodies*. Princeton, NJ: Princeton University Press.

Bartel, C. and Dutton, J. (2001) 'Ambiguous Organizational Memberships: Constructing Organizational Identities in Interactions with Others', in M. A. Hogg and D. J. Terry (eds) *Social Identity Processes in Organizational Contexts*, pp. 115–30. Philadelphia, PA: Psychology Press.

Becker, H. (1998) *Tricks of the Trade: How to Think About Your Research While You're Doing It*. Chicago: University of Chicago Press.

Beer, M. and Nohria, N. (eds). (2000) *Breaking the Code of Change*. Boston, MA: Harvard Business School Press.

Bendix, R. (1963) *Work and Authority in Industry: Ideologies of Management in the Course of Industrialization*. New York: Harper & Row.

Berthoin Antal, A. and Krebsbach-Gnath, C. (2001) 'Consultants as Agents of Organisational Learning', in M. Dierkes, A. Berthoin, J. Child and I. Nonaka (eds) *Handbook of Organizational Learning and Knowledge*, pp. 462–83. Oxford: Oxford University Press.

Blau, P. M. (1955) *The Dynamics of Bureaucracy: A Study of Interpersonal Relations in Two Government Agencies*. Chicago: University of Chicago Press.

Bolin, M. and Härenstam, A. (2008) 'An Empirical Study of Bureaucratic and Post-Bureaucratic Characteristics in 90 Workplaces', *Economic and Industrial Democracy* 29(4): 541–64.

Boltanski, L. and Chiapello, E. (2005a) *The New Spirit of Capitalism*. London: Verso.

Boltanski, L. and Chiapello, E. (2005b) 'The New Spirit of Capitalism', *International Journal of Politics, Culture, and Society* 18(3–4): 161–88.

Brech, E., Thomson, A. and Wilson, J. F. (2010) *Lyndall Urwick, Management Pioneer: A Biography*. Oxford: Oxford University Press.

Brint, S. (1996) *In an Age of Experts: The Changing Role of Professionals in Politics and Public Life*. Princeton, NJ: Princeton University Press.

Brocklehurst, M., Grey, C. and Sturdy, A. (2010) 'Management: The Work That Dares Not Speak Its Name', *Management Learning* 41(1): 7–19.

Brown, A. D. (2014) 'Identities and Identity Work in Organizations', *International Journal of Management Reviews*. doi: 10.1111/ijmr.12035.

Brown, P. and Hesketh, A. (2004) *The Mismanagement of Talent: Employability and Jobs in the Knowledge Economy*. Oxford: Oxford University Press.

Bryman, A. (2004) *Social Research Methods*. Oxford: Oxford University Press.

Buchanan, D. and Badham, R. (1999) 'Politics and Organizational Change: The Lived Experience', *Human Relations* 52(5): 609–29.

Buchanan, D. A., Addicott, R., Fitzgerald, L., Ferlie, E. and Baeza, J. I. (2007) 'Nobody in Charge: Distributed Change Agency in Healthcare', *Human Relations* 60(7): 1065–90.

Buchanan, D. A. and Fitzgerald, L. (2011) 'New Lock, New Stock, New Barrel, Same Gun: The Accessorized Bureaucracy of Health Care', in S. Clegg, M. Harris and H. Höpfl (eds) *Managing Modernity: Beyond Bureaucracy?*, pp. 56–80. Oxford: Oxford University Press.

Burns, T. (1954) 'The Directions of Activity and Communication in a Departmental Executive Group: A Quantitative Study in a British Engineering Factory with a Self-Recording Technique', *Human Relations* 7(1): 73–97.

Burns, T. (1957) 'Management in Action', *Operational Research Quarterly* 8(2): 45–60.

Butler, N. (2008) 'What Is Management Consultancy?', PhD thesis, School of Management, University of Leicester.

Byrne, J. A. (2012) 'B-Schools That Churn out Consultants', *Poets & Quants*, 22 June, http://poetsandquants.com/2012/06/22/b-schools-that-churn-out-consultants/.

Caldwell, R. (2001) 'Champions, Adapters, Consultants and Synergists: The New Change Agents in HRM', *Human Resource Management Journal* 11(3): 39–52.

Caldwell, R. (2003) 'The Changing Roles of Personnel Managers: Old Ambiguities, New Uncertainties', *Journal of Management Studies* 40(4): 983–1004.

Caldwell, R. (2005) 'Things Fall Apart? Discourses on Agency and Change in Organizations', *Human Relations* 58(1): 83–114.

Caldwell, R. (2008) 'HR Business Partner Competency Models: Re-Contextualising Effectiveness', *Human Resource Management Journal* 18(3): 275–94.

Carroll, T. and Moore, D. (2013) *The Transition from Management Consulting into Industry: Perspectives Before and After the Move*. Sydney: 325Consulting.

Chase, R. B. and Kumar, K. R. (2005) 'Operations Management Consulting', in L. Greiner and F. Poulfelt (eds) *The Contemporary Consultant: Handbook of Management Consulting*, pp. 115–31. Mason, OH: Thomson/South-Western.

Child, J. (1984) *Organization: A Guide to Problems and Practice*. London: Paul Chapman.

Christensen, C. M., Wang, D. and van Bever, D. (2013) 'Consulting on the Cusp of Disruption', *Harvard Business Review* 91(10): 106–14.

Cicourel, A. V. (1964) *Method and Measurement in Sociology*. New York: Free Press.

Clegg, S. (2012) 'The End of Bureaucracy?', *Research in the Sociology of Organizations* 35: 59–84.

Clegg, S. and Courpasson, D. (2004) 'Political Hybrids: Tocquevillean Views on Project Organizations', *Journal of Management Studies* 41(4): 525–47.

Clegg, S., Harris, M. and Höpfl, H. (eds). (2011) *Managing Modernity: Beyond Bureaucracy?* Oxford: Oxford University Press.

Clegg, S. R., Rhodes, C. and Kornberger, M. (2007) 'Desperately Seeking Legitimacy: Organizational Identity and Emerging Industries', *Organization Studies* 28(4): 495–513.

Courpasson, D. (2000) 'Managerial Strategies of Domination: Power in Soft Bureaucracies', *Organization Studies* 21(1): 141–61.

Czerniawska, F. (2011) 'Consultant-Managers: Something Else to Worry About', *The Source Blog*, 3 May, www.sourceforconsulting.com/blog/2011/05/03/consultant-managers-something-else-to-worry-about/.

Dalton, M. (1950) 'Conflicts between Staff and Line Managerial Officers', *American Sociological Review* 15(3): 342–51.

Daniel, C. A. (1998) *MBA: The First Century*. Cranberry, NJ: Associated University Presses.

Das, T. K. and Teng, B.-S. (1998) 'Between Trust and Control: Developing Confidence in Partner Cooperation in Alliances', *Academy of Management Review* 23(3): 491–512.

Daudigeos, T. (2013) 'In Their Profession's Service: How Staff Professionals Exert Influence in Their Organization', *Journal of Management Studies* 50(5): 722–49.

David, R. J. (2012) 'Institutional Change and the Growth of Strategy Consulting in the United States', in M. Kipping and T. Clark (eds) *The Oxford Handbook of Management Consulting*, pp. 71–92. Oxford: Oxford University Press.

David, R. J., Sine, W. D. and Haveman, H. A. (2013) 'Seizing Opportunity in Emerging Fields: How Institutional Entrepreneurs Legitimated the Professional Form of Management Consulting', *Organization Science* 24(2): 356–77.

Denis, J.-L., Langley, A. and Rouleau, L. (2007) 'Strategizing in Pluralistic Contexts: Rethinking Theoretical Frames', *Human Relations* 60(1): 179–215.

Diefenbach, T. and Sillince, J. A. A. (2011) 'Formal and Informal Hierarchy in Different Types of Organization', *Organization Studies* 32(11): 1515–37.

Donnelly, R. (2009) 'The Knowledge Economy and the Restructuring of Employment: The Case of Consultants', *Work Employment Society* 23(2): 323–41.

du Gay, P. (2000) *In Praise of Bureaucracy*. London: Sage.

du Gay, P. (2004) 'Against "Enterprise" (but Not against "Enterprise", for That Would Make No Sense)', *Organization* 11(1): 37–57.

Edersheim, E.H. (2004) *Mckinsey's Marvin Bower: Vision, Leadership and the Creation of Management Consulting*. New York: John Wiley & Sons.

Ekman, S. (2013) 'Authenticity at Work: Questioning the New Spirit of Capitalism from a Micro-Sociological Perspective', in P. du Gay and G. Morgan (eds) *New Spirits of Capitalism?: Crises, Justifications, and Dynamics*, pp. 294–316. Oxford: Oxford University Press.

Ellis, N. and Ybema, S. (2010) 'Marketing Identities: Shifting Circles of Identification in Inter-Organizational Relationships', *Organization Studies* 31(3): 279–305.

Engwall, L. (2012) 'Business Schools and Consultancies: The Blurring of Boundaries', in M. Kipping and T. Clark (eds) *The Oxford Handbook of Management Consulting*, pp. 365–85. Oxford: Oxford University Press.

Erturk, I., Froud, J., Johal, S. and Williams, K. (2005) 'Pay for Corporate Performance or Pay as Social Division? Rethinking the Problem of Top Management Pay in Giant Corporations', *Competition & Change* 9(1): 49–74.

Farrell, C. and Morris, J. (2003) 'The "Neo-Bureaucratic" State: Professionals, Managers and Professional Managers in Schools, General Practices and Social Work', *Organization* 10(1): 129–56.

Farrell, C. and Morris, J. (2013) 'Managing the Neo-Bureaucratic Organisation: Lessons from the UK's Prosaic Sector', *The International Journal of Human Resource Management* 24(7): 1376–92.

Faust, M. and Schneider, K. (2014) 'Functional Equivalents to External Consulting – a Case of a Reluctant German Corporation', in M. Faust (ed) *Globale Managementberatung*, pp. 155–79. Berlin: Rainer Hampp Verlag.

Fincham, R. (1999) 'The Consultant-Client Relationship: Critical Perspectives on the Management of Organizational Change', *Journal of Management Studies* 36(3): 335–51.

Fincham, R. (2003) 'The Agent's Agent: Power, Knowledge, and Uncertainty in Management Consultancy', *International Studies of Management and Organization* 32(4): 67–86.

Fincham, R. (2012) 'Expert Labour as a Differentiated Category: Power, Knowledge and Organisation', *New Technology, Work and Employment* 27(3): 208–23.

Fincham, R. and Clark, T. (2002) 'Introduction: The Emergence of Critical Perspectives on Consulting', in T. Clark and R. Fincham (eds) *Critical*

Consulting: New Perspectives on the Management Advice Industry, pp. 1–18. Oxford: Blackwell.

Fine, G. (1996) 'Justifying Work: Occupational Rhetorics as Resources in Restaurant Kitchens', *Administrative Science Quarterly* 41(1): 90–116.

Francis, H. and Keegan, A. (2006) 'The Changing Face of HRM: In Search of Balance', *Human Resource Management Journal* 16(3): 231–49.

Gable, G. (1996) 'A Multidimensional Model of Client Success When Engaging External Consultants', *Management Science* 42(8): 1175–98.

Gabriel, Y. (1998) 'The Hubris of Management', *Administrative Theory and Praxis* 20(3): 257–73.

Galal, K., Richter, A. and Wendlandt, V. (2012) 'IT Consulting and Outsourcing Firms: Evolution, Business Models and Future Prospects', in M. Kipping and T. Clark (eds) *The Oxford Handbook of Management Consulting*, pp. 117–36. Oxford: Oxford University Press.

Ganesh, S. (1978) 'Organizational Consultants: A Comparison of Styles', *Human Relations* 31(1): 1–28.

Garsten, C. (1999) 'Betwixt and Between: Temporary Employees as Liminal Subjects in Flexible Organizations', *Organization Studies* 20(4): 601–17.

Garvin, D. A. (2013) 'How Google Sold Its Engineers on Management', *Harvard Business Review* 91(12): 74–82.

Glückler, J. and Armbrüster, T. (2003) 'Bridging Uncertainty in Management Consulting: The Mechanisms of Trust and Networked Reputation', *Organization Studies* 24(2): 269–97.

Gouldner, A. W. (1955) *Patterns of Industrial Bureaucracy*. London: Routledge & Kegan Paul.

Gouldner, A. W. (1957) 'Cosmopolitans and Locals: Towards an Analysis of Latent Social Roles I', *Administrative Science Quarterly* 2(3): 281–306.

Grant, D., Hall, R., Wailes, N. and Wright, C. (2006) 'The False Promise of Technological Determinism: The Case of Enterprise Resource Planning Systems', *New Technology, Work and Employment* 21(1): 2–15.

Greenwood, R., Suddaby, R. and Hinings, C. R. (2002) 'Theorizing Change: The Role of Professional Associations in the Transformation of Institutionalized Fields', *Academy of Management Journal* 45(1): 58–80.

Grey, C. (1999) '"We Are All Managers Now"; "We Always Were": On the Development and Demise of Management', *Journal of Management Studies* 36(5): 561–85.

Guest, D. E. (1987) 'Human Resource Management and Industrial Relations', *Journal of Management Studies* 24(5): 503–21.

Guillén, M. (1994) *Models of Management. Work, Authority, and Organization in a Comparative Perspective.* Chicago: The University of Chicago Press.

Hales, C. (2002) '"Bureaucracy-Lite" and Continuities in Managerial Work', *British Journal of Management* 13(1): 51–66.

Hales, C. and Tamangani, Z. (1996) 'An Investigation of the Relationship between Organizational Structure, Managerial Role Expectations and Managers' Work Activities', *Journal of Management Studies* 33(6): 731–56.

Hales, C. P. (1986) 'What Do Managers Do? A Critical Review of the Evidence', *Journal of Management Studies* 23(1): 88–115.

Hancock, P. and Tyler, M. (eds). (2009) *The Management of Everyday Life.* Basingstoke: Palgrave/Macmillan.

Harding, N., Lee, H. and Ford, J. (2014) 'Who Is "the Middle Manager"?', *Human Relations* 67(10): 1213–37.

Harris, M., Clegg, S. and Höpfl, H. (2011) 'Managing Modernity: Beyond Bureaucracy?', in S. Clegg, M. Harris and H. Höpfl (eds) *Managing Modernity: Beyond Bureaucracy?,* pp. 1–10. Oxford: Oxford University Press.

Harrison, S. and Smith, C. (2003) 'Neo-Bureacracy and Public Management', *Competition and Change* 7(4): 243–54.

Hassard, J., Morris, J. and McCann, L. (2012) '"My Brilliant Career"? New Organizational Forms and Changing Managerial Careers in Japan, UK and USA', *Journal of Management Studies* 49(3): 571–99.

HBS. (2013) 'The HBS Case Method', www.hbs.edu/mba/academic-experience/Pages/the-hbs-case-method.aspx.

Heckscher, C. and Donnellon, A. (1994) *The Post-Bureaucratic Organization: New Perspectives on Organisational Change.* London: Sage.

Hekman, S. J. (1983) 'Weber's Ideal Type: A Contemporary Reassessment', *Polity* 16(1): 119–37.

Hernes, T. (2004) 'Studying Composite Boundaries: A Framework of Analysis', *Human Relations* 57(1): 9–29.

Hodgson, D. (2002) 'Disciplining the Professional: The Case of Project Management', *Journal of Management Studies* 39(6): 803–21.

Hodgson, D. and Cicmil, S. (2007) 'The Politics of Standards in Modern Management: Making "the Project" a Reality', *Journal of Management Studies* 44(3): 431–50.

Hodson, R. and Sullivan, T. A. (2002) *The Social Organization of Work.* Belmont, CA: Wadsworth.

Höpfl, H. (2006) 'Post-Bureaucracy and Weber's "Modern" Bureaucrat', *Journal of Organizational Change Management* 19(1): 8–21.

Hopper, K. and Hopper, W. (2009) *The Puritan Gift: Reclaiming the American Dream Amidst Global Financial Crisis*. London: I.B.Tauris.

Horne, J. H. and Lupton, T. (1965) 'The Work Activities of "Middle" Managers – An Exploratory Study', *Journal of Management Studies* 2(1): 14–33.

Hunter, I., Saunders, J., Boroughs, A. and Constance, S. (2006) *HR Business Partners*. Aldershot: Gower.

Inkson, K., Heising, A. and Rousseau, D. M. (2001) 'The Interim Manager: Prototype of the 21 St-Century Worker?', *Human Relations* 54(3): 259–84.

Jackall, R. (1988) *Moral Mazes: The World of Corporate Managers*. New York: Oxford University Press.

Jarzabkowski, P. and Spee, A. P. (2009) 'Strategy-as-Practice: A Review and Future Directions for the Field', *International Journal of Management Reviews* 11(1): 69–95.

Johnson, P., Wood, G., Brewster, C. and Brookes, M. (2009) 'The Rise of Post-Bureaucracy: Theorists' Fancy or Organizational Praxis?', *International Sociology* 24(1): 37–61.

Kanter, R. M. (1979) 'Power Failure in Management Circuits', *Harvard Business Review* 57(4): 65–75.

Kanter, R. M. (1989) *When Giants Learn to Dance: Mastering the Challenges of Strategy, Management and Careers in the 1990s*. New York: Simon & Schuster.

Karantinou, K. M. and Hogg, M. K. (2001) 'Exploring Relationship Management in Professional Services: A Study of Management Consultancy', *Journal of Marketing Management* 17(3–4): 263–86.

Kenton, B. and Moody, D. (2003) *The Role of the Internal Consultant*. Horsham: Roffey Park Institute Ltd.

Kenton, B. and Yarnall, J. (2005) *HR: The Business Partner*. Oxford: Elsevier Butterworth-Heinemann.

Khurana, R. (2007) *From Higher Aims to Hired Hands: The Social Transformation of American Business Schools and the Unfulfilled Promise of Management as a Profession*. Princeton, NJ: Princeton University Press.

Kipping, M. (2002) 'Trapped in Their Wave: The Evolution of Management Consultancies', in T. Clark and R. Fincham (eds) *Critical Consulting: New Perspectives on the Management Advice Industry*, pp. 28–49. Oxford: Blackwell.

Kipping, M. (2011) 'Hollow from the Start? Image Professionalism in Management Consulting', *Current Sociology* 59(4): 530–50.

Kipping, M. and Armbrüster, T. (2002) 'The Burden of Otherness: Limits of Consultancy Interventions in Historical Case Studies', in M. Kipping and L. Engwall (eds) *Management Consulting: Emergence and Dynamics of a Knowledge Industry*, pp. 203–21. Oxford: Oxford University Press.

Kipping, M. and Engwall, L. (eds). (2002) *Management Consulting: Emergence and Dynamics of a Knowledge Industry*. Oxford: Oxford University Press.

Kipping, M. and Wright, C. (2012) 'Consultants in Context: Global Dominance, Societal Effect and the Capitalist System', in M. Kipping and T. Clark (eds) *The Oxford Handbook of Management Consulting*, pp. 165–85. Oxford: Oxford University Press.

Kitay, J. and Wright, C. (2003) 'Expertise and Organizational Boundaries: The Varying Roles of Australian Management Consultants', *Asia Pacific Business Review* 9(3): 21–40.

Kitay, J. and Wright, C. (2004) 'Take the Money and Run? Organisational Boundaries and Consultants' Roles', *The Service Industries Journal* 24(3): 1–18.

Kitay, J. and Wright, C. (2007) 'From Prophets to Profits: The Occupational Rhetoric of Management Consultants', *Human Relations* 60(11): 1613–40.

Klein, J. A. (2004) *True Change: How Outsiders on the Inside Get Things Done in Organizations*. San Francisco, CA: Jossey-Bass.

Knights, D. and Willmott, H. (1989) 'Power and Subjectivity at Work: From Degradation to Subjugation in Social Relations', *Sociology* 23(4): 535–58.

Korczynski, M. (2001) 'The Contradictions of Service Work: Call-Centre as Customer-Oriented Bureaucracy', in A. Sturdy, I. Grugulis and H. Willmott (eds) *Customer Service: Empowerment and Entrapment*, pp. 79–101. Basingstoke: Palgrave/Macmillan.

Kotter, J. (1999) *What Leaders Really Do*. Boston, MA: Harvard Business School Press.

Kubr, M. (1996) *Management Consulting: A Guide to the Profession*. Geneva: ILO.

Kunda, G. and Ailon-Souday, G. (2005) 'Managers, Markets and Ideologies – Design and Devotion Revisited', in S. Ackroyd, R. Batt, P. Thompson and P. S. Tolbert (eds) *Oxford Handbook of Work and Organization*, pp. 200–19. Oxford: Oxford University Press.

Lacey, M. Y. (1995) 'Internal Consulting: Perspectives on the Process of Planned Change', *Journal of Organizational Change Management* 8(3): 75–84.

Law, M. (2009) 'Managing Consultants', *Business Strategy Review* 20(1): 62–66.

Lawrence, P. R. and Lorsch, J. W. (1967) *Organization and Environment: Managing Differentiation and Integration*. Boston, MA: Harvard University Press.

Lemann, N. (1999) 'The Kids in the Conference Room', *The New Yorker* 75(31): 209–16.

Lippitt, G. and Lippitt, R. (1986) *The Consulting Process in Action*. San Diego, CA: University Associates Inc.

Luthans, F. (1988) 'Successful vs. Effective Real Managers' *Academy of Management Perspectives*, 2(2): 127–132.

Maister, D. (1993) *Managing the Professional Service Firm*. New York: Free Press.

Malone, T. W. (2004) 'Bringing the Market Inside', *Harvard Business Review* 82(4): 106–14.

Marglin, S. (1974) 'What Do Bosses Do? The Origins and Functions of Hierarchy in Capitalist Production', *Review of Radical Political Economics* 660–112.

Marglin, S. (1979) 'Catching Flies with Honey: An Inquiry into Management Initiatives to Humanise Work', *Economic Analysis and Workers' Management* 13(4): 473–85.

Marsh, S. (2009) *The Feminine in Management Consulting – Power, Emotion and Values in Consulting Interactions*. Basingstoke: Palgrave/Macmillan.

Martin, B. (2005) 'Managers after the Era of Organizational Restructuring: Towards a Second Managerial Revolution?', *Work Employment Society* 19(4): 747–60.

Martin, B. and Wajcman, J. (2004) 'Markets, Contingency and Preferences: Contemporary Managers' Narrative Identities', *Sociological Review* 52(2): 240–64.

Martinko, M. J. and Gardner, W. L. (1990) 'Structured Observation of Managerial Work: A Replication and Synthesis', *Journal of Management Studies* 27(3): 329–57.

Matthaei, E. (2010) *The Nature of Executive Work: A Case Study*. Wiesbaden: Springer.

MCA. (2010) *The Value of Consulting: An Analysis of the Tangible Benefits of Using Management Consultancy*. London: MCA.

McDonald, D. (2013) *The Firm: The Story of McKinsey and Its Secret Influence on American Business*. New York: Simon and Schuster.

McDougald, M. S. and Greenwood, R. (2012) 'Cuckoo in the Nest? The Rise of Management Consulting in Large Accounting Firms', in M. Kipping and T. Clark (eds) *The Oxford Handbook of Management Consulting*, pp. 93–116. Oxford: Oxford University Press.

McGinn, D. (2013) 'Inside Consulting's Black Box', *Harvard Business Review* 91(9): 126–27.

McKenna, C. D. (2006) *The World's Newest Profession: Management Consulting in the Twentieth Century*. Cambridge: Cambridge University Press.

McSweeney, B. (2006) 'Are We Living in a Post-Bureaucratic Epoch?', *Journal of Organizational Change Management* 19(1): 22–37.

Menon, T. and Pfeffer, J. (2003) 'Valuing Internal vs. External Knowledge: Explaining the Preference for Outsiders', *Management Science* 49(4): 497–513.

Meriläinen, S., Tienari, J., Thomas, R. and Davies, A. (2004) 'Management Consultant Talk: A Cross-Cultural Comparison of Normalizing Discourse and Resistance', *Organization* 11(4): 539–64.

Merton, R. K. (1972) 'Insiders and Outsiders: A Chapter in the Sociology of Knowledge', *The American Journal of Sociology* 78(1): 9–47.

Merton, R. K. (1976) *Sociological Ambivalence and Other Essays*. New York: Free Press.

Meyerson, D. E. (2003) *Tempered Radicals: How People Use Difference to Inspire Change at Work*. Boston, MA: Harvard Business School Press.

Meyerson, D. E. and Scully, M. A. (1995) 'Tempered Radicalism and the Politics of Ambivalence and Change', *Organization Science* 6(5): 585–600.

Mintzberg, H. (1973) *The Nature of Managerial Work*. New York: Harper and Row.

Mintzberg, H. (1980) 'Structure in 5's: A Synthesis of the Research on Organization Design', *Management Science* 26(3): 322–41.

Mintzberg, H. (2004) *Managers Not MBAs: A Hard Look at the Soft Practice of Managing and Management Development*. San Francisco, CA: Berrett-Koehler.

Mohe, M. (2005) 'Generic Strategies for Managing Consultants: Insights from Clients' Companies in Germany', *Journal of Change Management* 5(3): 357–65.

Morris, J., Hassard, J. and McCann, L. (2008) 'The Resilience of "Institutionalized Capitalism"': Managing Managers under "Shareholder Capitalism" and "Managerial Capitalism"', *Human Relations* 61(5): 687–710.

Morris, T. (2000) 'From Key Advice to Execution? Consulting Firms and the Implementation of Strategic Decisions', in P. Flood, T. Dromgoole, S. Carroll and L. Gorman (eds) *Managing Strategic Implementation: An Organizational Behaviour Perspective*, pp. 125–37. Oxford: Blackwell.

Mueller, F. and Whittle, A. (2011) 'Translating Management Ideas: A Discursive Devices Analysis', *Organization Studies* 32(2): 187–210.

Muzio, D., Hodgson, D., Faulconbridge, J., Beaverstock, J. and Hall, S. (2011) 'Towards Corporate Professionalization: The Case of Project Management, Management Consultancy and Executive Search', *Current Sociology* 59(4): 443–64.

Nadler, D. A. and Slywotzky, A. J. (2005) 'Strategy and Organization Consulting', in L. Greiner and F. Poulfelt (eds) *The Contemporary Consultant: Insights from World Experts*, pp. 75–95. Mason, OH: Thomson/South-Western.

Neal, M. and Lloyd, C. (1998) 'The Role of the Internal Consultant', in P. Sadler (ed) *Management Consultancy: A Handbook of Best Practice*, pp. 432–46. London: Kogan Page.

Niece, J. M. and Trompeter, G. M. (2004) 'The Demise of Arthur Andersen's One-Firm Concept: A Case Study in Corporate Governance', *Business and Society Review* 109(2): 183–207.

Nolan, R. and Bennigson, L. (2005) 'Information Technology Consulting', in L. Greiner and F. Poulfelt (eds) *The Contemporary Consultant: Insights from World Experts*, pp. 55–73. Mason, OH: Thomson/South-Western.

Noordegraaf, M. (2000) 'Professional Sense-Makers: Managerial Competencies Amidst Ambiguity', *International Journal of Public Sector Management* 13(4): 319–32.

Nooteboom, B., Van Haverbeke, W., Duysters, G., Gilsing, V. and van den Oord, A. (2007) 'Optimal Cognitive Distance and Absorptive Capacity', *Research Policy* 36(7): 1016–34.

O'Mahoney, J. (2010) *Management Consultancy*. Oxford: Oxford University Press.

O'Mahoney, J., Heusinkveld, S. and Wright, C. (2013) 'Commodifying the Commodifiers: The Impact of Procurement on Management Knowledge', *Journal of Management Studies* 50(2): 204–35.

O'Mahoney, J. and Markham, C. (2013) *Management Consultancy*. Oxford: Oxford University Press.

O'Shea, J. and Madigan, C. (1997) *Dangerous Company: The Consulting Powerhouses and the Businesses They Save and Ruin*. New York: Times Business.

O'Reilly, D. and Reed, M. (2011) 'The Grit in the Oyster: Professionalism, Managerialism and Leaderism as Discourses of UK Public Services Modernization', *Organization Studies* 32(8): 1079–101.

OGC. (2006) *Delivering Value from Consultancy*. London: Office of Government Commerce.

Padavic, I. (2005) 'Laboring under Uncertainty: Identity Renegotiation among Contingent Workers', *Symbolic Interaction* 28(1): 111–34.

Pande, P. S., Neuman, R. P. and Cavanagh, R. R. (2000) *The Six Sigma Way: How GE, Motorola, and Other Top Companies Are Honing Their Performance*. New York: McGraw-Hill.

Parker, M. (2002) *Against Management: Organization in the Age of Managerialism*. Cambridge: Polity Press.

Paulsen, N. and Hernes, T. (eds). (2003) *Managing Boundaries in Organizations: Multiple Perspectives*. Basingstoke: Palgrave/Macmillan.

Peters, T. (1997) 'The Brand Called You', *Fast Company* 1083, www.fastcompany.com/28905/brand-called-you.

Pettigrew, A. M. (1973) *The Politics of Organisational Decision-Making*. London: Tavistock.

Pettigrew, A. M. (1975) 'Towards a Political Theory of Organizational Intervention', *Human Relations* 28(3): 191–208.

Pettigrew, A. M. (1985) *The Awakening Giant: Continuity and Change in Imperial Chemical Industries*. Oxford: Blackwell.

Pfeffer, J. and Fong, C. T. (2002) 'The End of Business Schools? Less Success Than Meets the Eye', *Academy of Management Learning & Education* 1(1): 78–95.

Pink, D. (2001) *Free Agent Nation: How America's New Independent Workers Are Transforming the Way We Live*. New York: Warner Business Books.

Poole, M., Mansfield, R. and Mendes, P. (2001) *Two Decades of Management*. London: The (UK) Institute of Management.

Poole, M., Mansfield, R. and Mendes, P. (2003) 'Britain's Managers over Twenty Years: A Focus on Ownership, Control and Stakeholder Interests', *Journal of General Management* 28(4): 1–14.

Ramsay, H. (1977) 'Cycles of Control: Worker Participation in Sociological and Historical Perspective', *Sociology* 11(3): 481–506.

Reed, M. (1996) 'Expert Power and Control in Late Modernity: An Empirical Review and Theoretical Synthesis', *Organization Studies* 17(4): 573–97.

Reed, M. (2011) 'The Post-Bureaucratic Organization and the Control Revolution', in S. Clegg, M. Harris and H. Höpfl (eds.) *Managing Modernity: Beyond Bureaucracy?*, pp. 230–56. Oxford: Oxford University Press.

Robertson, P. L. and Singleton, J. (2001) 'The Commonwealth as an Economic Network', *Australian Economic History Review* 41(3): 241–66.

Robinson, D. G. and Robinson, J. C. (2005) *Strategic Business Partner: Aligning People Strategies with Business Goals*. San Francisco, CA: Berrett-Koehler Publishers.

Rose, N. (1990) *Governing the Soul: The Shaping of the Private Self*. London: Routledge.

Ruef, M. (2002) 'The Interstices of Organizations: The Expansion of the Management Consulting Profession, 1933–1997', in K. Sahlin-Andersson and L. Engwall (eds) *The Expansion of Management Knowledge: Carriers, Flows, and Sources*, pp. 74–95. Stanford, CA: Stanford University Press.

Santos, F. M. and Eisenhardt, K. M. (2005) 'Organizational Boundaries and Theories of Organization', *Organization Science* 16(5): 491–508.

Sayles, L. R. (1964) *Managerial Behavior: Administration in Complex Organizations*. New York: McGraw Hill.

Schein, E. (1969) *Process Consultation: Its Role in Organization Development*. Reading, MA: Addison-Wesley.

Schein, E. (1971) 'The Individual, the Organization, and the Career: A Conceptual Scheme', *The Journal of Applied Behavioral Science* 7(4): 401–26.

Schein, E. (1987) *Process Consultation: Lessons for Managers and Consultants*. Reading, MA: Addison-Wesley.

Schein, E. (1997) 'The Concept of "Client" from a Process Consultation Perspective: A Guide for Change Agents', *Journal of Organizational Change Management* 10(3): 202–16.

Schein, E. (2009) *Helping: How to Offer, Give and Receive Help*. San Francisco, CA: Berrett-Koehler.

Scott, B. (2000) *Consulting on the Inside: An Internal Consultant's Guide to Living and Working inside Organizations*. Alexandria, VA: American Society for Training and Development.

Selim, G., Woodward, S. and Allegrini, M. (2009) 'Internal Auditing and Consulting Practice: A Comparison between UK/Ireland and Italy', *International Journal of Auditing* 13(1): 9–25.

Shenhav, Y. A. (1999) *Manufacturing Rationality: The Engineering Foundations of the Managerial Revolution*. Oxford: Oxford University Press.

Stewart, R. (1991) *Managing Today and Tomorrow*. London: Macmillan.

Stonequist, E. (1937) *The Marginal Man: A Study in Personality and Culture Conflict*. New York: Russell and Russell.

Storey, J., Salaman, G. and Platman, K. (2005) 'Living with Enterprise in an Enterprise Economy: Freelance and Contract Workers in the Media', *Human Relations* 58(8): 1033–54.

Sturdy, A. (1997a) 'The Dialectics of Consultancy', *Critical Perspectives on Accounting* 8 511–35.

Sturdy, A. (1997b) 'The Consultancy Process – An Insecure Business?', *Journal of Management Studies* 34(3): 389–413.

Sturdy, A. (2009) 'Popular Critiques of Consultancy and a Politics of Management Learning?', *Management Learning* 40(4): 457–63.

Sturdy, A. (2011) 'Consultancy's Consequences? A Critical Assessment of Management Consultancy's Impact on Management', *British Journal of Management* 22(3): 517–30.

Sturdy, A., Clark, T., Fincham, R. and Handley, K. (2004) '*Both* Cosmopolitans and Locals? Multiplicity, Complexity, Fluidity and Exclusion in Management Consultant – Client Relationships'. Paper presented at the 2004 EGOS Colloquium, Ljubljana, Slovenia, July.

Sturdy, A. and Grey, C. (2003) 'Beneath and Beyond Organizational Change Management: Exploring Alternatives', *Organization* 10(4): 651–62.

Sturdy, A., Handley, K., Clark, T. and Fincham, R. (2009) *Management Consultancy: Boundaries and Knowledge in Action*. Oxford: Oxford University Press.

Sturdy, A., Schwarz, M. and Spicer, A. (2006) 'Guess Who's Coming to Dinner? Structures and Uses of Liminality in Strategic Management Consultancy', *Human Relations* 59(7): 929–60.

Sturdy, A. and Wright, C. (2008) 'A Consulting Diaspora? Enterprising Selves as Agents of Enterprise', *Organization* 15(3): 427–44.

Sturdy, A. and Wright, C. (2011) 'The Active Client: The Boundary-Spanning Roles of Internal Consultants as Gatekeepers, Brokers and Partners of Their External Counterparts', *Management Learning* 42(5): 485–503.

Sturdy, A., Wright, C. and Wylie, N. (2012) 'Management as Consultancy? Internal Consultants and Change'. Paper presented at the JMS/SAMS International Conference on the Evolution and Future of Management, St. Anne's College, Oxford, 26–28 March.

Sturdy, A., Wright, C. and Wylie, N. (2014) 'Managers as Consultants: Neo-Bureaucracy and Its Tensions'. Paper presented to the 32nd International Labour Process Conference, Kings College London, 7–9 April.

Sturdy, A., Wright, C. and Wylie, N. (forthcoming) 'Managers as Consultants: The Hybridity and Tensions of Neo-Bureaucratic Management', *Organization*.

Sturdy, A. and Wylie, N. (2011) 'Internal Consultants as Agents of Change', ESRC Research Report RES-000-22-1980/A, www.cass.city.ac.uk/__data/assets/pdf_file/0007/107179/InternalConsultants.pdf.

Sturdy, A., Wylie, N. and Wright, C. (2010) 'Management Consultancy without Consulting Firms or Consultants'. Paper presented to the 26th EGOS Colloquium, Lisbon, Portugal, 28 June–3 July.

Sturdy, A., Wylie, N. and Wright, C. (2013) 'Management Consultancy and Organizational Uncertainty: The Case of Internal Consultancy', *International Studies of Management and Organization* 43(3): 58–73.

Styhre, A. (2008) 'Management Control in Bureaucratic and Postbureaucratic Organizations', *Group & Organization Management* 33(6): 635–56.

Tengblad, S. (2004) 'Expectations of Alignment: Examining the Link between Financial Markets and Managerial Work', *Organization Studies* 25(4): 583–606.

Tengblad, S. (2006) 'Is There a "New Managerial Work"? A Comparison with Henry Mintzberg's Classic Study 30 Years Later', *Journal of Management Studies* 43(7): 1437–61.

Tengblad, S. (2012) *The Work of Managers: Towards a Practice Theory of Management*. Oxford: Oxford University Press.

Tengblad, S. and Vie, O. E. (2012) 'Management in Practice: Overview of Classic Studies on Managerial Work', in S. Tengblad (ed) *The Work of Managers: Towards a Practice Theory of Management*, pp. 18–44. Oxford: Oxford University Press.

Thomas, A. B. (2003) *Controversies in Management: Issues, Debates, Answers*. London: Routledge.

Thomas, R. and Linstead, A. (2002) 'Losing the Plot? Middle Managers and Identity', *Organization* 9(1): 71–93.

Thrift, N. (2005) *Knowing Capitalism*. London: Sage.

Trethewey, A. and Ashcraft, K. L. (2004) 'Practicing Disorganization: The Development of Applied Perspectives on Living with Tension', *Journal of Applied Communication Research* 32(2): 81–88.

Trinca, H. (2002) 'Is Management Consultancy Dead?', *Australian Financial Review*, 17 August, p. 21.

Tsoukas, H. (1994) 'What Is Management? An Outline of a Metatheory', *British Journal of Management* 5(4): 289–301.

Tushman, M. L. (1977) 'Special Boundary Roles in the Innovation Process', *Administrative Science Quarterly* 22(4): 587–605.

Tushman, M. L. and Scanlan, T. J. (1981) 'Characteristics and External Orientations of Boundary Spanning Individuals', *Academy of Management Journal* 24(1): 83–98.

Ulrich, D. (1998) 'A New Mandate for Human Resources', *Harvard Business Review* 76(1): 119–27.

Ulrich, D. and Brockbank, W. (2005) *The HR Value Proposition*. Harvard, MA: Harvard Business School Publishing.

Van Maanen, J. (1988) *Tales of the Field: On Writing Ethnography*. Chicago: University of Chicago Press.

Van Maanen, J. and Schein, E. H. (1979) 'Toward a Theory of Organizational Socialization', in B. M. Staw (ed) *Research in Organizational Behavior*, pp. 209–64. Greenwich, CT: JAI Press.

Van Maanen, J., Sørensen, J. B. and Mitchell, T. R. (2007) 'The Interplay between Theory and Method', *Academy of Management Review* 32(4): 1145–54.

Vie, O. E. (2010) 'Have Post-Bureaucratic Changes Occurred in Managerial Work?', *European Management Journal* 28(3): 182–94.

Visscher, K. (2006) 'Capturing the Competence of Management Consulting Work', *Journal of Workplace Learning* 18(4): 248–60.

Watson, T. (1994) *In Search of Management: Culture, Chaos and Control in Managerial Work*. London: Thompson Business Press.

Webb, J. (2004) 'Organizations, Self-Identities and the New Economy', *Sociology* 38(4): 719–38.

Werr, A. and Pemer, F. (2007) 'Purchasing Management Consulting Services: From Management Autonomy to Purchasing Involvement', *Journal of Purchasing and Supply Management* 13(2): 98–112.

Werr, A., Stjernberg, T. and Docherty, P. (1997) 'The Functions of Methods of Change in Management Consulting', *Journal of Organizational Change Management* 10(4): 288–307.

Whittington, R. (1992) 'Putting Giddens into Action', *Journal of Management Studies* 29(6): 693–712.

Whyte, W. H. (1956) *The Organization Man*. New York: Doubleday.

Wickham, P. A. (1999) *Management Consulting*. London: Financial Times/Pitman.

Willmott, H. (1984) 'Images and Ideals of Managerial Work: A Critical Examination of Conceptual and Empirical Accounts', *Journal of Management Studies* 21(3): 349–68.

Willmott, H. (1996) 'A Metatheory of Management: Omniscience or Obfuscation? A Comment', *British Journal of Management* 7(4): 323–27.

Wood, P. (ed). (2002) *Consultancy and Innovation: The Business Service Revolution in Europe*. London: Routledge.

Worren, N. A. M., Ruddle, K. and Moore, K. (1999) 'From Organizational Development to Change Management: The Emergence of a New Profession', *Journal of Applied Behavioral Science* 35(3): 273–86.

Wright, C. (2008) 'Reinventing Human Resource Management: Business Partners, Internal Consultants and the Limits to Professionalisation', *Human Relations* 61(8): 1063–86.

Wright, C. (2009) 'Inside Out? Organizational Membership, Ambiguity and the Ambivalent Identity of the Internal Consultant', *British Journal of Management* 20(3): 309–22.

Wright, C. and Kipping, M. (2012) 'The Engineering Origins of Consulting – and Their Long Shadow', in T. Clark and M. Kipping (eds) *The Oxford Handbook of Management Consulting*, pp. 29–49. Oxford: Oxford University Press.

Wright, C. and Kitay, J. (2002) '"But Does It Work?" Perceptions of the Impact of Management Consulting', *Strategic Change* 11(5): 271–78.

Wright, C., Sturdy, A. and Wylie, N. (2012) 'Management Innovation through Standardization: Consultants as Standardizers of Organizational Practice', *Research Policy* 41(3): 652–62.

Wylie, N., Sturdy, A. and Wright, C. (2014) 'Change Agency in Occupational Context: Lessons for HRM', *Human Resource Management Journal* 24(1): 95–110.

Zabusky, S. E. and Barley, S. R. (1997) '"You Can't Be a Stone If You're Cement": Reevaluating the Emic Identities of Scientists in Organizations', *Research in Organizational Behavior* 19: 361–404.

Index

Printed in the United States
by Baker & Taylor

Printed in the United States
By Bookmasters